Fresh Ways with Picnics & Barbecues

Time-Life Books Inc.
is a wholly owned subsidiary of
TIME INCORPORATED

Editor-in-Chief: Jason McManus
Chairman and Chief Executive Officer: J. Richard Munro
President and Chief Operating Officer: N. J. Nicholas, Jr.
Editorial Director: Richard B. Stolley

THE TIME INC. BOOK COMPANY

President and Chief Executive Officer: Kelso F. Sutton
President, Time Inc. Books Direct: Christopher T. Linen

TIME® LIFE BOOKS

COVER

Lighter versions of the traditional delights of the American backyard barbecue make summertime indulgence almost guilt-free. Grilled steak, barbecued chicken, cabbage salad, garlic potato fans and corn on the cob, fresh blueberries and iced peach yogurt combine here for a tempting outdoor feast with a reduced calorie count, low sodium, and little saturated fat. This is one of four complete menus—with recipes for all dishes—that appear on pages 106-127.

Library of Congress Cataloging in Publication Data
Fresh ways with picnics & barbecues / by the editors of Time-Life Books.
p. cm. — (Healthy home cooking)
Includes index.
ISBN 0-8094-6083-1. — ISBN 0-8094-6084-X (lib. bdg.)
1. Outdoor cookery. 2. Barbecue cookery.
I. Time-Life Books. II. Title: Fresh ways with picnics and barbecues. III. Series.
TX823.F74 1989 89-4384
641.5'78—dc19 CIP

For information on and a full description of any Time-Life Books series, please call 1-800-621-7026 or write:
Reader Information
Time-Life Customer Service
P.O. Box C-32068
Richmond, Virginia 23261-2068

First printing. Printed in U.S.A.
Published simultaneously in Canada.
School and library distribution by Silver Burdett Company, Morristown, New Jersey 07960.

HEALTHY HOME COOKING

SERIES DIRECTOR: Jackie Matthews
Studio Stylist: Liz Hodgson

Editorial Staff for *Fresh Ways with Picnics & Barbecues:*
Editor: Frances Dixon
Researchers: Heather Campion, Eva Reynolds
Designer: Paul Reeves
Sub-Editors: Wendy Gibbons, Eugénie Romer
Indexer: Myra Clark

PICTURE DEPARTMENT:
Administrator: Patricia Murray
Picture Coordinator: Amanda Hindley

EDITORIAL PRODUCTION:
Chief: Maureen Kelly
Assistant: Samantha Hill
Editorial Department: Theresa John, Debra Lelliott

U.S. Edition:
Assistant Editor: Barbara Fairchild Quarmby
Copy Coordinator: Anne Farr
Picture Coordinator: Betty H. Weatherley

Editorial Operations
Copy Chief: Diane Ullius
Production: Celia Beattie
Library: Louise D. Forstall

Correspondents: Elisabeth Kraemer-Singh (Bonn); Christina Lieberman (New York); Maria Vincenza Aloisi (Paris); Ann Natanson (Rome).

THE CONTRIBUTORS

LISA CHERKASKY has worked as a chef at numerous restaurants in Washington, D.C., and in Madison, Wisconsin, including nationally known Le Pavillon and Le Lion d'Or. A graduate of The Culinary Institute of America at Hyde Park, New York, she has also taught classes in French cooking technique.

SILVIJA DAVIDSON studied at Leith's School of Food and Wine in London and specializes in the development of recipes from Latvia, as well as other international cuisines.

JOANNA FARROW, a home economist and recipe writer who contributes regularly to food magazines, is especially interested in the decorative presentation of food. Her books include *Creative Cake Decorating* and *Novelty Cakes for Children.*

ANTONY KWOK, originally a fashion designer from Hong Kong, has won several awards for his Asian-inspired style of cooking and was the *London Standard* Gastronomic Seafish Cook of 1986.

JANE SUTHERING is a writer and home economist who has concentrated on the development of healthful recipes and vegetarian dishes. She is consultant to a major British health-food restaurant chain, and has created the recipes for all eight of their cookbooks.

ROSEMARY WADEY is food editor of *Home and Country* magazine and a former head of the Food Advisory Department at the Good Housekeeping Institute. An established writer with 25 titles to date, her books include *Cooking for Two* and *The Pastry Book.*

The following people also have contributed recipes to this volume: Pat Alburey, Jane Bird, Maddalena Bonino, Gail Duff, Anne Gains, Yvonne Hamlett, Carole Handslip, Cristine McKie, Norma MacMillan, Sally Major, Roselyne Masselin, Louise Steele, and Susie Theodorou.

THE COOKS

The recipes in this book were prepared for photographing by Pat Alburey, Allyson Birch, Jane Bird, Antony Kwok, Lesley Sendall, Jane Suthering, Michelle Thompson, Rosemary Wadey, and Steven Wheeler. *Studio Assistant:* Rita Walters.

THE CONSULTANT

PAT ALBUREY is a home economist with a wide experience in preparing foods for photography, teaching cooking, and creating recipes. She has written a number of cookbooks, and she was the studio consultant for the Time-Life Books series The Good Cook. She has created a number of the recipes in this volume.

THE NUTRITION CONSULTANT

PATRICIA JUDD trained as a dietitian and worked in hospital nutrition before returning to college to earn her M.Sc. and Ph.D. degrees. She has since lectured in Nutrition and Dietetics at London University.

Nutritional analyses for *Fresh Ways with Picnics & Barbecues* were derived from McCance and Widdowson's *The Composition of Food* by A. A. Paul and D. A. T. Southgate, and other current data.

Other Publications:

AMERICAN COUNTRY
VOYAGE THROUGH THE UNIVERSE
THE THIRD REICH
THE TIME-LIFE GARDENER'S GUIDE
MYSTERIES OF THE UNKNOWN
TIME FRAME
FIX IT YOURSELF
FITNESS, HEALTH & NUTRITION
SUCCESSFUL PARENTING
UNDERSTANDING COMPUTERS
LIBRARY OF NATIONS
THE ENCHANTED WORLD
THE KODAK LIBRARY OF CREATIVE PHOTOGRAPHY
GREAT MEALS IN MINUTES
THE CIVIL WAR
PLANET EARTH
COLLECTOR'S LIBRARY OF THE CIVIL WAR
THE EPIC OF FLIGHT
THE GOOD COOK
WORLD WAR II
HOME REPAIR AND IMPROVEMENT
THE OLD WEST

This volume is one of a series of illustrated cookbooks that emphasize the preparation of healthful dishes for today's weight-conscious, nutrition-minded eaters.

Fresh Ways with Picnics & Barbecues

BY

THE EDITORS OF TIME-LIFE BOOKS

TIME-LIFE BOOKS / ALEXANDRIA, VIRGINIA

Contents

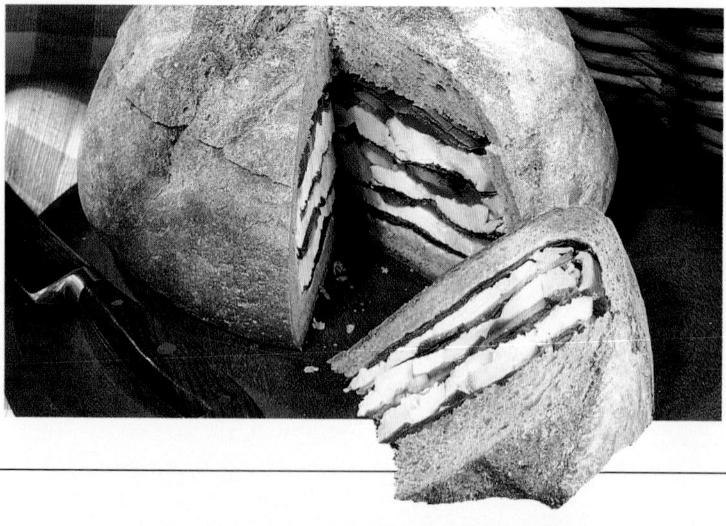
Whole-Wheat Loaf Filled with Smoked Chicken Salad

Fresh Fruit in a Watermelon Bowl

Aromatic Leg of Lamb

Grilled Vegetables

Caribbean Fish Barbecue

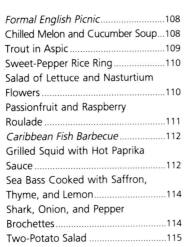

Golden Chicken Salad in a Spaghetti Squash

Food, Friends, and Fresh Air

There is no setting more conducive to the enjoyment of fine food than the great outdoors, the natural environment that is itself the source of all that is good to eat. Out in the open air, appetite is sharpened, and the flavors of fresh ingredients simply prepared are heightened and imbued with a special magic.

As with all meals, the more care that is taken in preparation, the more rewarding will be the results. The choice of dishes, the order in which they will be prepared, their packing and serving—all these considerations must be well thought out before the countdown begins. But beyond these common sense procedures, there are no absolute laws governing the delightful alchemy of outdoor eating. Invite 4 friends or 40. Spread a blanket on the grass and serve sandwiches and lemonade, or set up tables and lay out a princely feast of delicacies on a starched damask cloth. Whether you choose to entertain at a formal garden party or a backyard barbecue, informality and good humor will prevail, and you will find even your starchiest guest relaxing under the open sky.

Picnic or barbecue?

To cook or not to cook is one of the very first questions to be asked by anyone planning to entertain outdoors. Few people can resist the taste of fresh food—meat, poultry, fish, or vegetables—grilled over charcoal in the open air. Cooking over a fire, however, involves time preparing the coals and attending the grill, time that might be spent chatting with your guests if all the food has been prepared ahead of time. Furthermore, outdoor cooking restricts your choice of location. Most barbecue equipment cannot conveniently be carried for long distances and is unsuitable for many sites that are otherwise ideal for picturesque picnics: The rowboat and the rocky ledge are out-of-bounds for a barbecue. When entertaining nearer home, the arguments for outdoor cooking become increasingly persuasive. On the deck or in the backyard, with your kitchen close at hand and a volunteer to help at the grill, cooking over coals may seem the only way to match the mood of a warm summer night.

Cold food is by no means second best. For those who think of picnics in terms of hastily assembled sandwiches from home or stodgy carry-out food, a carefully planned picnic array of cold dishes comes as a revelation. Soups, salads, pâtés, terrines, cold meats, quiches, cakes, ice cream—no other social occasion can so comfortably encompass both elegance and informality as a picnic.

Whatever the menu, there is a sense of celebration about any outdoor meal, a festive atmosphere that tempts even the most weight-conscious guest to come back for a second—and perhaps a third—helping. Eating outdoors gives many people a feeling that they are free of restrictions, and that their diets and calorie charts no longer apply. While the enjoyment of food is always to the good, overeating is never to be encouraged. To prevent backsliding, the most important step you can take is to ensure that all the dishes you offer are prepared with Healthy Home Cooking's nutritional guidelines in mind. Use fresh ingredients to prepare dishes that are low in sodium, cholesterol, and saturated fats, then relax and enjoy your party.

Fresh Ways with Picnics and Barbecues explores the world of healthful outdoor eating at all levels—from simple sandwiches to cold stuffed beef tenderloin; from grilled homemade sausages to spit-roasted leg of lamb. Separate chapters are devoted to picnic food and to grilled specialties, but this is not to imply that picnics and barbecues are in any way mutually exclusive. Many dishes can be precooked on a grill and eaten cold; and a picnic can be enhanced by hot foods prepared on a hibachi or other small, portable grill. Chapter 3 offers a selection of menus that show how dishes and techniques can be imaginatively combined to suit different outdoor occasions. A fourth chapter describes ways in which a cook preparing food for a picnic or barbecue can make use of a versatile ally, the microwave oven.

Planning and packing for picnics

No one knows exactly how or where the word "picnic" first arose. In its earliest sense, some 200 years ago, it described a meal to which each guest contributed a dish. By the mid-19th century the picnic had moved outdoors and acquired its modern meaning. One vestige of its original sense remains, however: A picnic today is often a multicoursed affair, as if several cooks still had a hand in its preparation.

The number of courses and the fact that they must all be packed and transported safely to the picnic site make careful planning essential. Fortunately, most picnic dishes can be prepared a day in advance and stored in the refrigerator overnight—some even improve with keeping. Sandwiches, however, are best made with bread bought on the morning of the picnic and then assembled just before packing. Salad ingredients and dressings should be packed separately and combined immediately before serving, unless a recipe gives instructions otherwise. Terrines, pâtés, and cold roast meat can often be presliced for convenience before packing. Transfer chilled soups directly from the refrigerator to thermoses; soups intended to be served hot should be reheated and poured into thermoses when all the other food and equipment are ready to go.

Rigid containers with tightfitting lids are the picnic packer's best friend. To save space and prevent food from drying out, choose one that most nearly matches the shape and size of the food you are packing. Cake pans, lined with wax paper, serve as useful alternatives. A light wrapping of aluminum foil helps keep sandwiches and presliced food, such as roast meat, moist and compact; alternatively, seal in the flavor and freshness of meat, terrines, or pâtés by wrapping them first in a layer of wax paper, and then covering them tightly in plastic wrap. Large or awkwardly shaped dishes for which you can find no container or pan should be covered with foil or plastic wrap and packed securely and conspicuously at the top of the picnic basket or cooler.

If space is at a premium and you are unable to take a salad bowl with you, make sure that one of your salad containers is large enough to accommodate all the assembled ingredients. A screw-top jar is ideal for salad dressing, but be sure that the lid does not leak, and place it in a plastic bag closed with a twist tie before committing it to the cooler. Plastic bags with twist ties are also useful for crudités and other ingredients that will not crush easily.

Picnic drinks are heavy and awkward to carry for any distance. If you have to walk to reach your picnic site, stick to a simple selection of beverages—mineral water, perhaps, to be served with slices of lime or lemon, and thermoses of iced tea or coffee. Wrap wine bottles in several layers of newspaper; this will protect them from damage and serve as insulation for chilled wine. Or you may prefer wines that come vacuum-sealed in cardboard boxes. Beer, sparkling wines, and carbonated drinks are explosive immediately after a hot, bumpy journey; allow them to rest in a cool place for a while before opening them—or leave them at home for a backyard barbecue.

To keep food and drink cool and secure while traveling to the picnic site, the ideal container is an insulated cooler. Commercially sealed plastic containers of refrigerant gel kept in the freezer overnight are useful for packing around food that must remain chilled and also are handy for picnic foods that have a long, hot journey ahead of them.

If you lack such specialized picnic equipment, a sturdy cardboard box with homemade insulation will serve almost as well. Wrap and pack your food items directly from the refrigerator, then wrap the individual items in newspaper and pack them, surrounded by crumpled newspaper, in the carrying carton. The crumpled newspaper will both keep the food cool and act as a shock absorber. Bubble-wrap plastic packing material and even folded newspapers also serve as effective insulation.

For the outdoor concert or the fashionable sports event, when cardboard packing boxes would appear unseemly, a picnic hamper provides a distinguished note. Hampers are light, rigid carrying cases, generally made of woven willow. They are available empty or fully equipped with food and drink containers, cutlery, and tableware. Knives, forks, and plates conveniently strap to the inside of the cover. However, the traditional, airy hamper provides no insulation for chilled food, and may not be spacious enough to contain all the paraphernalia for a special picnic. Be prepared to supplement your elegant picnic with food from a cooler or cardboard box.

Sturdy paper or plastic plates and cups are adequate for many picnics, but the tone of the occasion—and some say the taste of the food—is improved by pottery or china tableware. Stack china plates securely, interleaved with table napkins or tissue paper to keep them from rattling. Plastic eating utensils are widely available but are not strong enough for all types of picnic food. If weight is not a factor, use stainless-steel cutlery instead. Wrap it in paper towels or table napkins.

Before leaving home, make a list of all the equipment you will need and check that everything is packed. As well as plates and cutlery, you will normally require a cutting board and a sharp knife, serving utensils, a tablecloth, napkins, paper towels, and a large plastic bag for trash. A damp cloth or sponge for wiping hands is also useful. Depending upon your beverages, take a bottle opener or a corkscrew. Consider whether folding lawn chairs and a card table are appropriate for the occasion. Finally, check the weather forecast: Umbrellas, sunscreen, and insect repellent may well be in demand.

Cooking over coals

Because so many barbecues take place just a few steps away from the kitchen, the problems of packing and transportation generally do not arise. The food itself, however, still requires preparation. Cold accompaniments such as salads should be made in advance. The tenderness and flavor of the lean cuts of meat used

The Key to Better Eating

Healthy Home Cooking addresses the concerns of today's weight-conscious, health-minded cooks by offering recipes developed within strict nutritional guidelines.

The chart at right shows the National Research Council's Recommended Dietary Allowances of calories and protein for healthy men, women, and children, along with the council's recommendations for the "safe and adequate" intake of sodium. Although the council has not established recommendations for either cholesterol or fat, the chart includes what the National Institutes of Health and the American Heart Association consider the daily maximum amounts for healthy members of the population. The Heart Association, among other groups, has pointed out that Americans derive about 40 percent of their calories from fat; this, it believes, should be cut to less than 30 percent.

The volumes in the Healthy Home Cooking series do not purport to be diet books, nor do they focus on health foods. Rather, the books express a common-sense approach to cooking that uses salt, sugar, cream, butter, and oil in moderation while including other ingredients that also contribute flavor and satisfaction. The portions themselves are modest in size.

The recipes make few unusual demands. Naturally they call for fresh ingredients, suggesting substitutes should these be unavailable. (Only the original ingredient is calculated in the nutrient analysis, however.) The majority of the ingredients can be found in any well-stocked supermarket; the occasional exceptions can be bought in specialty or ethnic food stores.

Recommended Dietary Guidelines

		Average Daily Intake		Maximum Daily Intake			
		CALORIES	PROTEIN *grams*	CHOLESTEROL *milligrams*	TOTAL FAT *grams*	SATURATED FAT *grams*	SODIUM *milligrams*
Children	7-10	2400	22	240	80	27	1800
Females	11-14	2200	37	220	73	24	2700
	15-18	2100	44	210	70	23	2700
	19-22	2100	44	300	70	23	3300
	23-50	2000	44	300	67	22	3300
	51-75	1800	44	300	60	20	3300
Males	11-14	2700	36	270	90	30	2700
	15-18	2800	56	280	93	31	2700
	19-22	2900	56	300	97	32	3300
	23-50	2700	56	300	90	30	3300
	51-75	2400	56	300	80	27	3300

About cooking times

To help the cook plan ahead effectively, Healthy Home Cooking takes time into account in all of its recipes. While recognizing that everyone cooks at a different speed and that stoves and ovens may differ somewhat in their temperatures, the series provides approximate "working" and "total" times for every dish. Working time stands for the minutes actively spent on preparation; total time includes unattended cooking time, as well as any time devoted to marinating, soaking, cooling, or chilling. Because the recipes emphasize fresh foods, the dishes may take a bit longer to prepare than those that call for canned or packaged products, but the difference in flavor, and often in added nutritional value, should compensate for the little extra time involved.

for recipes in this volume are often improved by letting the meat sit overnight in an acidic marinade. Take meat out of the refrigerator an hour or two before you are ready to cook it, to allow it to reach room temperature; chilled meat can easily burn on the outside before it is sufficiently cooked.

The preparation of the fire for cooking will depend on the type of fuel and grill that you use. The most commonly used fuel for outdoor cooking is charcoal, which can be burned either in a permanent outdoor fireplace of brick or stone or on a portable grill. A wide range of the latter is available from hardware and garden stores, especially in spring and summer; they vary widely in size, sophistication, and expense, but all are similar in principle. The charcoal-fueled portable grill consists essentially of a metal firebox, usually mounted on legs in order to stand at a convenient height, and a chromeplated rack for cooking the food. The firebox often has adjustable vents for controlling combustion; many models include a grate to promote circulation of air under the fuel. The height of the rack can in most cases be adjusted to control the cooking temperature.

Choose a grill adequate for the number of people you intend to entertain. A circular grill 18 inches across will normally suffice for eight guests. Then decide what other features you need—and can afford. A simple windscreen, attached to the firebox rim, is a welcome aid if you are cooking in an exposed location. Collapsible legs make a grill convenient for taking on picnics; alternatively, choose a tabletop model such as the popular hibachi.

Most barbecue grills can be fitted with an electrically driven rotisserie, which brings back the romance of spit-roasting with little of the work.

With the exception of the cast-iron hibachi, most grills are made of sheet metal. Since this must be thick enough to withstand long exposure to high heat, choose a model made of 20-gauge steel or heavier. A porcelain enamel finish is more durable than heat-resistant paint, with which less-expensive models are sometimes finished.

Two types of charcoal are generally available for outdoor cooking. Briquettes are nuggets of pulverized and compressed charcoal; lump charcoal consists simply of unprocessed charcoal pieces. Briquettes take about 45 minutes to reach the correct temperature—15 minutes or so longer than lump charcoal—but they burn hotter and last nearly twice as long. Use enough charcoal to form a bed of coals about 2 inches deep and at least 1 inch wider all around than the area taken up by the food.

A barbecue fire can be lighted with paper and dry sticks, but solid or liquid fire starters speed up the operation. Do not use kerosene or gasoline, which are dangerously flammable and can spoil the flavor of food.

To start the fire, stack the charcoal in a pyramid and use the fire starter as directed. (Never add more liquid fire starter after the charcoal has been ignited.) When the flames have subsided and a white film of ash covers the coals, rake them into an even bed ready for cooking. Check the temperature by holding your hand at rack level. If you are forced to withdraw your hand within two to three seconds, the fire is hot enough to sear meat; if you are able to tolerate about four seconds, the fire is medium hot.

Control the cooking temperature of a grill by raising or lowering the rack. Most of the recipes in this volume are cooked over medium-hot coals, unless otherwise specified. Opening the firebox vents will increase the heat, as will raking the coals together into a compact bed. If it is necessary to replenish the fire, add fresh charcoal around the edges. Toward the end of the cooking time, small branches of rosemary, bay, or sage placed on top of the coals will impart a delicious flavor to any grilled food.

The simplest alternative to charcoal as an outdoor cooking fuel is hardwood. Over glowing wood embers, the food may be cooked on a metal rack supported by homemade walls of bricks. Well-seasoned oak, mesquite, beech, and ash are among the best woods; fruitwoods such as cherry and apple release a delicately scented smoke that flavors the food. Pine, spruce, and other softwoods are not recommended; they burn too quickly and can taint the food with their resinous fumes. The principal disadvantages of wood as a cooking fuel are that it burns at a faster rate than charcoal, and that maintaining the fire in the right condition—a glowing bed but no flame—requires skill and constant attention.

At the other end of the scale—centuries away from the wood fire—are gas and electric grills, which require neither wood nor charcoal. Instead, they heat a layer of volcanic rock until it glows like a bed of coals. This heat source gives off no aroma of its own, but fat and juices dripping from the meat create an aromatic smoke that flavors the food. Gas and electric grills require only 10 minutes to heat and are extremely easy to control. For some outdoor cooks, however, they take away half of the fun of a barbecue by removing nearly all of the effort.

Whichever type of fuel or fire you use, make sure that equipment is close at hand before beginning to cook. Turn meat with tongs; a fork will pierce the surface and allow juices to escape. Use a basting brush made with natural bristle—not nylon or plastic, which may melt. Douse flareups caused by dripping fat with a squeeze bottle of water.

After the barbecue, allow the ashes to cool completely before disposing of them. If you are using a portable grill, do not extinguish hot coals with cold water, as this may cause the firebox to warp. The twilight of a barbecue, however, need not be wasted. The embers are ideal for toasted marshmallows, a delicacy that can be prepared—and best appreciated—by children.

1 Individual quiches, filled with mussels and leeks in a golden saffron custard, make an appealing and colorful picnic lunch (recipe, page 52).

The Pleasures of Picnics

A picnic, the most movable of feasts, is defined by its setting, not by what food it consists of. As long as it is eaten outdoors, it may be a snack or a banquet: fruit and cheese or an eight-course meal. The only restrictions are that the food must be convenient to transport and easy both to serve and to eat. The almost infinite range of possibilities is reflected in the 53 recipes in this chapter, which are designed to tempt even the most agoraphobic guest into the open air.

Sandwiches, the ultimate outdoor convenience food, need never be dull. Experiment with fillings and vary the bread—try sourdough, black rye, or poppy seed, for instance. The sandwich ideas on pages 20 to 21 are imaginative meals in themselves. Several other recipes extend the concept of bread and filling: For a change, try the Mediterranean lamb baguettes *(page 23)*—French bread filled with seasoned chopped lamb—or sample the mushroom-stuffed tenderloin of beef enclosed in a hollowed-out loaf of Italian bread *(page 22)*. For guests who prefer to make their own open-face sandwiches or salads, there are a number of recipes for cold meats, roulades, and terrines that can be sliced at the picnic site.

Any food that is wrapped in pastry lends itself to outdoor eating. Round-steak turnovers *(page 49)* are particularly convenient for picnic menus, and international variations on this theme include Indian samosas *(page 48)*, baked rather than deep-fried to keep the fat content low. Greek phyllo pastry, available in ready-made sheets, provides a neat, crisp, low-calorie wrapping for dishes such as mushroom strudel *(page 53)* and salmon phyllo parcels *(page 54)*.

Soup may not be a traditional picnic food, but it is easy to transport and to serve. In anticipation of hot summer afternoons, two of the recipes in this chapter are for chilled soups *(pages 12 and 14)*; a third is for a warming saffron and pumpkin soup, which is served with a cheese and herb bread *(page 13)*.

Salads also have a place in the picnic basket. Pack green, leafy ingredients separately and toss them with the dressing and other ingredients just before serving. The taste and texture of a freshly made salad is well worth any extra effort and brings a welcome change of pace to the conventional picnic menu.

Chilled Snow-Pea Soup

Serves 6
Working time: about 40 minutes
Total time: about 3 hours and 30 minutes
(includes chilling)

Calories **70**
Protein **3g.**
Cholesterol **0mg.**
Total fat **4g.**
Saturated fat **1g.**
Sodium **70mg.**

2 tbsp. polyunsaturated margarine
¾ lb. snow peas, stems and strings removed
8 scallions, trimmed and chopped
one 3-oz. potato, peeled and grated
4 tsp. unbleached all-purpose flour
2½ cups unsalted chicken stock (recipe, page 139)
⅛ tsp. salt
freshly ground black pepper
1¼ cups skim milk
10 fresh basil leaves

Melt the margarine in a heavy-bottomed saucepan over medium heat. Set aside four of the snow peas; add the remaining snow peas to the pan, with the scallions and potato. Stir the vegetables for one minute, then add the flour and stir for one minute more. Gradually mix in the stock, and bring it to a boil, stirring continuously. Add the salt and some freshly ground black pepper. Cover the pan, lower the heat, and simmer the mixture for 15 minutes, stirring it occasionally. Remove the pan from the heat.

Purée the mixture in a food processor or blender with the skim milk. Press the purée through a sieve. Finely chop four of the basil leaves and stir them into the soup; reserve the remaining basil leaves for garnish. Allow the soup to cool, then chill it in the refrigerator for at least two hours.

Blanch the reserved snow peas in a saucepan of boiling water. Drain them, refresh them under cold running water, and drain them again thoroughly. Cut the snow peas into thin, diagonal strips.

Pour the soup into a chilled thermos. Pack the snow-pea strips and reserved basil leaves in a small, airtight container or plastic bag. Transport the soup and garnish to the picnic in a cooler.

Garnish each serving with a few slivers of snow pea and a basil leaf.

Saffron and Pumpkin Soup with Parmesan Bread

Serves 8
Working time: about 45 minutes
Total time: about 1 hour and 30 minutes

:alories **210**
rotein **10g.**
:holesterol **5mg.**
otal fat **3g.**
aturated fat **1g.**
odium **280mg.**

¼ tsp. saffron threads, or ⅛ tsp. powdered saffron
¼ tsp. salt
3 cups unsalted vegetable stock (recipe, page 139)
1½ lb. pumpkin or other winter squash, peeled, seeded, and cut into 2-inch cubes
2 strips of orange zest, each about 1 inch long
¼ tsp. freshly grated nutmeg or ground nutmeg
ground white pepper
4 tsp. freshly grated Parmesan cheese for garnish
Parmesan bread
2 cups unbleached all-purpose flour
¾ cup whole-wheat flour
1 tsp. baking soda
¼ cup freshly grated Parmesan cheese
1 tbsp. finely chopped fresh marjoram
1 tsp. dark brown sugar
1½ cups buttermilk

First make the bread. Preheat the oven to 400° F., and lightly grease and flour a baking sheet and an 8-inch round cake pan. Sift the all-purpose flour, the whole-wheat flour, and the baking soda into a mixing bowl, then upend the sifter and rap it on the inside of the bowl to release the bran into the mixture. Stir in the Parmesan cheese and marjoram. In a separate bowl, dissolve the sugar in a little of the buttermilk, then stir in the rest of the buttermilk. Make a well in the center of the dry ingredients and pour the buttermilk into the well. Stir the mixture quickly but thoroughly with a wooden spoon to make a moist dough. Sprinkle the dough with a little flour, gather it up with well-floured hands, and place it in the center of the baking sheet. Shape the dough into a flat round, about 7 inches in diameter. Mark the round into eighths with a sharp knife, scoring about halfway through the dough.

Invert the greased and floured cake pan over the dough, and bake it in the oven for 15 minutes. Remove the pan, and continue baking the bread until it is brown on the bottom and a skewer inserted in the center comes out clean—about 10 minutes more. Let the bread cool on a wire rack.

Meanwhile, prepare the soup. Using a mortar and pestle, grind the saffron threads with the salt; if you are using powdered saffron, stir it into the salt. Bring the stock to a boil in a large, heavy-bottomed saucepan, then add the pumpkin, orange zest, saffron, and salt. Cover the pan, lower the heat, and simmer the pumpkin until it is completely tender—20 to 30 minutes. Remove and discard the orange zest. Lift out the pumpkin cubes with a slotted spoon, and purée them in a food processor with a little of the cooking liquid. Add the remaining liquid and blend it in. Season the soup with the nutmeg and pepper, and pour it immediately into a preheated thermos.

Carry the Parmesan cheese for the garnish in a small screw-top jar, and wrap the bread loosely in paper towels or wax paper. Serve each portion of soup sprinkled with ½ teaspoon of the cheese, and break the bread into eight wedges.

EDITOR'S NOTE: *The bread may be made up to 24 hours in advance of the picnic. Wrap it tightly in foil as soon as it is cool, and store it in the refrigerator.*

Carrot and Cardamom Soup

Serves 8
Working time: about 35 minutes
Total time: about 3 hours (includes chilling)

Calories **75**
Protein **3g.**
Cholesterol **trace**
Total fat **2g.**
Saturated fat **1g.**
Sodium **275mg.**

8 cardamom pods
2 tsp. virgin olive oil
1 onion, coarsely chopped
2 celery stalks, coarsely sliced
1½ lb. carrots (6 to 8 medium), cut into chunks
3 cups unsalted chicken or vegetable stock (recipes, page 139)
¼ lb. cucumber (about ½), peeled and cut into chunks
¾ cup plain low-fat yogurt
½ tsp. salt
freshly ground black pepper
1 tsp. sugar
2 slices whole-wheat bread, crusts removed
celery leaves for garnish
ice cubes for garnish (optional)

Wrap the cardamom pods in a double layer of paper towels and crush them lightly with a rolling pin, to split them. Heat the oil in a large, heavy-bottomed saucepan over medium heat. Add the onion, celery, carrots, and split cardamom pods, and cook the mixture, stirring it occasionally, until the vegetables begin to soften—about three minutes. Stir in 2 cups of the stock, and bring the liquid to a boil. Lower the heat, cover the pan, and simmer the vegetables until the carrots are soft—8 to 10 minutes. Remove the pan from the heat, and let the mixture cool for about 10 minutes.

Purée the cucumber chunks with the cooked vegetable mixture in a food processor or blender. Pour the purée into a bowl and add the remaining stock, then stir in ½ cup of the yogurt, the salt, some pepper, and the sugar. Pass the soup through a coarse sieve to remove the cardamom pods. Refrigerate the soup in a tightly covered container until it is thoroughly chilled—at least two hours, or overnight.

Toast the bread on both sides, then cut it into ¼-inch dice. Place the diced toast, the celery leaves, and the remaining yogurt in separate, small containers. Pour the soup into a chilled thermos, and place some ice cubes, if you are using them, in a well-insulated ice bucket with a tightfitting lid. Place everything in a cooler.

To serve, pour the soup into individual bowls and add a few cubes of ice to each bowl, if you wish. Swirl a spoonful of yogurt on the surface of each portion. Garnish the soup with the celery leaves, and serve with the diced whole-wheat toast.

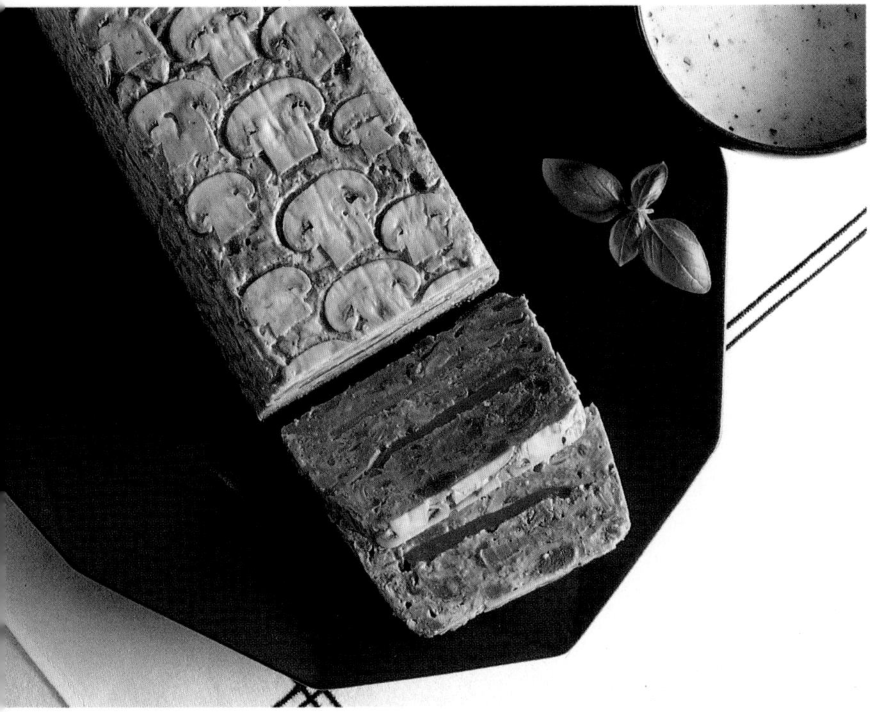

Mushroom Loaf with Basil Mayonnaise

Makes 12 slices
Working time: about 1 hour
Total time: about 12 hours (includes chilling)

Per slice:
Calories **160**
Protein **12g.**
Cholesterol **40mg.**
Total fat **8g.**
Saturated fat **2g.**
Sodium **130mg.**

3 lb. mushrooms with stems, wiped clean
2 tbsp. polyunsaturated margarine
1 large onion, finely chopped
2 large garlic cloves, finely chopped
3 oz. dried ceps (glossary), rinsed thoroughly to remove all grit, soaked in 1 cup warm water for one hour
10 oz. skinned and boned chicken breast, diced
4 thick slices white bread, crusts removed (about ½ oz.), soaked in 6 tbsp. skim milk
2 tbsp. sour cream or crème fraîche (glossary)
2 tbsp. chopped fresh parsley
¼ tsp. salt
freshly ground black pepper
2 large sweet red peppers, peeled (technique, page 138), seeded, and deribbed, trimmed into large rectangles
2 large sweet yellow peppers, peeled (technique, page 138), seeded, and deribbed, trimmed into large rectangles

Basil mayonnaise

1 egg yolk
2 tbsp. safflower oil
3 tbsp. Parmesan cheese, freshly grated
½ cup loosely packed fresh basil leaves, chopped
1 tbsp. skim milk
1 tbsp. plain low-fat yogurt

Reserve six whole mushrooms, and coarsely slice the remainder. Set the mushrooms aside.

Melt the margarine in a large, heavy-bottomed saucepan over medium heat, and sauté the onion and garlic until they are translucent—three to five minutes. Increase the heat to high and add the sliced mushrooms. Sauté the mushrooms, turning them constantly, until they start to release their liquid—two to three minutes. Coarsely chop the ceps and add them to the pan with their soaking liquid. Mix them in well, and boil the mixture rapidly until almost all the liquid in the pan has evaporated and the mushrooms are barely moist—15 to 20 minutes. Remove the pan from the heat and set it aside to cool.

Put the diced chicken breast into a food processor and blend it to a smooth paste. Add the soaked bread and process for 30 seconds, then pour in the sour cream or crème fraîche and process the mixture for 10 seconds more. Fold in the cooled sautéed mushrooms together with the parsley, the salt, and some pepper.

Preheat the oven to 400° F., and line a loaf pan 11 by 4 by 3 inches with parchment paper. Slice the six reserved mushrooms, and arrange the slices in the bottom of the loaf pan in three parallel lines.

Divide the mushroom and chicken mixture into three equal portions. Spoon the first portion into the loaf pan, being careful not to disturb the mushroom slices below; level the surface. On top of this layer place the trimmed red-pepper rectangles, laying them along the length of the pan but keeping them ½ inch in from the sides; trim them further if necessary. (Leaving the border free will prevent the loaf from breaking into layers when it is served.)

Spoon the second portion of the mushroom mixture over the red peppers, smoothing it evenly, and place the trimmed yellow peppers on top of the mixture exactly as you did the red peppers. Top the yellow-pepper rectangles with the final portion of mushroom mixture, smoothing the surface as before.

Place the loaf pan in a roasting pan and pour in sufficient boiling water to come two-thirds of the way up the sides of the loaf pan. Bake the loaf until it is firm to the touch—about 40 minutes—then remove the roasting pan from the oven and allow the loaf to cool in the water bath. Remove the loaf pan from the water bath and refrigerate the loaf overnight in its pan.

To make the basil mayonnaise, whisk the egg yolk in a small bowl until it is thick and creamy, then gradually add the oil in a thin stream, whisking continuously as you do so. Using a mortar and pestle, mash the cheese into the basil, then add this to the egg mixture with the milk and yogurt. Stir the sauce well, and refrigerate it.

When you are ready to go to the picnic, transfer the mayonnaise to a container with a tightfitting lid and pack it, upright, in a cooler. Cover the loaf, still in its pan, with foil, and pack it in the cooler too. To serve the loaf, turn it out onto a flat platter or board and peel off the lining paper. Cut the loaf into slices and serve it with the basil mayonnaise.

Game Terrine Scented with Orange Zest

Serves 10
Working time: about 1 hour
Total time: about 2 days (includes marinating and chilling)

Calories **170**
Protein **26g.**
Cholesterol **50mg.**
Total fat **7g.**
Saturated fat **2g.**
Sodium **175mg.**

1 lb. loin of venison, trimmed of fat and sinew, and cut into 1½-by-½-inch strips
2 oz. thinly sliced bacon
¾ lb. pork tenderloin, trimmed of fat and ground
3 tbsp. fresh white breadcrumbs
1 tsp. chopped fresh thyme
¼ tsp. finely grated orange zest
¼ tsp. freshly grated nutmeg or ground nutmeg
¼ tsp. salt
ground white pepper
12 juniper berries

Spiced port marinade

½ cup ruby port
½ orange, zest only, cut off in strips
4 black peppercorns
¼ tsp. ground mace
2 sprigs thyme
1 bay leaf

First prepare the marinade. Put the port into a small, nonreactive saucepan, and add the orange zest, peppercorns, mace, thyme, and bay leaf. Set the pan over very low heat, and simmer the contents until only 2 to 3 tablespoons of liquid remain—about 10 minutes. Strain the marinade and allow it to cool; reserve the bay leaf for garnish.

Put the strips of venison into a bowl, add the cooled marinade, and toss them together. Cover the bowl and let the meat marinate in the refrigerator for 24 to 72 hours, turning the pieces occasionally.

At the end of the marinating period, lift out the venison pieces with a slotted spoon, and pat them dry with paper towels. Reserve the unabsorbed marinade. Select ¼ cup of irregularly shaped venison strips and set them aside.

Cut one slice of bacon in half crosswise and reserve it for garnish. Combine the rest of the bacon with the ¼ cup of venison strips, and dice both finely. Put the diced meat into a bowl, and add the reserved marinade, the ground pork, breadcrumbs, thyme, orange zest, nutmeg, salt, and white pepper. Stir the ingredients together well.

Preheat the oven to 325° F. Line the bottom and sides of a loaf pan 7½ by 3¾ by 2 inches with parchment paper. Using the back of a tablespoon, press one-third of the pork mixture into the bottom of the pan. Press four juniper berries into the mixture. Arrange about half of the venison strips over the pork layer, placing them end to end, lengthwise, in the pan. Cover the venison strips with another third of the pork mixture, and add four more juniper berries. Repeat the process with the remaining venison strips and pork mixture, shaping the top layer of pork so that it rises slightly in the center. Decorate the terrine by pressing into its surface the reserved bay leaf and bacon slices, and the remaining four juniper berries.

Cover the terrine tightly with a double layer of foil, lightly oiling the section that will come in contact with the terrine. Place the loaf pan in a roasting pan, and pour in sufficient boiling water to come two-thirds of the way up the sides of the loaf pan. Bake the terrine until the juices run clear when a skewer is inserted in its center—one to one and a half hours.

Remove the terrine from its water bath, and loosen the foil around the edges of the pan. Arrange weights totaling about 3½ pounds—either weights from a kitchen scale or unopened cans of food—evenly over the surface of the terrine to compress it, and let it cool to room temperature. When the terrine is cool, remove the weights. Chill the terrine in the refrigerator for at least 24 hours.

Transport the terrine to the picnic in its pan, wrapped in foil and packed inside a cooler. To serve the terrine, turn it out onto a wooden board and slice it with a sharp, serrated knife.

SUGGESTED ACCOMPANIMENTS: *a salad of oakleaf lettuce leaves and orange wedges; crusty bread; red-currant jelly.*

Duck with Blackberries in Port Jelly

Serves 6
Working time: about 50 minutes
Total time: about 6 hours (includes chilling)

Calories **185**
Protein **17g.**
Cholesterol **100mg.**
Total fat **8g.**
Saturated fat **2g.**
Sodium **125mg.**

½ lb. fresh or frozen blackberries
⅔ cup port
1 tsp. light brown sugar
1¼ lb. duck-breast fillets, skinned, all fat removed
¼ tsp. salt
½ tbsp. virgin olive oil
1 large sprig thyme
½ cup unsalted chicken stock (recipe, page 139)
2½ tsp. powdered gelatin
oakleaf lettuce leaves, washed and dried, for garnish
extra blackberries for garnish
6 thyme flowers for garnish (optional)

Put the blackberries into a nonreactive saucepan with the port and sugar. Place the pan over medium heat, and bring the liquid just to a boil. Immediately remove the pan from the heat and set it aside.

Season the duck fillets with the salt. Heat the oil in a heavy-bottomed skillet over medium heat, and add the duck fillets. Sauté them quickly for about one minute on each side to seal them, then add the thyme sprig to the pan.

Lay a flat plate on top of the duck breasts and place a heavy weight on top of the plate. Lower the heat, and cook the duck fillets for about 12 minutes, turning them over after six minutes, until they are cooked through but still slightly pink in the center. Remove the pan from the heat and allow the fillets to cool for at least 45 minutes.

Place a fine sieve on top of a large measuring cup. Pour the blackberries and their juice into the sieve, and allow them to drain; there should be about ¾ cup of liquid in the cup. Strain the juices from the duck fillets into the cup, then stir in the stock.

Put 2 tablespoons of cold water into a small bowl, and sprinkle the gelatin evenly over the surface. Let it stand for about five minutes to allow the gelatin to soften and swell. Set the bowl in a saucepan of gently simmering water, and stir the mixture until the gelatin has completely dissolved. Stir the gelatin solution into the port liquid in the cup.

Rinse out six ½-cup ramekins or other small molds. Pour a little of the port jelly into the bottom of each ramekin, and place them in the refrigerator until the jelly has set—about 20 minutes. Meanwhile, cut the cooled duck breasts into ⅛-inch-thick slices.

Place three blackberries in a row down the center of each ramekin, and place a small slice of duck on each side of the berries. Continue adding blackberries and duck slices to the ramekins in layers, dividing them equally among the six. Pour enough port jelly into each ramekin to completely cover the meat and blackberries. Let the jellies set in the refrigerator for at least four hours, or overnight.

To transport the jellies to the picnic site, cover each ramekin with a double layer of plastic wrap, and stand the ramekins upright in a covered container; pack the garnishes in separate containers. Place all the containers in a cooler. Take a thermos of hot water and a bowl to the picnic with you. To unmold the jellies, pour the hot water into the bowl and briefly dip the bottoms of the ramekins in the water. Invert the jellies onto serving plates. Garnish each plate with a lettuce leaf and a few blackberries, and if you wish, place a thyme flower on top of each jelly.

Chicken and Walnut Mousses

Serves 4
Working time: about 35 minutes
Total time: about 3 hours and 15 minutes
(includes chilling)

Calories **225**
Protein **37g.**
Cholesterol **90mg.**
Total fat **7g.**
Saturated fat **2g.**
Sodium **195mg.**

4 chicken breasts, skinned, boned, and sliced (about 1 lb.)
1 onion, coarsely chopped
⅔ cup plain low-fat yogurt
1 garlic clove, crushed
¼ tsp. ground coriander
⅛ tsp. salt
freshly ground black pepper
2 egg whites
4 pickled walnuts, 2 coarsely chopped, 2 halved for garnish, or 8 walnut halves, 4 coarsely chopped, 4 reserved for garnish

Preheat the oven to 350° F. Lightly oil four ½-cup ramekins or other small, flameproof molds.

Put half of the chicken and half of the onion into a food processor and process them until they are completely smooth—one to two minutes. Transfer the purée to a bowl, then process the remaining chicken and onion and add it to the bowl. Add the yogurt, garlic, coriander, salt, and some freshly ground black pepper, and beat the mixture until it is smooth.

In a separate bowl, beat the egg whites until they form stiff peaks. Stir 2 tablespoons of the egg whites into the chicken purée to lighten the mixture, then fold in the remaining egg white using a rubber spatula.

Fill each ramekin halfway to the top with the mousse. Divide the chopped walnuts into four equal portions and sprinkle a portion into each ramekin. Fill the ramekins with the remaining mousse.

Set the ramekins in a baking pan and pour in sufficient boiling water to come two-thirds of the way up the sides of the ramekins. Place the baking pan in the oven and bake the mousses until they are firm to the touch—35 to 40 minutes. Remove the ramekins from the pan and allow them to cool to room temperature, then chill them for at least two hours.

To transport the mousses to the picnic, cover each ramekin with a double layer of plastic wrap and place the ramekins upright in a covered container. Put the walnut halves into a separate, small, covered container. Pack the containers in a cooler.

To serve, run a knife around the edge of each ramekin, and carefully turn the mousses out onto individual serving plates. Garnish the top of each one with a walnut half.

SUGGESTED ACCOMPANIMENT: *mixed bean salad.*

EDITOR'S NOTE: *Pickled walnuts are available at some gourmet groceries.*

Cucumber Dip

Serves 6
Working time: about 15 minutes
Total time: about 1 hour and 45 minutes (includes chilling)

Calories **60**
Protein **1g.**
Cholesterol **15mg.**
Total fat **5g.**
Saturated fat **3g.**
Sodium **25mg.**

½ cucumber, peeled, seeded, and grated
½ tsp. salt
⅔ cup sour cream
1 cup loosely packed watercress, leaves only, washed, dried, and finely chopped
2 scallions, trimmed and finely chopped
1 fresh green chili pepper, very finely chopped (cautionary note, page 63)
freshly ground black pepper

Place the cucumber in a shallow bowl, sprinkle it with the salt, and let it stand for 30 minutes. Rinse the salt off under cold running water, and drain the cucumber well; lightly squeeze out any excess water.

Put the cucumber into a bowl with the sour cream, watercress, scallions, chopped chili pepper, and black pepper, and mix everything together well. Let the dip rest in the refrigerator for at least one hour before transferring it to a container with a tightfitting lid. Keep the dip in its container in the refrigerator until you are ready to go to the picnic. Pack the container upright in a cooler.

SUGGESTED ACCOMPANIMENT: *a selection of crunchy fresh vegetables.*

Red-Pepper Dip

Serves 6
Working time: about 15 minutes
Total time: about 1 hour and 15 minutes (includes chilling)

Calories **40**
Protein **3g.**
Cholesterol **trace**
Total fat **3g.**
Saturated fat **1g.**
Sodium **130mg.**

2 sweet red peppers (about 7 oz. each)
½ cup plain low-fat yogurt
½ tsp. salt
¼ tsp. cayenne pepper

Place the peppers 2 inches below a preheated broiler and roast them, turning them frequently, until their skin is blistered on all sides. Transfer the peppers to a bowl and cover the bowl with plastic wrap; the trapped steam will loosen the skin. Using a small, sharp knife, peel off the pepper skin in sections *(page 138, Steps 1 and 2)*. Seed and derib the peeled peppers, and chop the flesh coarsely.

Place the chopped red peppers in a food processor and blend them until they are smooth. Put the pepper purée into a bowl and stir in the yogurt. Add the salt and cayenne pepper, mixing well. Let the dip rest in the refrigerator for at least one hour before transferring it to a container with a tightfitting lid. Keep the dip in its container in the refrigerator until you are ready to go to the picnic. Pack it upright in a cooler.

SUGGESTED ACCOMPANIMENT: *a selection of crunchy fresh vegetables.*

Melon and Prosciutto on Poppy-Seed Rolls

Makes 6 filled rolls
Working (and total) time: about 20 minutes

6 crusty poppy-seed rolls
6 tbsp. cream cheese
6 slices peeled melon (about 1½ oz.)
12 thin cucumber slices, halved
6 paper-thin slices prosciutto (about 1½ oz.)
12 sprigs watercress

Per filled roll:
Calories **218**
Protein **7g.**
Cholesterol **50mg.**
Total fat **9g.**
Saturated fat **4g.**
Sodium **468mg.**

Cut the poppy-seed rolls in half and spread 1 tablespoon of cream cheese evenly on each bottom half. On each roll, arrange a melon slice and four pieces of cucumber on top of the cheese, and lay a slice of prosciutto on top of the melon. Add two sprigs of watercress to each roll and replace the top halves.

Spicy Cod and Corn on Sourdough Bread

Makes 6 sandwiches
Working time: about 30 minutes
Total time: about 1 hour and 30 minutes

4½ oz. cod fillet
1¼ cups unsalted vegetable stock (recipe, page 139)
1 tbsp. mayonnaise
2 tbsp. sour cream
½ tsp. garam masala (glossary)
½ tsp. ground turmeric
12 slices whole-wheat sourdough bread
3 oz. frozen corn, blanched in boiling water and drained thoroughly
6 unskinned almonds, cut into slivers with a sharp knife
tiny cress or radish sprouts (glossary)

Per sandwich:
Calories **200**
Protein **11g.**
Cholesterol **13mg.**
Total fat **7g.**
Saturated fat **1g.**
Sodium **350mg.**

Place the fish fillet in a wide, shallow pan, and pour in sufficient vegetable stock to cover it. Cover the pan, and bring the liquid slowly to the simmering point. Simmer the cod until the flesh flakes easily with a fork—three to four minutes. Transfer the cod to a plate and allow it to cool. Flake the fish gently.

Place the mayonnaise and sour cream in a small bowl, and stir in the garam masala and turmeric. Spread this mixture evenly over six of the bread slices. Divide the flaked cod and the corn among the six covered slices, and sprinkle on a few almond slivers. Top each slice with some cress or radish sprouts, and cover it with a second slice of bread.

Chicken, Celery, and Pistachio English Muffins

Makes 6 filled muffins
Working (and total) time: about 25 minutes

6 whole-wheat English muffins
6 tbsp. plain low-fat yogurt
6 oz. skinned cooked chicken breast, cut into strips
1 tbsp. grainy mustard
6 iceberg lettuce leaves, washed and dried
2 small celery stalks, trimmed and thinly sliced
18 pistachios, finely sliced
cayenne pepper for garnish

Per filled muffin:
Calories **200**
Protein **15g.**
Cholesterol **20mg.**
Total fat **4g.**
Saturated fat **1g.**
Sodium **360mg.**

Cut the whole-wheat muffins in half, and spread 1 tablespoon of the yogurt on each bottom muffin half. Spread the strips of chicken breast evenly with the grainy mustard.

Place a lettuce leaf on top of each covered muffin half and divide the chicken strips, celery slices, and pistachios among them. Garnish the filling with a light dusting of cayenne pepper and replace the top halves of the English muffins.

Cottage Cheese, Shrimp, and Red-Pepper Sandwiches

Makes 6 sandwiches
Working (and total) time: about 25 minutes

¾ cup low-fat cottage cheese
1 tbsp. tomato paste
ground white pepper
12 slices whole-wheat bread
3 oz. peeled cooked small shrimp
6 mushrooms, wiped clean and thinly sliced
½ sweet red pepper, peeled (technique, page 138), seeded, deribbed, and sliced into 6 rings
6 chives, finely cut

Per sandwich:
Calories **160**
Protein **12g.**
Cholesterol **30mg.**
Total fat **3g.**
Saturated fat **1g.**
Sodium **450mg.**

Place the cottage cheese in a bowl, and stir in the tomato paste and some white pepper. Spread the cottage cheese mixture evenly over six of the slices of whole-wheat bread, and divide the shrimp, sliced mushrooms, and pepper rings among the covered slices. Scatter some cut chives over the filling, and press a second slice of bread gently on top.

Chinese-Style Beef Sandwiches

Makes 6 sandwiches
Working (and total) time: about 30 minutes

1 whole-wheat baguette, about 2 feet long, cut into 6 equal pieces
3 tbsp. polyunsaturated margarine
1½ tsp. finely chopped fresh ginger
2 tbsp. low-sodium soy sauce
6 slices cold cooked lean beef (about 6 oz.)
1 slice fresh pineapple, peeled, cored, and chopped
1½ oz. (⅓ cup) peanuts, coarsely chopped
3 scallions, trimmed, white parts sliced, green parts cut lengthwise into slivers

Per sandwich:
Calories **335**
Protein **16g.**
Cholesterol **20mg.**
Total fat **14g.**
Saturated fat **4g.**
Sodium **480mg.**

Cut the six baguette pieces in half. In a small bowl, blend together the margarine, fresh ginger, and soy sauce, and spread this mixture evenly over the bottoms of the baguette pieces. Place a slice of beef on each bottom half, then cover the halves with the pineapple, peanuts, and scallions. Replace the top halves of the baguette pieces.

Avocado and Mozzarella Salad on Pumpernickel Bread

Makes 6 sandwiches
Working (and total) time: about 25 minutes

1 small avocado, halved, pitted, and peeled
2 tbsp. fresh lemon juice
ground white pepper
6 fresh basil leaves, shredded
12 slices pumpernickel bread
1½ oz. low-fat mozzarella, sliced
1 large tomato, halved, seeded (technique, page 138, Step 2), and cut into 12 pieces
1 small onion, cut into rings
1 large black olive, pitted and thinly sliced

Per sandwich:
Calories **225**
Protein **8g.**
Cholesterol **5mg.**
Total fat **6g.**
Saturated fat **2g.**
Sodium **400mg.**

Put the avocado into a bowl and mash it with a fork. Add the lemon juice, some ground white pepper, and the shredded basil leaves, and mix these ingredients in thoroughly with the fork.

Spread six pieces of bread evenly with the avocado mixture, then top each one with a sixth of the cheese, tomato, onion, and olive slices. Press a second piece of bread gently onto each filled base.

EDITOR'S NOTE: *The fillings featured on these pages may be teamed with any bread of your choice; each recipe provides sufficient filling for six sandwiches or rolls. Once prepared, the filled sandwiches and rolls should be loosely wrapped in wax paper or plastic wrap and chilled until required. To avoid crushing them, carry them to the picnic site in rigid containers, packed upright inside a cooler.*

Mushroom-Stuffed Beef Tenderloin in a Crusty Loaf

Serves 12
Working time: about 1 hour
Total time: about 11 hours (includes chilling)

Calories **240**
Protein **23g.**
Cholesterol **45mg.**
Total fat **13g.**
Saturated fat **3g.**
Sodium **265mg.**

2½ lb. beef tenderloin in one piece, trimmed of fat
½ lb. oyster or other wild mushrooms, wiped clean and finely sliced
1 tsp. unsalted butter
⅛ tsp. salt
1 tbsp. Dijon mustard
1 tbsp. finely chopped fresh tarragon
freshly ground black pepper
1¼ lb. large spinach leaves, stemmed
1 loaf Italian bread (about 14 oz.)
2 tsp. safflower oil
3 tbsp. sour cream
1½ tbsp. grainy mustard

First make a pocket in the tenderloin. Slice into the meat from one side, cutting about two-thirds of the way through the meat and stopping about ½ inch short of each end. Place the tenderloin on a work surface with the cut side up. Using a meat mallet or a rolling pin, lightly pound the edges of the meat to open up the pocket a little. Set the tenderloin aside while you prepare the mushroom stuffing.

Place the mushrooms, butter, salt, and Dijon mustard in a nonstick saucepan. Cover the pan and cook these ingredients over low heat for about five minutes, until the mushrooms begin to give up their juices. Remove the lid and cook for 5 to 10 minutes more, until all the moisture has evaporated. Cool the mushroom mixture a little, then stir in the tarragon.

Sprinkle the cut surfaces of the meat generously with black pepper, and pack the mushroom stuffing into the prepared pocket. Close up the slit and tie the tenderloin neatly with string at ½-inch intervals. Grind a little more pepper over the tenderloin. Preheat the oven to 475° F.

Cook the spinach leaves in a saucepan of rapidly boiling water until they are just tender—about 30 seconds. Drain the spinach, refresh it under cold running water, and drain it again thoroughly, pressing out as much water as possible without tearing the leaves. Place the leaves on paper towels to dry. When they are dry, lay them out on a large piece of plastic wrap, overlapping them, to form a rectangle large enough to wrap around the tenderloin.

Slice through the loaf of Italian bread on one of its long sides, cutting about halfway through and leaving the other side intact to serve as a hinge. Open out the loaf a little and hollow it to make a cavity; you will need to remove about 1½ cups of crumbs to make sufficient space for the wrapped tenderloin.

Brush the tenderloin all over with the oil and place it in a roasting pan. Roast the tenderloin for 25 minutes for medium-rare meat; for well-done meat, cook it for 10 minutes more. Remove the meat from the oven and allow it to rest for 15 minutes. Cut off and discard the string, and place the tenderloin in the center of the spinach rectangle. Blend the sour cream and grainy mustard, and spread this mixture all over the tenderloin. Using the plastic wrap to lift them, wrap the spinach leaves around the coated tenderloin. Place the wrapped tenderloin inside the hollowed-out loaf, and close up the loaf firmly.

Wrap the stuffed loaf in aluminum foil and place it in a large loaf pan or terrine into which it will fit snugly; if necessary, pack the pan with crumpled foil. Place a brick or a similar weight on top of the loaf, and let it cool completely. Chill the loaf in the refrigerator, still weighted if space allows, for at least eight hours, or overnight.

Transport the loaf to the picnic wrapped in its foil and packed inside a cooler. Cut it into slices with a sharp, long-bladed knife.

SUGGESTED ACCOMPANIMENT: *cherry tomatoes.*

Mediterranean Lamb Baguettes

Makes 24 slices
Working time: about 30 minutes
Total time: about 3 hours (includes chilling)

Per slice:
Calories **95**
Protein **7g.**
Cholesterol **20mg.**
Total fat **4g.**
Saturated fat **2g.**
Sodium **115mg.**

3 small baguettes (about ¼ lb. each)
1 tbsp. virgin olive oil
1 large garlic clove, finely chopped
1 lb. lean lamb from the leg or loin, trimmed of fat and ground or very finely chopped
1 tbsp. tomato paste
4 sun-dried tomatoes (glossary), softened in hot water and finely chopped
¼ lb. zucchini (1 small), blanched and coarsely grated
4 black olives, pitted and finely chopped
2 tbsp. capers, rinsed
1 tsp. finely chopped fresh summer savory, or ½ tsp. dried summer savory
¼ tsp. salt
freshly ground black pepper
3 tbsp. unsalted butter, softened
summer savory sprigs for garnish (optional)

Cut each baguette lengthwise along one side, leaving the other side intact. Open up the baguettes and hollow them out, reserving the crumbs.

Heat the oil in a heavy-bottomed skillet, add the garlic, and cook it over medium heat until it is soft—about five minutes. Add the lamb and cook it, stirring frequently, until no trace of pink remains—about 15 minutes. Stir in the tomato paste and the chopped sun-dried tomatoes, then add the zucchini, olives, and capers. Stir well, reduce the heat to low, and cook the ingredients for two minutes more. Finally, add the savory, the salt, and some freshly ground black pepper, and cook the mixture for 30 seconds more. Remove the pan from the heat, and allow the contents to cool to room temperature—about 20 minutes.

Meanwhile, if the reserved breadcrumbs are not already fairly fine, process them in a blender or food processor until they are fine.

When the lamb mixture has cooled, stir in the breadcrumbs. Open up the baguette shells, and butter the inside of each one. Divide the stuffing among the baguettes, packing it firmly into the hollowed-out cavities. Close the loaves, completely surrounding the filling, and wrap each one tightly in aluminum foil. Chill the stuffed baguettes in the refrigerator for at least two hours.

Transport the baguettes to the picnic still wrapped in their foil and packed inside a cooler, and slice them just before serving. Alternatively, preslice the baguettes at home, then re-form them and wrap them tightly in foil again. Garnish the slices with a few sprigs of summer savory, if you wish.

SUGGESTED ACCOMPANIMENT: *a salad of plum tomatoes, romaine lettuce, and capers, dressed with an olive oil and red wine vinaigrette.*

EDITOR'S NOTE: *Select light brown, soft baguettes for this recipe. Wrapped, stuffed baguettes will keep well in the refrigerator for up to 48 hours. They may also be frozen for up to two months. To thaw a stuffed baguette, remove it from the freezer and allow it to stand, wrapped in its foil covering, at room temperature for two hours. Place the thawed baguette, still in its foil, in a preheated 425° F. oven for 10 to 15 minutes to warm it.*

Crab and Avocado Stacked Sandwiches

Serves 6
Working time: about 35 minutes
Total time: about 2 hours (includes chilling)

Calories **270**
Protein **14g.**
Cholesterol **30mg.**
Total fat **10g.**
Saturated fat **2g.**
Sodium **520mg.**

1 small unsliced pumpernickel sandwich loaf, crusts removed
1 small unsliced whole-wheat sandwich loaf, crusts removed
1 small unsliced white sandwich loaf, crusts removed

Crab filling

⅓ cup plain low-fat yogurt
6 oz. crabmeat, picked over
1 tbsp. tomato paste
½ tsp. dark brown sugar
1 tsp. sherry vinegar
⅛ tsp. cayenne pepper

Avocado filling

1 cup loosely packed watercress leaves, blanched, drained, and squeezed dry
one ¼-lb. avocado, peeled and pitted, sprinkled with 1 tsp. fresh lemon juice to prevent discoloration
⅓ cup plain low-fat yogurt
1 tbsp. finely chopped fresh lemon balm (glossary), optional
ground white pepper

Cut off and discard the rounded tops of the loaves. Slice each loaf lengthwise into three equal rectangles. Trim all the bread rectangles so that they are exactly the same size, and set them aside.

To prepare the crab filling, mix the yogurt with the crabmeat, tomato paste, brown sugar, vinegar, and cayenne pepper. Chill the mixture in the refrigerator until it is firm—about one hour.

For the avocado filling, chop the watercress leaves finely and place them in a food processor. Add the avocado, and process the mixture until it is smooth. Add the yogurt, lemon balm, if you are using it, and some white pepper, and apply a few quick, short bursts of power to amalgamate the ingredients. Chill the mixture until it is firm—30 minutes to one hour.

Divide the crab filling among the three pumpernickel rectangles, and spread it right up to the edges. Spread the avocado filling over the whole-wheat bread rectangles in the same way. Lay each whole-wheat slice on a pumpernickel slice, filling side up, and top the stacks with the white bread slices. Wrap the sandwich loaves in plastic wrap or wax paper, and chill them for at least 30 minutes. Pack the loaves in a cooler to transport them to the picnic.

Unwrap the sandwich loaves just before they are to be served, and cut them into slices using a sharp, serrated bread knife.

Whole-Wheat Loaf Filled with Smoked Chicken Salad

Serves 8
Working time: about 1 hour
Total time: about 9 hours (includes chilling)

Calories **190**
Protein **22g.**
Cholesterol **45mg.**
Total fat **5g.**
Saturated fat **2g.**
Sodium **400mg.**

1 round whole-wheat loaf, about 7 inches in diameter

1 tbsp. unsalted butter, softened

1 bunch sorrel leaves, stemmed, deveined, washed, and dried

4 garlic cloves, crushed

1 lb. boned and skinned cooked smoked chicken breasts, cut crosswise into thin slices, or one 3-lb. cooked smoked chicken, skinned and boned, meat cut into thin slices, or 1 lb. cooked smoked turkey breast, cut into thin slices

4 firm small tomatoes (about 9 oz.), thinly sliced

¼ cucumber, thinly sliced

½ tsp. salt

freshly ground black pepper

Cut a lid, about 5 inches in diameter, from the top of the loaf. Scoop out most of the crumbs from the center, leaving a crusty shell about ½ inch thick. Using the back of a spoon, spread the butter inside the shell and on the underside of the lid.

Lay about one-quarter of the sorrel leaves in the bottom of the hollowed-out loaf, and spread them with one-quarter of the crushed garlic. Pack one-third of the sliced chicken or turkey on top, followed by one-third of the tomato and cucumber slices. Season with a little of the salt and plenty of black pepper. Repeat the layers with the remaining ingredients, finishing with a layer of sorrel and garlic.

Place the buttered lid over the top layer of filling, and wrap the loaf in foil. Set a breadboard on top of the loaf, and weight it down with a brick or several unopened cans of food. Chill the loaf overnight.

Transport the filled loaf to the picnic, still wrapped in its foil, inside a cooler. To serve, remove the foil and cut the loaf into wedges, using a sharp knife.

EDITOR'S NOTE: *The bread removed from the center of the loaf may be used to make fresh breadcrumbs.*

Cheese and Bacon Whole-Wheat Bars

Serves 6
Working time: about 30 minutes
Total time: about 1 hour and 30 minutes
(includes cooling)

Calories **315**
Protein **12g.**
Cholesterol **30mg.**
Total fat **10g.**
Saturated fat **6g.**
Sodium **315mg.**

1½ oz. lean bacon, finely chopped
1 cup whole-wheat flour
1¼ cups unbleached all-purpose flour
3 tsp. baking powder
⅛ tsp. salt
3 tbsp. unsalted butter
1½ oz. sharp cheddar cheese, finely grated (about ½ cup)
1 tbsp. finely grated Parmesan cheese
1 tbsp. chopped fresh oregano, or 1 tsp. dried oregano
1 tbsp. fresh lemon juice
⅔ cup skim milk

Salad filling

½ cup plain low-fat yogurt
¼ head crisp lettuce, sliced
¼ cucumber, thinly sliced
6 scallions, sliced

Preheat the oven to 450° F., and grease and flour a baking sheet.

Put the bacon into a heavy-bottomed, nonstick skillet and cook it over medium heat, stirring frequently, until it is lightly browned—two to three minutes. Transfer the bacon to paper towels to drain and cool.

Put the whole-wheat flour into a mixing bowl and sift in the all-purpose flour, baking powder, and salt. Using your fingertips, rub in the butter until the mixture resembles fine breadcrumbs. Stir in the bacon, the cheddar and Parmesan cheeses, and the oregano. Add the lemon juice to the milk, and using a wooden spoon, gradually mix sufficient liquid into the dry ingredients to make a soft, but not sticky, dough.

Transfer the dough to a floured work surface, and with floured hands, shape it into a rectangle measuring about 10 by 4 inches. Using a metal spatula, lift the dough onto the prepared baking sheet. With a sharp knife, mark the top of the dough rectangle crosswise into six bars, cutting down about ¼ inch into the dough. Bake the dough until it is well risen, firm to the touch, and a light golden brown—about 20 minutes. Allow the bread to cool on a wire rack.

Cut the bread into the six marked bars and split each one in half. Fill the bars with the yogurt and the lettuce, cucumber, and scallion slices. Wrap the filled bars individually in foil or plastic wrap, and pack them in a covered container. Put the container into a cooler to take to the picnic site.

EDITOR'S NOTE: *The baked bread may be frozen, unfilled, for up to two months. Cover the bread tightly in plastic wrap and foil before putting it into the freezer. Thaw it at room temperature for two hours.*

Turkey and Ham Rolls

Makes 8 filled rolls
Working time: about 45 minutes
Total time: about 2 hours and 15 minutes
(includes rising and cooling)

Per filled roll:
Calories **250**
Protein **19g.**
Cholesterol **30mg.**
Total fat **4g.**
Saturated fat **1g.**
Sodium **370mg.**

1 tsp. virgin olive oil
1 onion, chopped
¾ lb. lean boneless turkey, coarsely chopped
⅓ cup dry white wine
6 oz. celeriac, peeled and coarsely grated
6 oz. lean cooked ham, trimmed of fat and cut into ¼-inch dice
1 tbsp. chopped fresh thyme, or 1 tsp. dried thyme leaves
3 tbsp. chopped fresh parsley
2 tbsp. grated horseradish
freshly ground black pepper

Sesame rolls

3 cups unbleached all-purpose flour
½ tsp. sugar
½ tsp. salt
1½ tsp. fast-rising dry yeast
½ cup skim milk
1 egg white
skim milk for glazing
4 tsp. sesame seeds

First make the dough for the rolls. In a large bowl, mix together the flour, sugar, salt, and yeast. Heat the milk in a saucepan until it is hot to the touch—about 110° F.—then pour it into the dry ingredients together with the egg white. Stir to create a soft dough, adding a little warm water if the mixture is too dry. Turn the dough onto a floured surface, and with well-floured hands, knead it gently until it is smooth—about 10 minutes. Place the dough in a clean bowl, cover it with plastic wrap, and let it rise in a warm place until it has doubled in size—about 30 minutes.

Meanwhile, prepare the turkey and ham filling. Heat the oil in a heavy-bottomed saucepan, add the onion, and cook it over medium heat until it is soft—about three minutes. Add the turkey and cook it, stirring continuously, for about five minutes, or until it is cooked through. Blend the turkey and onion mixture with the wine in a food processor until it is finely chopped but not puréed. Transfer the mixture to a bowl and beat in the celeriac, ham, thyme, parsley, horseradish, and some black pepper. Let the mixture cool completely.

Lightly grease a large baking sheet. On a floured work surface, punch down the risen dough to its original size and divide it into eight equal pieces. Roll out one piece into a round about 6 inches in diameter. Brush the edges of the round with water and spoon one-eighth of the turkey filling into the center. Bring the edges of the dough up over the filling and pleat and press them together neatly to seal the filling inside the roll. Place the filled roll, seam side down, on the baking sheet. Use the remaining dough and filling to make another seven rolls and place them on the baking sheet, leaving a ¼-inch gap between the rolls. Cover the filled rolls with lightly greased plastic wrap and let them rise for 20 minutes. Meanwhile, preheat the oven to 400° F.

Glaze the tops of the rolls lightly with skim milk and sprinkle them with the sesame seeds. Bake the rolls until they turn a deep golden color—about 20 minutes. Cool them on a wire rack.

Take the rolls to the picnic site wrapped in foil inside a covered container. Carry the container in a cooler.

SUGGESTED ACCOMPANIMENT: *a salad of shredded cabbage and flat-leaf parsley, dressed with sour cream.*

Individual Tomato Pizzas

Serves 4
Working time: about 45 minutes
Total time: about 3 hours (includes rising and cooling)

Calories **345**
Protein **10g.**
Cholesterol **55mg.**
Total fat **9g.**
Saturated fat **3g.**
Sodium **135mg.**

2 cups unbleached all-purpose flour
¼ tsp. salt
1 tbsp. unsalted butter
1 tsp. fast-rising dry yeast
1 tbsp. safflower oil
½ lb. onions (2 medium), thinly sliced
2 garlic cloves, crushed
1 lb. tomatoes (3 medium), peeled (technique, page 138) and sliced
1 tbsp. tomato paste
1 tbsp. chopped fresh basil, or 1 tsp. dried basil
1 tsp. chopped fresh marjoram, or ¼ tsp. dried marjoram
3 oz. mushrooms, trimmed and sliced (about 1¼ cups)
freshly ground black pepper
¼ sweet green pepper, seeded and deribbed, blanched for two minutes and cut into long, narrow strips
4 quail eggs, hard-boiled, each cut into 4 slices (optional)
1 large black olive, pitted and cut into thin slivers

Sift the flour and ⅛ teaspoon of salt into a mixing bowl, and using your fingertips, rub in the butter until the mixture resembles fine breadcrumbs. Sprinkle in the dry yeast, and mix it in thoroughly. Heat some water in a small pan until it is hot to the touch—about 110° F. Using a wooden spoon, mix sufficient warm water—about ½ cup—into the dry ingredients to form a pliable dough. Turn out the dough onto a lightly floured surface, and knead it for 5 to 10 minutes, until it is smooth. Put the dough into a large, oiled plastic bag, and fold over the top of the bag but do not seal it. Set the dough aside in a warm place to rise for about one hour, until it has doubled in size.

Meanwhile, prepare the topping. Heat the oil in a heavy-bottomed saucepan, and sauté the onions and garlic over low heat until the onions are soft but only very lightly colored—about five minutes. Add the tomatoes and tomato paste, and continue cooking until the tomatoes have broken down—five to eight minutes more. Add the basil, the marjoram, the mushrooms, the remaining salt, and some pepper, and cook the mixture for one to two minutes more, until the mushrooms are soft. Set the filling aside to cool.

Lightly oil four 6- to 7-inch pie or tart pans, and place them on a baking sheet. Punch down the risen dough, and knead it again until it is smooth. Divide the dough into quarters. Keeping the unrolled dough covered with plastic wrap while you are working to prevent it from drying out, roll out each piece of dough in turn into a round about ¼ inch thick, and use the rounds to line the pie pans. Divide the cooled tomato mixture among the rounds, spreading it in an even layer. Set the pizzas aside to rise in a warm place, uncovered, until they are puffy—10 to 15 minutes. Meanwhile, preheat the oven to 425° F.

Bake the pizzas until their edges are lightly browned—about 20 minutes. Remove the pizzas from their pans and let them cool on a wire rack. When they are cool—after about one hour—arrange the strips of blanched green pepper, the slices of quail egg, if you are using them, and the olive slivers in a decorative pattern on top of the pizzas. Return the pizzas to their pans, and wrap each one loosely in a sheet of wax paper to transport to the picnic.

Artichoke Filled with Seafood in a Dill Dressing

Serves 4
Working time: about 1 hour
Total time: about 4 hours (includes marinating)

Calories **230**
Protein **28g.**
Cholesterol **100mg.**
Total fat **11g.**
Saturated fat **3g.**
Sodium **480mg.**

1 garlic clove, halved
3 tbsp. fresh lemon juice
4 medium artichokes
½ lb. salmon trout fillets or salmon fillet
4 large scallops, bright white connective tissue removed
1 shallot, thinly sliced
3 tbsp. dry vermouth
1 tsp. safflower oil
freshly ground black pepper
2 sprigs thyme
¼ lb. crabmeat, picked over and flaked
2 tsp. chopped fresh dill
1 lemon, finely grated zest of one half, the other half sliced for garnish
4 thin slices smoked salmon (about 2 oz.)
dill sprigs for garnish (optional)

Pour 1 gallon of water into a large, nonreactive saucepan, and add the garlic and 1 tablespoon of the lemon juice. Using a stainless-steel knife, cut off and discard the top third and the stem of an artichoke; trim away the small or discolored leaves at the base, and use kitchen scissors to trim off the prickly tips of the leaves. Rinse the artichoke well, then drop it immediately into the pan of acidulated water. Prepare the remaining artichokes in the same way.

Bring the pan of artichokes to a boil, cover the pan, and simmer the artichokes until they are tender—40 to 45 minutes. Drain the artichokes and refresh them under cold running water, then drain them again and leave them upside down on a clean dishtowel.

Meanwhile, preheat the oven to 375° F. and lightly oil a sheet of aluminum foil measuring about 14 by 12 inches. Place the salmon trout fillets or salmon fillet and scallops on the sheet of foil with the shallot, 1 tablespoon of the lemon juice, 2 tablespoons of the vermouth, the oil, some pepper, and the sprigs of thyme. Wrap the foil over to enclose the fish in a parcel. Place the parcel on a baking sheet and put it in the oven for 15 minutes. Let the fish cool in the foil.

Open the cooled foil parcel carefully and drain off and reserve the cooking liquid. Skin the fish and remove any bones, then flake the flesh into neat pieces; place the flaked fish in a bowl. Slice the scallops and add them to the bowl, together with the crabmeat. Strain the reserved cooking liquid, and mix into it the remaining lemon juice and vermouth, the chopped dill, and the lemon zest. Add this mixture to the fish and toss the ingredients lightly. Cover the bowl and marinate the fish in the refrigerator for at least two hours, stirring it gently from time to time.

Form the smoked salmon slices into neat rolls. Remove the choke from each cooled artichoke by spreading apart the top leaves and pulling out the smaller inner leaves, then scraping away the hairy choke with a teaspoon, to expose the artichoke heart. Spoon the marinated fish mixture into the prepared artichokes, and top each one with a smoked salmon roll. Cover the filled artichokes loosely with plastic wrap and chill them until they are needed.

Pack the artichokes, wedged upright, in a covered container. Cut the lemon slices in half and pack them and the dill sprigs, if you are using them, in a separate small, covered container. Transport both containers to the picnic in a cooler.

To serve, garnish the filled artichokes with the halved lemon slices and, if desired, the dill sprigs.

Ginger and Cilantro Fish Balls

Makes 16 fish balls
Working time: about 35 minutes
Total time: about 2 hours (includes chilling)

Per fish ball:
Calories **70**
Protein **11g.**
Cholesterol **25mg.**
Total fat **3g.**
Saturated fat **1g.**
Sodium **150mg.**

1½-inch piece fresh ginger, finely chopped
3 shallots, finely chopped
2 tbsp. dry vermouth
1 tbsp. fresh lemon juice
½ lb. thinly sliced smoked halibut or smoked cod fillet
1 lb. fresh cod fillet, skinned, chopped into 1-inch cubes, and chilled
1½ egg whites, chilled
¼ tsp. salt
1 tbsp. chopped cilantro
ground white pepper
2 tbsp. safflower oil
16 small sprigs cilantro
1 lemon, cut into wedges, for garnish (optional)
salad greens for garnish

Put the ginger and shallots into a small, nonreactive saucepan with the vermouth and lemon juice. Simmer the mixture over low heat until only half of the liquid remains—about two minutes. Allow the mixture to cool while you prepare the fish.

Select the best slices of smoked halibut or smoked cod and cut from them 16 ribbons, each measuring about 3 inches by ½ inch. Store the fish ribbons in the refrigerator until you are ready to use them. Dice the rest of the smoked fish finely.

Put the diced smoked fish and the ginger and shallot mixture in the refrigerator, together with a food processor bowl and blade and a mixing bowl. Chill them for at least 30 minutes.

Using the chilled equipment, process the diced smoked fish with the cubed fresh cod, the egg whites, and the salt until the mixture forms a coarse-textured ball. Transfer the ball to the mixing bowl. Add the chopped cilantro and some white pepper, and mix them in well. Cover the bowl with plastic wrap and return it to the refrigerator for 30 minutes.

Line a steamer with a sheet of aluminum foil large enough to form a cover when the edges are folded over. Oil the foil with a little of the safflower oil.

Divide the chilled fish mixture into 16 portions. Lightly oil your hands and a board with the remaining safflower oil, and roll each portion into a ball on the board. Wrap a ribbon of smoked fish around each ball, and arrange the balls in the foil-lined steamer with the ribbon ends underneath. Place a sprig of cilantro on top of each ball, and fold the aluminum foil over the fish balls to cover them.

Pour enough water into a saucepan to fill it to a depth of 1 inch, and bring the water to a boil. Cover the steamer, and place it over the pan of boiling water. Lower the heat, and steam the balls until they are spongy and firm to the touch—10 to 15 minutes. Remove the foil package from the steamer, and transfer the fish balls to a plate to cool.

Pack the fish balls in a covered container with the lemon wedges, if you are using them; put the salad greens into a plastic bag and secure it with a twist tie. Transport them to the picnic site inside a cooler. Serve the fish balls on a bed of greens.

Seafood and Tagliatelle Salad

Serves 8
Working time: about 45 minutes
Total time: about 1 hour

alories **315**
rotein **26g.**
holesterol **302mg.**
otal fat **7g.**
aturated fat **1g.**
odium **420mg.**

2 lb. very small squid, cleaned and skinned, tentacles reserved
2 tsp. white wine vinegar
12 black peppercorns
2 bay leaves
1 tsp. salt
¾ lb. green tagliatelle
½ lb. peeled cooked small shrimp
1 sweet red pepper, seeded, deribbed, and cut into long julienne
8 large cooked shrimp, peeled, heads and tails left on

Lemon vinaigrette

¼ tsp. salt
2½ tbsp. fresh lemon juice
½ lemon, grated zest only
3 tbsp. virgin olive oil
¼ garlic clove, very finely chopped
¼ tsp. very finely chopped chili pepper (cautionary note, page 63)
2 tbsp. chopped fresh parsley

First make the lemon vinaigrette. Put the salt, lemon juice and zest, olive oil, garlic, chili pepper, and chopped parsley into a screw-top jar, and shake the jar well to combine the ingredients. Refrigerate the vinaigrette until it is needed.

Slice the squid pouches into rings, and cut the tentacles in half crosswise. Bring 1 quart of water to a boil in a nonreactive saucepan with the vinegar, peppercorns, bay leaves, and salt. Add the squid to the pan, and cook it in the boiling water for 30 seconds. Drain it well and set it aside to cool; discard the bay leaves and peppercorns.

Add the tagliatelle to 2 quarts of boiling water with 1 teaspoon of salt. Start testing the pasta after six minutes, and cook it until it is al dente. Drain the pasta and rinse it under cold running water, then drain it well again.

Place the squid, pasta, small shrimp, red-pepper strips, and vinaigrette in a large bowl, and toss them until they are thoroughly combined.

Carry the salad and the garnish of large shrimp to the picnic in separate covered containers inside a cooler, so that both are kept as cold as possible until you are ready to serve the salad. Serve the salad accompanied by the large shrimp.

Chicken, Mango, and Penne Salad

Serves 6
Working time: about 40 minutes
Total time: about 1 hour (includes cooling)

Calories **435**
Protein **30g.**
Cholesterol **60mg.**
Total fat **8g.**
Saturated fat **5g.**
Sodium **160mg.**

4 chicken breasts, skinned and boned (about 1 lb.)
2 tsp. low-sodium soy sauce
¾ lb. penne (or other short, tubular pasta)
½ lb. snow peas, stems and strings removed
2 large mangoes

Cilantro and coconut dressing

¾ cup plain low-fat yogurt
1 tbsp. chopped cilantro
¼ tsp. salt
freshly ground black pepper
3 tbsp. unsweetened coconut flakes

First make the dressing. In a bowl, mix together the yogurt, cilantro, salt, pepper, and coconut flakes. Set the dressing aside.

Put the chicken breasts into a saucepan with 2½ cups of water and the soy sauce; slowly bring the liquid to a simmer. Partially cover the pan, and poach the chicken until the flesh is firm and opaque all the way through when pierced with the tip of a sharp knife—7 to 10 minutes. Remove the chicken breasts from the liquid with a slotted spoon, and set them aside to cool. When they are cool, carve them into slices.

Meanwhile, bring 3 quarts of water to a boil in a large saucepan. Add 2 teaspoons of salt and the penne. Start testing the pasta after eight minutes, and cook it until it is al dente. Drain the pasta, refresh it under cold running water, and drain it again thoroughly. Blanch the snow peas in boiling water, then refresh them under cold running water and drain them well. Peel the mangoes and cut the flesh into slices.

Toss the chicken, penne, and snow peas in the dressing, and pack the mixture in a tightly covered container. Put the mango slices into another covered container. Transport both containers to the picnic site in a cooler, and combine their contents when serving.

Minted Potato and Turkey Salad

Serves 4
Working time: about 30 minutes
Total time: about 40 minutes

Calories **275**
Protein **21g.**
Cholesterol **40mg.**
Total fat **9g.**
Saturated fat **2g.**
Sodium **55mg.**

1 lb. small new potatoes, scrubbed and cut into ½-inch chunks
6 oz. broccoli florets (about 2 cups)
1 red-skinned tart apple
10 oz. cooked skinless turkey breast, cut into ½-inch cubes
¼ lb. carrots (about 2 medium), julienned
3 scallions, trimmed and sliced diagonally into 1-inch pieces
mint sprigs for garnish

Lemon vinaigrette

2 tbsp. safflower oil
2 tbsp. fresh lemon juice
1 tbsp. white wine vinegar
½ lemon, grated zest only
½ tsp. grainy mustard
1 garlic clove, crushed
⅛ tsp. salt
freshly ground black pepper
½ tsp. sugar

Bring a large saucepan of water to a boil, and simmer the potatoes until they are tender but not too soft—about 10 minutes.

Meanwhile, prepare the vinaigrette. In a small, nonreactive bowl, whisk together the oil, 1 tablespoon of the lemon juice, the vinegar, lemon zest, mustard, garlic, salt, plenty of black pepper, and the sugar.

Drain the potatoes well and put them into a large mixing bowl. While the potatoes are still hot, add the dressing and toss them well. Let the potatoes cool.

Parboil the broccoli florets in boiling water for one to two minutes, then drain them, rinse them under cold running water, and drain them again very thoroughly. Quarter and core the apple, cut it into thin slices, and toss the slices in the remaining tablespoon of lemon juice. Add the broccoli florets, apple slices, turkey cubes, carrot sticks, and scallions to the cooled potatoes. Toss all the ingredients together and transfer them to a container with a tightfitting lid. Put the mint sprigs into a plastic bag, and take a small pair of scissors to the picnic as well.

At the picnic, transfer the salad to a serving bowl. Use the scissors to cut one or two mint sprigs into strips over the salad. Finally, garnish the salad with a few whole mint sprigs.

Sesame Chicken Breasts

Serves 8
Working time: about 30 minutes
Total time: about 4 hours and 15 minutes
(includes chilling)

Calories **245**
Protein **21g.**
Cholesterol **50mg.**
Total fat **9g.**
Saturated fat **2g.**
Sodium **205mg.**

2½ cups dry white wine
2 tsp. sugar
1 tbsp. powdered gelatin
1 lb. cooked beets, peeled, sliced, and cut into 1½-inch-long batons
8 small chicken breast halves, skinned and boned (about ¼ lb. each)
6 tbsp. sesame seeds, toasted
½ tsp. ground cardamom
2 tsp. ground cumin
1½ tsp. chili powder
½ tsp. salt
freshly ground black pepper
1 egg white
8 tsp. sour cream for garnish

Put the wine and sugar into a nonreactive saucepan, and bring the wine just to a boil. Pour it into a flameproof bowl and sprinkle on the gelatin, whisking well until the gelatin has dissolved. Let the gelatin solution cool slightly, then stir in the beets. Turn the mixture into a 1-quart container with a tightfitting lid. Refrigerate it, covered, for at least three hours, or overnight, until the gelatin has set.

Preheat the oven to 350° F., and lightly oil a shallow baking dish.

Wipe the chicken breasts on paper towels. Mix together the sesame seeds, cardamom, cumin, chili powder, salt, and some black pepper, and spread this mixture out on a plate. In a small bowl, lightly beat the egg white. Dip each chicken breast into the egg white, then coat it in the sesame-seed mixture, pressing the seeds and spices on with the back of a spoon. Place the breasts, skinned side up, in the baking dish and bake them until they are just cooked through—about 25 minutes. (The juices should run clear when a skewer is inserted in the thickest part of a breast.) Let them cool.

Pack the chicken breasts in a covered container, and spoon the sour cream into another covered container. Cover the jellied beets, and transport all three containers to the picnic in a cooler.

At the picnic site, cut each chicken breast into slices. Serve the chicken with the jellied beets, and garnish each portion of beets with a teaspoon of sour cream.

EDITOR'S NOTE: *To toast sesame seeds, warm them in a heavy-bottomed skillet over medium-low heat until they are golden—about three minutes.*

Summer Lamb with Fava Bean and Nectarine Salad

Serves 8
Working time: about 35 minutes
Total time: about 14 hours (includes marinating)

Calories **250**
Protein **29g.**
Cholesterol **65mg.**
Total fat **12g.**
Saturated fat **4g.**
Sodium **130mg.**

1¾ lb. loin of lamb, trimmed of fat and sinew
2 tsp. virgin olive oil
1½ tsp. pink peppercorns, rinsed, dried, and crushed
¼ tsp. salt
1 tsp. ground cinnamon
1 tsp. ground cumin
½ tsp. ground mace

Fava bean and nectarine salad

14 oz. (about 2½ cups) shelled fresh young fava beans, skinned, or frozen young fava beans, thawed and skinned, or fresh or frozen lima beans
2 nectarines
2 tsp. tarragon vinegar
1 tsp. honey
⅛ tsp. salt
8 fresh mint leaves, finely chopped
1 tbsp. finely chopped fresh tarragon
1 tbsp. virgin olive oil
¼ cup plain low-fat yogurt
pink peppercorns, rinsed and dried, for garnish

Brush the lamb all over with the olive oil, rub it with the crushed peppercorns, and sprinkle it with the salt. Stir together the cinnamon, cumin, and mace, and pat the meat all over with the mixture. Put the lamb into the refrigerator and let it marinate, loosely covered, for about 12 hours, to allow the flavors to develop.

Remove the lamb from the refrigerator 30 minutes before you plan to cook it, and place it in a roasting pan. Preheat the oven to 450° F. Roast the lamb, on the top shelf of the oven, for six to nine minutes for rare to medium meat; turn it over once during roasting. Remove the meat from the oven, cover it loosely with aluminum foil, and let it cool to room temperature. When it has cooled, pour off and reserve the roasting juices. Wrap the meat tightly in the foil, and chill it until it is needed.

To make the salad, cook the fava or lima beans in rapidly boiling water until they are just tender—6 to 10 minutes. Drain them, and set them aside to cool. Slice each nectarine lengthwise into 16 wedge-shaped segments. Put the beans and nectarines into separate lidded containers.

To make the dressing, put the tarragon vinegar into a small, nonreactive bowl. Stir in the honey and salt, then add the chopped mint, the chopped tarragon, the oil, the yogurt, and the reserved roasting juices. Whisk the dressing until all the ingredients are thoroughly amalgamated. Stir the dressing into the beans, and put the lid on the container.

Pack the foil-wrapped meat and the containers of beans and nectarines inside a cooler. Combine the dressed beans and sliced nectarines at the picnic site, just before serving. If possible, slice the meat there too, on a board and using a sharp knife. Alternatively, the meat may be sliced beforehand, then reassembled into one piece and wrapped tightly in foil. Take a small, sealed container of pink peppercorns with you, and garnish each serving with two or three of them.

Pork and Prune Loaf with Minted Onion Relish

Serves 6
Working time: about 45 minutes
Total time: about 8 hours and 45 minutes
(includes cooling and chilling)

Calories **325**
Protein **38g.**
Cholesterol **80mg.**
Total fat **8g.**
Saturated fat **3g.**
Sodium **225mg.**

1 onion, finely chopped
¾ cup fresh whole-wheat breadcrumbs
½ cup pitted prunes, chopped
⅛ tsp. salt
¼ tsp. pumpkin-pie spice
freshly ground black pepper
1 egg white, lightly beaten
2 pork tenderloins (about ¾ lb. each), trimmed of fat and connective tissue

Minted onion relish

1 tart apple, peeled, cored, and cut into pieces
4 onions, sliced
⅓ cup white wine vinegar
2 tbsp. light brown sugar
3 tbsp. chopped fresh mint, plus mint sprigs for garnish

To make the stuffing for the pork loaf, combine the chopped onion, breadcrumbs, and chopped prunes in a mixing bowl. Add the salt, pumpkin-pie spice, and some freshly ground black pepper, then stir in the lightly beaten egg white.

Preheat the oven to 375° F. Place the pork tenderloins on a board and cut a 4- to 5-inch "tail" off the narrow end of each tenderloin. Using a long, sharp knife, slit each larger piece of meat lengthwise, leaving a hinge at one side so that the upper and lower halves remain attached. Slit the two tails in the same way.

Open out one of the larger pieces of tenderloin and spread half of the stuffing over it. Open out the two tenderloin tails and arrange them on top of the stuffing, overlapping their narrow ends if necessary. Spread the remaining stuffing over the tails, then open out the last piece of tenderloin and lay it on top. Tie the layered meat with string at 1-inch intervals, then wrap it in a sheet of foil. Put the foil parcel into a baking dish, and bake it for one and a half hours. Leave the meat in its foil to cool for four to six hours, and then refrigerate it for at least two hours, or overnight.

To make the relish, put the apple and sliced onions into a food processor and chop them finely. Transfer them to a nonreactive saucepan and add the vinegar. Cook the mixture over low heat, stirring frequently, until it is soft and thick—about 20 minutes. Add the sugar and continue cooking until all the liquid has been absorbed—about 10 minutes. Stir in half of the chopped mint and cook for one minute more. Allow the relish to cool to room temperature, and then stir in the remaining mint. Pack the relish in a container with a tightfitting lid, and put the mint sprigs into a small plastic bag.

Cut the chilled pork loaf into 12 slices; it can then be reassembled, wrapped in foil, and carried to the picnic site in a covered container, inside a cooler. Serve the slices with the relish, garnished with sprigs of mint.

SUGGESTED ACCOMPANIMENT: *crisp lettuce leaves.*

Spiced Beef Tenderloin

Serves 12
Working time: about 1 hour
Total time: about 7 hours and 30 minutes
(includes cooling and chilling)

Calories **290**
Protein **30g.**
Cholesterol **65mg.**
Total fat **14g.**
Saturated fat **5g.**
Sodium **240mg.**

1½ oz. pine nuts (6 tbsp.)
2 tbsp. virgin olive oil
1 large onion, finely chopped
3 garlic cloves, crushed
2 tsp. ground coriander
1½ tsp. ground cardamom
1 tsp. ground cumin
3 tsp. paprika
1¼ tsp. salt
⅛ tsp. cayenne pepper
freshly ground black pepper
1 cup raisins
½ lb. mushrooms, chopped
one 3-lb. piece beef tenderloin, trimmed of fat and sinew
2 tbsp. black peppercorns, coarsely crushed
¼ cup finely chopped fresh parsley

First make the stuffing. Put the pine nuts into a dry skillet and cook them over medium heat, shaking the pan frequently, for 30 seconds, or until they are lightly browned all over.

Heat 1 tablespoon of the olive oil in a large, heavy-bottomed skillet over medium heat. Add the chopped onion and cook it until it is soft but not browned—about five minutes. Stir in the garlic, coriander, cardamom, cumin, 2 teaspoons of the paprika, ¾ teaspoon of the salt, the cayenne, and plenty of freshly ground black pepper. Continue cooking for two minutes, then stir in the raisins and mushrooms. Cook the mixture, stirring frequently, until the raisins are plump—10 to 15 minutes more. Remove the pan from the heat, stir in the pine nuts, and allow the stuffing to cool for about 30 minutes.

Preheat the oven to 425° F. Make an incision lengthwise through the center of the tenderloin by inserting a long, thin-bladed carving knife in the meat from the middle of one end and pressing it in as far as possible. Withdraw the knife, and insert a well-scrubbed, round sharpening steel into the slit. Gently rotate the steel, and work it up and down and from side to side until you have created a hole 1 to 2 inches wide. To ensure that the hole is uniform down the length of the tenderloin, it may be necessary to repeat the process from the other end.

With your fingers, carefully push the cooled stuffing into the tenderloin until the hole is completely and compactly filled. Tie the stuffed tenderloin at 1-inch intervals along its length. Season the meat with the remaining salt, and coat it evenly with the crushed black peppercorns.

Heat the remaining tablespoon of oil in a large, heavy roasting pan over medium heat. Lightly brown the tenderloin all over in the hot oil, then transfer the roasting pan to the oven. Cook the tenderloin for 30 minutes for medium-rare meat, basting it every 10 minutes with the pan juices. For well-done meat, cook the tenderloin for 10 minutes more.

Allow the tenderloin to cool at room temperature for one hour, then cover it loosely with foil and refrigerate it for at least four hours, or overnight.

Before packing the tenderloin to take to the picnic, remove the string. Coat the meat evenly with the chopped parsley and sprinkle it lightly with the remaining teaspoon of paprika. Wrap the meat in foil and pack it in a long container. Place the container in a cooler for transport to the picnic.

At the picnic site, set the tenderloin on a board, and use a sharp carving knife to slice the meat.

Stuffed Pork Tenderloin with Peppered Pear Salad

Serves 4
Working time: about 1 hour and 20 minutes
Total time: about 9 hours (includes cooling and chilling)

Calories **315**
Protein **28g.**
Cholesterol **60mg.**
Total fat **12g.**
Saturated fat **3g.**
Sodium **280mg.**

3½ oz. dried pears (about ½ cup)
1 pork tenderloin (about ¾ lb.), trimmed of fat and connective tissue
¼ tsp. salt
freshly ground black pepper
⅛ tsp. ground allspice
2 tsp. grainy mustard
½ tsp. ground cinnamon
¼ tsp. green peppercorns, rinsed and dried
1 tbsp. finely chopped fresh tarragon, or 1 tsp. dried tarragon
½ tsp. virgin olive oil
2 tsp. honey
1 tsp. dry mustard

Peppered pear salad

1 tbsp. honey
3½ tsp. fresh lemon juice
3-inch piece cinnamon stick
1 tsp. green peppercorns, rinsed and dried
4 allspice berries
2 fresh pears
1½ tbsp. virgin olive oil
⅛ tsp. salt
1 lettuce heart, leaves washed and dried
1 cup loosely packed watercress leaves, washed and dried
8 nasturtium flowers for garnish (optional)

Soak the dried pears in 1½ cups of hot water until they are soft—about 20 minutes. Meanwhile, prepare the meat. Using a long, sharp knife, cut the tenderloin lengthwise to a depth of about 1½ inches. Lift the upper section, and deepen the lengthwise cut to within about ⅓ inch of the opposite side. Open out the meat and place it on a sheet of plastic wrap. Cover the tenderloin with a second sheet of plastic wrap. Using the flat side of a meat mallet, pound the tenderloin until it is as thin as possible. Sprinkle the surface with the salt, pepper, and allspice, and set the meat aside.

Remove the dried pears from their soaking liquid; retain the liquid. Pat the pears dry and dice them finely. Mix the diced pears with the grainy mustard, cinnamon, green peppercorns, and tarragon, and spread the mixture along the center of the flattened tenderloin. Close up the tenderloin tightly and tie it with string at 1-inch intervals.

Preheat the oven to 375° F. Brush a heavy, nonstick skillet with the olive oil, and brown the stuffed tenderloin lightly on all sides over a fairly high heat. Brush the meat all over with the honey, sprinkle it with the dry mustard, and wrap it in a double thickness of foil. Roast it in the oven for 40 minutes, then allow it to cool in the foil for four to six hours, until it reaches room temperature. Tighten the foil around the meat and chill it for at least two hours, or until it is needed.

To prepare the salad, put the reserved pear-soaking water into a nonreactive saucepan and add the honey, 3 teaspoons of the lemon juice, the cinnamon stick, peppercorns, and allspice berries. Bring the mixture to a boil, then lower the heat and simmer it for five minutes. Meanwhile, peel and quarter the fresh pears; do not core them yet or they will break up during cooking. Add the pears to the pan, cover them, and simmer them very gently until they are tender—6 to 10 minutes, depending on the ripeness of the pears.

Carefully remove the pears with a slotted spoon and set them aside. Strain the poaching liquid through a fine sieve, return it to the saucepan, and boil it rapidly until only 1½ to 2 tablespoons remain. Allow the liquid to cool, then transfer it to a screw-top jar and shake it with the olive oil, the remaining ½ teaspoon of lemon juice, and the salt.

To pack the salad for carrying to the picnic site, carefully core the pears and put them into a nonreactive container with a lid. Pour a little of the dressing over them—leave the remaining dressing in its jar. Place the lettuce leaves on top of the pears, followed by the watercress leaves. Cover the container. Pack the nasturtium flowers for garnish, if you are using them, in a separate container.

To prepare the meat for the picnic, cut the stuffed tenderloin into 12 slices, then reassemble the roll and rewrap it tightly in foil. Pack it in a container and carry it to the picnic inside a cooler.

Arrange three slices of stuffed tenderloin on each plate. Accompany each serving with two pear quarters and a portion of the dressed green salad, and garnish the plate with two nasturtium flowers, if you wish. Serve the remaining dressing separately.

Marinated Steak Salad with Vegetable Bâtons

Serves 6
Working time: about 45 minutes
Total time: about 6 hours (includes marinating)

Calories **290**
Protein **34g.**
Cholesterol **80mg.**
Total fat **13g.**
Saturated fat **5g.**
Sodium **110mg.**

1 tbsp. safflower oil
1 lb. 10 oz. beef tenderloin, trimmed of fat and sinew
½-inch piece fresh ginger, peeled and finely chopped
2 garlic cloves, crushed
5 tbsp. rice wine or sherry
3 tbsp. low-sodium soy sauce
freshly ground black pepper
½ lb. carrots (about 3 medium)
½ cucumber
2 celery stalks
8 oz. canned bamboo shoots

Preheat the oven to 425° F.

Pour the oil into a large, shallow, flameproof casserole or roasting pan set over high heat. When the oil is hot, sear the meat until it is well browned on all sides—three to five minutes. Place the casserole in the oven and cook the tenderloin, uncovered, for 15 minutes for rare meat, or for up to 30 minutes for medium-rare meat. Remove the tenderloin from the oven, and let it rest and cool for 30 minutes.

In a shallow, nonreactive container, mix together the ginger, garlic, rice wine or sherry, soy sauce, and a grinding of black pepper, to make a marinade. Slice the meat as thinly as possible across the grain, and place the slices in the marinade. Cover the container with a lid or with foil and let the meat marinate in the refrigerator for at least four hours, or overnight, turning it from time to time.

On the day of the picnic, cut the carrots, cucumber, celery, and bamboo shoots into bâtons 1½ to 2 inches long. Combine the prepared vegetables, and put them into a covered container or a plastic bag secured with a twist tie. Pack the containers of vegetables and marinated meat in a cooler.

To serve, transfer the vegetables to individual plates. Lift the slices of beef from the marinade and lay them over the vegetables.

Pasta, Corn, and Leek Salad

Serves 6 as a side dish
Working time: about 20 minutes
Total time: about 30 minutes

Calories **260**
Protein **10g.**
Cholesterol **0mg.**
Total fat **4g.**
Saturated fat **1g.**
Sodium **110mg.**

3 oz. pasta spirals
4 ears of corn, husked, or 1 lb. frozen corn kernels
2 cups white parts of leek, cut into thin rounds
2 large tomatoes, cut into thin wedges
2 black olives, pitted and diced

Mustard-basil dressing

1 tbsp. fresh lemon juice
1 tsp. Dijon mustard
⅓ cup low-fat yogurt
¼ tsp. salt
freshly ground black pepper
¼ cup chopped fresh basil

Cook the pasta spirals in 1 quart of boiling water with 1 teaspoon of salt. Start testing the pasta after six minutes, and continue cooking it until it is al dente. Refresh the pasta under cold running water and drain it thoroughly.

If you are using fresh corn, cook it in a saucepan of boiling water for 6 to 10 minutes, until it is just tender. Refresh the ears under cold running water and drain them well. Using a sharp knife, cut off the corn kernels. If you are using frozen corn, blanch it in boiling water and drain it thoroughly.

Parboil the leeks until they are just tender but still have bite—one to two minutes. Refresh them under cold running water and drain them well.

For the dressing, blend the lemon juice and mustard into the yogurt, then stir in the salt, some pepper, and the basil. Transfer the pasta, corn, and leeks to a lidded, nonreactive container, pour on the dressing, and toss the salad gently to combine the ingredients. Cover the salad and chill it until it is needed.

Put the container of dressed salad into a cooler. Pack the tomato wedges and olive dice in separate small containers, and put these in the cooler too. To serve, arrange the tomato wedges around the edge of a serving bowl, pile the salad in the center, and sprinkle the olive dice over the top.

Artichoke and Asparagus Salad

Serves 8 as a side dish
Working time: about 45 minutes
Total time: about 1 hour

:alories **55**
'rotein **3g.**
:holesterol **trace**
otal fat **3g.**
aturated fat **1g.**
odium **105mg.**

1 lemon, cut in half
4 artichokes
1 lb. thin asparagus, trimmed
1 head red-leaf lettuce, leaves separated, washed, and dried, and torn into large pieces
4 heads Bibb lettuce, cut into 1-by-½-inch chunks, washed and dried

Orange-hazelnut vinaigrette

2 tbsp. fresh orange juice
1½ tbsp. hazelnut oil
1 tsp. grainy mustard
½ orange, grated zest only
½ tsp. salt
freshly ground black pepper

Fill a large, nonreactive pan with water. Squeeze the juice from one lemon half into the pan, then add the lemon half itself.

Remove two or three outer layers of leaves from one of the artichokes to expose the tender, yellow-green inner leaves. Using a stainless-steel knife, slice through the artichoke about 1½ inches above the rounded base and discard the top. Cut off the stem flush with the rounded end of the artichoke, and rub the base with the cut surface of the second lemon half. Pare off the dark green bases of the leaves, then trim away the light green parts from the upper half of the artichoke, moistening the cut surfaces with the lemon half as you work. With a teaspoon, scrape out and discard the hairy choke from the center of the vegetable. Drop the artichoke heart that remains into the pan of acidulated water to preserve its color. Prepare the remaining artichokes in the same way.

Bring the pan of artichoke hearts to a boil, and simmer them until they can be pierced easily with the tip of a sharp knife—10 to 12 minutes. Refresh the artichoke hearts under cold running water, then cut each one into 16 pieces.

While the artichokes are cooking, cook the asparagus in a large, shallow pan of boiling water to cover until it is tender—one to two minutes. Refresh the asparagus under cold running water and drain it thoroughly. Cut the spears diagonally into 1-inch pieces, keeping the tips intact.

Put the red-leaf and Bibb lettuce, the artichoke hearts, and the asparagus into a lidded container, and chill them in the refrigerator until they are needed. Put all the ingredients for the vinaigrette into a screw-top jar, and shake them together well. Store the jar of vinaigrette in the refrigerator.

Pack the container of salad and the jar of vinaigrette inside a cooler. At the picnic site, transfer the salad to a bowl. Pour on the dressing and toss the salad gently just before serving.

Pear, Fennel, and Watercress Salad

Serves 4
Working (and total) time: about 40 minutes

Calories **195**
Protein **6g.**
Cholesterol **10mg.**
Total fat **11g.**
Saturated fat **3g.**
Sodium **305mg.**

2½ oz. light rye or other whole-grain bread (about 2 to 3 slices), crusts removed, cut into ½-inch cubes

2 large ripe pears, cored, diced, and placed in acidulated water

2 oz. Edam cheese, cut into bâtons

¼ lb. fennel bulbs (about 2 small), trimmed and thinly sliced

1½ cups loosely packed watercress, washed and dried, divided into sprigs

Lemon dressing

¼ thin-skinned lemon, coarsely chopped

½ tsp. grainy mustard

1 tbsp. honey

2 tbsp. virgin olive oil

Preheat the oven to 350° F. Arrange the bread cubes on a baking sheet and toast them in the oven until they are golden brown and crisp—about 20 minutes. Let the croutons cool.

To prepare the dressing, put the chopped lemon, the mustard, the honey, and the oil in a food processor or blender. Add 2 tablespoons of water and process the ingredients until they form a creamy purée.

Drain the pears, and place them in a large mixing bowl with the cheese and fennel. Add the lemon dressing and combine everything thoroughly. Transfer the dressed ingredients to a large, nonreactive container with a tightfitting lid. Pack the croutons and watercress in separate containers.

At the picnic site, add the watercress and croutons to the dressed salad, and toss all the ingredients together. Serve the salad at once.

EDITOR'S NOTE: *The cheese bâtons and fennel slices can be prepared and dressed up to 12 hours in advance and stored in the refrigerator.*

Mushroom Ratatouille Salad

Serves 8 as a side dish
Working time: about 30 minutes
Total time: about 2 hours and 15 minutes
(includes cooling)

Calories **75**
Protein **3g.**
Cholesterol **0mg.**
Total fat **4g.**
Saturated fat **1g.**
Sodium **110mg.**

1½ lb. eggplant, cut into ¾-inch pieces
1½ tsp. salt
2 tbsp. virgin olive oil
2 large onions, cut into thin rings
4 garlic cloves, crushed
¼ cup white wine
½ lb. large mushrooms, sliced
3 tbsp. chopped fresh oregano
2 sweet yellow peppers, blanched and cut into 2½-inch-long strips
1 lb. plum tomatoes (about 6), peeled, seeded (technique, page 138), and coarsely chopped into ½-inch pieces
freshly ground black pepper
3 tbsp. chopped fresh parsley

In a bowl, toss the eggplant pieces with 1 teaspoon of the salt. Place the eggplant in a colander and weight it down with a plate small enough to rest on top of the pieces. Let the eggplant drain for 30 minutes to eliminate its natural bitterness. Rinse the eggplant under cold running water to rid it of the salt, and drain it well. Pat the pieces dry on paper towels.

Heat the oil in a large, nonreactive saucepan. Add the onions and cook them over low heat, stirring occasionally, until they are soft but not brown—about eight minutes. Mix in the crushed garlic and cook for one minute more.

Add the eggplant pieces to the pan, pour in the wine, and cook them, uncovered, for 15 minutes. Stir in the mushrooms and oregano, cover the pan, and cook the mixture for five minutes more.

Remove the lid from the saucepan and add the yellow peppers, the tomatoes, the remaining salt, and some freshly ground black pepper. Heat everything through for two minutes, stir in the parsley, and set the pan aside to allow the salad to cool.

Transfer the salad to a covered, nonreactive container to take to the picnic.

Salad of Red Leaves, Beans, and Roots

Serves 12 as a side dish
Working time: about 40 minutes
Total time: about 3 hours

alories **100**
rotein **4g.**
holesterol **5mg.**
otal fat **6g.**
aturated fat **2g.**
odium **75mg.**

6 oz. dried red kidney beans (about ¾ cup), picked over
½ lb. red cabbage, finely shredded
1 small red onion, quartered and finely sliced
2 medium beets, peeled and grated
1 head radicchio, leaves washed and dried
1 oz. Stilton cheese, crumbled
1 tsp. poppy seeds

Walnut vinaigrette

1 tsp. grainy mustard
⅛ tsp. hot red-pepper sauce
⅛ tsp. salt
freshly ground black pepper
2 tbsp. red wine vinegar
¼ cup walnut oil

Rinse the kidney beans under cold running water, then put them into a large saucepan with enough cold water to cover them by about 3 inches. Discard any beans that float to the surface. Cover the saucepan, leaving the lid ajar, and slowly bring the liquid to a boil.

Lower the heat and simmer the beans until they are tender—about one hour. Check the water level from time to time and add more hot water if necessary. Drain and rinse the beans when they are cooked. Dry them thoroughly.

Put the shredded red cabbage into a large bowl with the kidney beans, onion, and beets. Mix these ingredients together well. Next, make the dressing. In a small, nonreactive bowl, whisk together the mustard, hot red-pepper sauce, salt, pepper, vinegar, and walnut oil. Pour the dressing over the salad and toss it well. Transfer the salad to a covered, nonreactive container, and chill it until you are ready to leave for the picnic. Place the radicchio leaves in a plastic bag, and the Stilton in a small, sealed container, and chill these too. Fold the poppy seeds in a sheet of paper towel.

At the picnic, line a large salad bowl with the radicchio leaves. Pile the salad in the center, and sprinkle the Stilton and poppy seeds over the top.

EDITOR'S NOTE: *This salad may also be made with canned red kidney beans; rinse the beans thoroughly before use.*

Green and White Rice Salad

Serves 12 as a side dish
Working time: about 25 minutes
Total time: about 45 minutes

alories **105**
rotein **2g.**
holesterol **0mg.**
otal fat **5g.**
aturated fat **1g.**
odium **123mg.**

2 cups unsalted vegetable stock (recipe, page 139)
¾ cup long-grain rice
14 oz. fresh peas, shelled (about 2½ cups), or ¼ lb. frozen peas, thawed
½ cucumber, cut into ¼-inch dice
1 small zucchini, trimmed and julienned
6 scallions, trimmed and thinly sliced diagonally
1 tbsp. finely cut chives
3 tbsp. chopped fresh parsley
1 large head Bibb lettuce, leaves washed and dried

Tarragon vinaigrette

½ tsp. Dijon mustard
⅛ tsp. salt
freshly ground black pepper
2 tbsp. tarragon vinegar
¼ cup walnut or virgin olive oil

Bring the stock to a boil in a small saucepan and add the rice. Lower the heat to a simmer and cook the rice, covered, until it is just tender and all the stock has been absorbed—15 to 20 minutes. Set the rice aside to cool.

Blanch the fresh peas in boiling water for about 30 seconds; if you are using frozen peas, add them to boiling water and just bring the water back to a boil. Drain the peas, refresh them under cold running water, and drain them again.

Transfer the cooled rice to a large bowl, add the peas, cucumber, and zucchini, and mix the ingredients together well. Stir in the scallions, chives, and parsley.

To make the dressing, whisk the mustard, salt, pepper, vinegar, and oil together in a small, nonreactive bowl. Pour the dressing over the salad, and toss it thoroughly. Place the dressed salad in a covered, nonreactive container to take to the picnic, and chill it until you are ready to leave. Place the lettuce leaves in a plastic bag and chill them too.

At the picnic, line a large serving bowl with the lettuce leaves and pile the salad in the center.

Asparagus and Walnut Frittata

A FRITTATA IS AN OPEN ITALIAN OMELET THAT MAY BE MADE WITH ALMOST ANY VEGETABLE OR HERB FILLING. UNLIKE A FRENCH OMELET, WHICH HAS A MOIST, CREAMY FILLING AND IS USUALLY FOLDED FOR SERVING, A FRITTATA IS COOKED UNTIL IT IS FIRM. THE COMBINATION OF WHOLE EGGS AND EGG WHITES USED HERE PRODUCES A LIGHT RESULT AND A FAT AND CHOLESTEROL COUNT LOWER THAN THAT OF A FRITTATA BASED ON WHOLE EGGS.

Serves 6
Working and (total time): about 30 minutes

Calories **150**
Protein **10g.**
Cholesterol **120mg.**
Total fat **10g.**
Saturated fat **3g.**
Sodium **205mg.**

10 oz. asparagus, trimmed
3 eggs
3 egg whites
1½ oz. Parmesan cheese, freshly grated
1½ oz. walnuts (6 tbsp.), toasted and chopped
2 oz. day-old whole-wheat bread (about 2 slices), crusts removed, soaked for 10 minutes in ¼ cup skim milk
1 tbsp. chopped fresh basil
⅛ tsp. salt
freshly ground black pepper
1 tsp. virgin olive oil or safflower oil

Bring a large, shallow pan of water to a boil. Cook the asparagus in the boiling water for one to two minutes, then drain it, refresh it under cold running water, and drain it again well. Cut the asparagus into 2-inch pieces and set them aside.

Whisk the whole eggs and egg whites with the Parmesan and the chopped walnuts. Add the soaked bread, the basil, and the asparagus pieces to the egg mixture, and season it with the salt and some pepper. Mix the ingredients well.

Heat the oil in a heavy-bottomed, nonstick skillet over medium heat and pour in the mixture; distribute the asparagus pieces evenly in the pan and flatten the mixture with the back of a wooden spoon. Cook the frittata over medium heat until the underside is firm—five to eight minutes. Invert the frittata onto a large plate, then slide it back into the pan and cook the second side for five to eight minutes, or until it, too, is firm and golden brown. Slide the frittata back onto the plate and let it cool.

When you are ready to go to the picnic, wrap the frittata in wax paper and pack it in a rigid container. Serve the frittata cut into wedges.

SUGGESTED ACCOMPANIMENT: *a salad of mixed lettuce leaves dressed with a light vinaigrette.*

EDITOR'S NOTE: *To toast walnuts, spread them out on a baking sheet and place them in a 350° F. oven for five minutes, stirring them occasionally. The frittata may also be served hot.*

Chinese Chicken Pancakes

Makes 12 pancakes
Working (and total) time: about 1 hour and 45 minutes

Per pancake:
Calories **125**
Protein **9g.**
Cholesterol **30mg.**
Total fat **3g.**
Saturated fat **trace**
Sodium **35mg.**

1½ cups unbleached all-purpose flour
1 tbsp. sesame oil
10 oz. skinned and boned chicken breasts
2 shallots, one sliced, the other quartered, sliced lengthwise, and separated into slivers
¼ tsp. five-spice powder (glossary)
ground white pepper
1 tsp. safflower oil
1 large garlic clove, very finely chopped
1 large carrot, halved crosswise and julienned
1-inch piece fresh ginger, finely chopped
1 tbsp. light brown sugar
2 tsp. low-sodium soy sauce
1 tbsp. dry sherry
1 tbsp. malt vinegar or white vinegar
1 tbsp. tomato paste
½ cup unsweetened pineapple juice
2 tsp. cornstarch
½ cup fresh bean sprouts
4 scallions, halved lengthwise and shredded into fine slivers
1 sweet red pepper, seeded, deribbed, and cut into thin strips
6 canned water chestnuts, sliced
12 long chives

Place the flour in a bowl, add ¾ cup boiling water, and mix well with a wooden spoon to form a dough. Let the dough cool for two minutes, then knead it on a lightly floured surface until it is smooth. Form the dough into a long roll and cut it into 12 equal pieces. Shape each piece into a ball. Using a floured rolling pin, roll out each ball on a well-floured surface into a 6-inch round: Flatten the ball with the rolling pin, rotating the dough to keep its circular shape, then roll it out, turning it and pulling it into shape as necessary. Brush off the excess flour from the pancakes, then lightly brush one side of each pancake with a little of the sesame oil and sandwich them together in pairs, oiled side out.

In a heavy-bottomed, nonstick skillet over medium heat, cook one pair of pancakes for one and a half to two minutes on each side, flattening them with a spatula as they cook. Remove them from the pan and gently pull the two pancakes apart, then lay them on a plate oiled side up. Cook the remaining pairs of pancakes in the same way, separating them when they are cooked and stacking them on the plate. Let the pancakes cool, then cover them and chill them until they are needed.

Put the chicken breasts into a small pan with 1 cup of cold water, the sliced shallot, the five-spice powder, and some white pepper. Cover the pan and bring the liquid to a boil, then lower the heat and simmer the chicken gently for 15 minutes. Remove the pan from the heat, turn the chicken pieces over, then set them aside to cool in their cooking liquid.

Remove the cooled chicken from the pan and cut it into long, thin strips; strain and reserve ½ cup of the cooking liquid. Cover the chicken strips and chill them until they are needed.

To make the sauce, heat the safflower oil in a heavy-bottomed, nonstick skillet over medium heat. Add the garlic, shallot slivers, carrot, and ginger, and sauté these ingredients gently for three minutes. In a bowl, mix together the sugar, soy sauce, sherry, vinegar, tomato paste, and pineapple juice, and add the mixture to the skillet. Blend the cornstarch to a smooth paste with 3 tablespoons of the reserved chicken-cooking liquid, and add the remaining liquid to the pan. Bring the contents of the pan to a boil over medium heat, stir in the cornstarch mixture, and simmer the mixture, stirring constantly, until the sauce thickens and clears—about two minutes. Pour the sauce into a bowl and set it aside to cool.

Meanwhile, put the bean sprouts into a flameproof bowl, pour on sufficient boiling water to cover them, and let them soften for 15 seconds. Drain the bean sprouts and refresh them under cold running water, then drain them again thoroughly.

Lay the pancakes, oiled side up, on the work surface. Spread the center of each one with a little of the sauce. Place a bundle of bean sprouts, chicken strips, scallion slivers, red-pepper strips, and water chestnut slices on the sauced area of each pancake, allowing the strips of filling to overhang one edge of the pancake a little. Fold the opposite edge of each pancake over the filling, then fold over the two side sections, enclosing the filling but keeping one end of the pancake open. Tie each filled pancake with a chive to hold it together.

Wrap the pancakes individually in foil or plastic wrap and arrange them in a rigid container. Pack the remaining sauce in a portable container to serve with the pancakes as a dipping sauce. Transport the pancakes and sauce in a cooler.

EDITOR'S NOTE: *For best results, cook the pancakes, chicken, and sauce a day in advance, then assemble and wrap the pancakes on the day of the picnic.*

Baked Vegetable Samosas

UNLIKE TRADITIONAL SAMOSAS, WHICH ARE DEEP-FRIED IN OIL, THESE HEALTHFUL ALTERNATIVES ARE OVEN BAKED. TO FURTHER REDUCE THE FAT AND CALORIES, THE FILLING IS ENCASED IN A SPECIAL LIGHT PASTRY THAT HAS ONLY HALF THE USUAL FAT CONTENT OF SHORTCRUST.

Makes 8 samosas
Working time: about 1 hour
Total time: about 1 hour and 25 minutes

Per samosa:
Calories **170**
Protein **5g.**
Cholesterol **30mg.**
Total fat **7g.**
Saturated fat **2g.**
Sodium **70mg.**

1 potato (about 3½ oz.), peeled and quartered
1 small carrot, quartered lengthwise
1 tsp. safflower oil
2 tsp. fresh lemon juice
1 leek (about 3 oz.), trimmed, washed thoroughly to remove all grit, and finely shredded
1½ oz. frozen peas (about ⅓ cup)
1 fresh hot green chili pepper, seeded and finely chopped (cautionary note, page 63)
¾ tsp. cumin seeds
½ tsp. ground turmeric
¾ tsp. ground coriander
1 small egg, beaten, for glazing
1 tbsp. poppy seeds

Shortcrust pastry

1 cup plus 2 tbsp. unbleached all-purpose flour
6 tbsp. whole-wheat flour
3 tbsp. polyunsaturated margarine
3½ tbsp. skim milk

Bring a saucepan of water to a boil. Add the potat and carrot, lower the heat, and simmer them for 1 minutes. Drain the vegetables, return them to the par and shake them over low heat for a few seconds to dr them off. Allow them to cool a little, then chop ther and set them aside.

Put the oil, lemon juice, leek, peas, chili, cumir turmeric, and coriander into a small, heavy-bottomed nonreactive saucepan. Add 1 tablespoon of water an cook the mixture over low heat for three minutes stirring it frequently. Stir in the potato and carrot, an transfer the vegetables to a plate to cool.

Meanwhile, prepare the pastry. Put the all-purpos flour and the whole-wheat flour into a mixing bow and rub in the margarine with your fingertips until th mixture resembles fine breadcrumbs. Make a well i the center and pour in the milk. Using a woode spoon, mix the ingredients together to form a firn dough. Gather the dough into a ball and knead it o a lightly floured surface until it is smooth. Divide th dough into four equal portions. Form each portion int a ball, then roll out each ball into a round, about inches in diameter. Using a small plate as a guide, trin the edges of the rounds neatly to size, then cut eacl round in half.

Preheat the oven to 375° F. Lightly grease a bakin sheet. Divide the spiced vegetable mixture evenl among the semicircles of dough, mounding it on on half of the semicircle only and leaving a narrow borde free of filling. Lightly dampen the edges of each semi circle with water, then fold the unfilled section o dough over the filling, and press the edges togethe firmly to form neat, triangular parcels. Decorate eacl rounded edge by gently pressing the tip of a pointe knife into the edge.

Brush the samosas lightly with the beaten egg, an sprinkle poppy seeds in two parallel lines across eacl one. Arrange them on the baking sheet. Bake th samosas until they are golden brown—20 to 25 min utes. Cool them on a wire rack.

Pack the cold samosas in a covered container t transport them to the picnic.

SUGGESTED ACCOMPANIMENTS: *scallions and hot lime pickle*

EDITOR'S NOTE: *Chopped onion may be substituted for th leek, if preferred.*

Round-Steak Turnovers

Serves 4
Working time: about 50 minutes
Total time: about 2 hours and 50 minutes
(includes cooling)

Calories **365**
Protein **15g.**
Cholesterol **20mg.**
Total fat **16g.**
Saturated fat **4g.**
Sodium **230mg.**

1 tsp. virgin olive oil
¼ lb. potatoes, peeled and cut into ¼-inch dice (about ¾ cup)
1 medium carrot, cut into ¼-inch dice
3 oz. rutabaga, peeled and cut into ¼-inch dice (about ¾ cup)
1 onion, finely chopped
¼ cup lean round steak, trimmed of fat and connective tissue, and cut into ½-inch dice
1 tbsp. chopped fresh oregano, or 1 tsp. dried oregano
3 tbsp. unsalted veal stock (recipe, page 139) or water
¼ tsp. salt
freshly ground black pepper
1 egg white, beaten

Shortcrust pastry

1½ cups unbleached all-purpose flour
⅛ tsp. salt
4 tbsp. polyunsaturated margarine

Heat the olive oil in a large, heavy-bottomed skillet over medium heat. Add the potatoes, carrots, rutabaga, and onion, and cook the vegetables until they just begin to soften—about 10 minutes. Remove the pan from the heat and allow the vegetables to cool.

Meanwhile, make the pastry. Sift the flour and salt into a mixing bowl, and rub in the margarine with your fingertips until the mixture resembles fine breadcrumbs. Make a well in the center and pour in 3 tablespoons of cold water. Using a wooden spoon, mix the ingredients together to form a firm dough. Gather the dough into a ball and knead it on a lightly floured surface until it is smooth. Divide the dough into four equal portions. Form each portion into a ball, then roll out each ball into a round, about 6 inches in diameter. Using a small plate as a guide, trim the edges of the rounds neatly to size.

Add the diced round steak to the cooled vegetables, then stir in the oregano, the veal stock or water, salt, and some freshly ground black pepper. Place a quarter of the steak and vegetable mixture in the center of each round, and brush the edges with a little of the beaten egg white. Taking one round at a time, carefully bring two opposite sides together until they meet in the center of the filling; press the edges firmly, to seal them. Shape the pastry neatly around the filling, and crimp the joined edges by pinching them between your thumb and forefinger.

Place the turnovers on a baking sheet and refrigerate them for 20 minutes. While the turnovers are chilling, preheat the oven to 425° F.

Brush each turnover with beaten egg white, then bake them until they are golden brown—25 to 30 minutes. Cool the turnovers on a wire rack for at least an hour before packing them in a covered container.

SUGGESTED ACCOMPANIMENTS: *celery sticks; tomatoes.*

Individual Smoked Trout Flans

Makes 6 flans
Working time: about 25 minutes
Total time: about 1 hour and 10 minutes

Per flan:
Calories **160**
Protein **22g.**
Cholesterol **55mg.**
Total fat **15g.**
Saturated fat **3g.**
Sodium **210mg.**

1½ cups whole-wheat flour
6 tbsp. polyunsaturated margarine, chilled
14 oz. skinned smoked trout fillets
½ cup skim milk
3 tbsp. grated horseradish
⅓ cup plain low-fat yogurt
¼ lb. cucumber (1 small), peeled, seeded, and finely diced
1 tbsp. chopped fresh tarragon
1 lemon, finely grated zest and juice
freshly ground black pepper
2 egg whites
6 lemon wedges for garnish
6 sprigs tarragon for garnish

First make the pastry. Put the flour into a large bowl, and rub the margarine into the flour with your fingertips until the mixture resembles fine breadcrumbs. Using a wooden spoon, stir in 3 tablespoons of cold water to make a firm dough. Turn the dough onto a lightly floured surface and knead it until it is smooth. Divide the dough into six portions. Roll out the portions into thin rounds, and use them to line six fluted tart molds about 4 inches in diameter and 1 inch deep. Prick the bottoms and sides of the pastry shells with a fork, and chill them for 20 minutes while you preheat the oven to 400° F.

Meanwhile, place the trout fillets in a large saucepan with the skim milk, and poach them gently until the fish is tender and flakes easily with a fork—about 10 minutes. Drain the fillets and discard the milk; allow the fish to cool.

Bake the pastry shells until the pastry is crisp and lightly browned—20 to 25 minutes. Lower the oven temperature to 325° F.

Flake the smoked trout and put it into a mixing bowl. Add the horseradish, yogurt, cucumber, chopped tarragon, lemon zest and juice, and some black pepper, and mix well. In a separate bowl, beat the egg whites lightly until they begin to form soft peaks. Using a rubber spatula, fold them into the fish mixture. Fill the pastry shells with the fish mixture and bake the flans until they are set in the center—about 15 minutes. Allow the flans to cool completely in their molds, then refrigerate them until they are needed.

When you are ready to go to the picnic, wrap the flans—still in their molds—in several thicknesses of wax paper. Pack them in a covered container and place the container in a cooler. Put the lemon wedges and tarragon sprigs into small plastic bags, and place them in the cooler too.

At the picnic site, remove the flans from their molds, and serve each one garnished with a lemon wedge and a sprig of tarragon.

Zucchini and Camembert Quiche

Serves 8
Working time: about 30 minutes
Total time: about 1 hour and 35 minutes

Calories **250**
Protein **8g.**
Cholesterol **70mg.**
Total fat **13g.**
Saturated fat **3g.**
Sodium **3mg.**

1¼ lb. zucchini (about 4 medium), sliced
1 tsp. polyunsaturated margarine
1 onion, finely chopped
1½ tbsp. chopped fresh basil, or 1½ tsp. dried basil
4½ oz. firm Camembert, rind removed, cut into small pieces
1¼ cups skim milk
2 eggs, beaten
⅛ tsp. salt
freshly ground black pepper
Shortcrust pastry
1¾ cups unbleached all-purpose flour
⅛ tsp. salt
6 tbsp. polyunsaturated margarine, chilled

Preheat the oven to 350° F. Put the zucchini into a lightly oiled baking dish, cover them with foil, and bake them until they are tender—about 20 minutes.

Meanwhile, sift the flour and salt for the pastry into a large bowl, then rub in the margarine with your fingertips until the mixture resembles fine breadcrumbs. Using a wooden spoon, stir in 3 to 4 tablespoons of cold water to make a firm dough. Turn out the dough onto a lightly floured surface and knead it until it is smooth. Roll out the dough, and use it to line a quiche dish 9 inches in diameter and 1 inch deep. Prick the bottom and sides of the pastry shell with a fork, and chill the pastry shell for 20 minutes. Meanwhile, increase the oven temperature to 400° F.

Bake the pastry shell for 15 minutes, then remove it from the oven and set it aside. Lower the oven temperature to 350° F.

Melt the margarine in a heavy-bottomed skillet, and sauté the onion until it is transparent and tender—five to six minutes. Add the chopped basil and cook for one minute more.

Spread half of the onion mixture in the bottom of the quiche shell and cover it with half of the zucchini, then add the remaining onions, followed by the rest of the zucchini. Sprinkle the diced Camembert on top. In a separate bowl, whisk together the milk, eggs, salt, and some freshly ground black pepper. Pour this mixture over the layered vegetables. Bake the quiche until it is set and golden brown —30 to 40 minutes. Allow it to cool completely.

Transport the quiche in its dish, covered with foil. Cut it into wedges for serving.

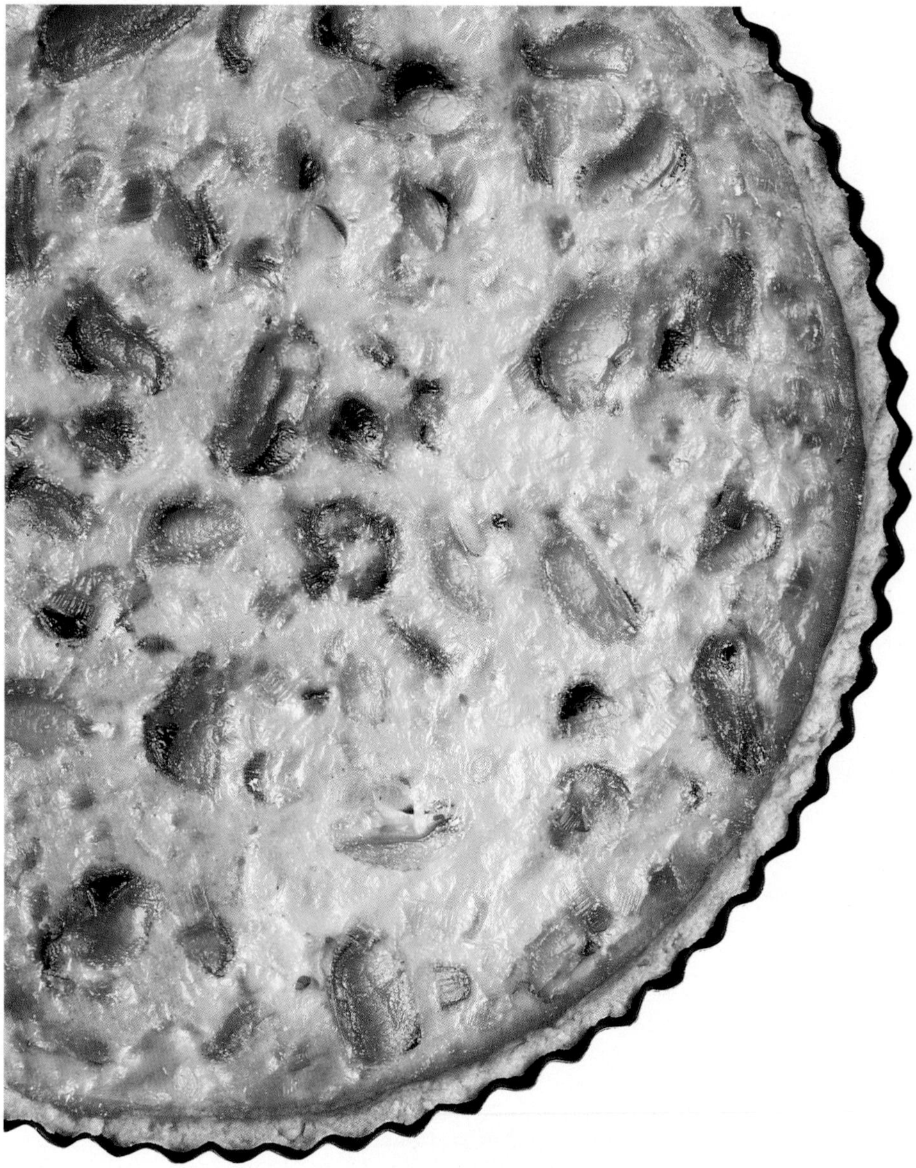

Mussel and Leek Quiche

Serves 12
Working time: about 40 minutes
Total time: about 3 hours

Calories **150**
Protein **10g.**
Cholesterol **80mg.**
Total fat **6g.**
Saturated fat **2g.**
Sodium **135mg.**

3 lb. mussels, scrubbed and debearded
6 oz. small leeks, trimmed to leave 2 inches of green stem, sliced into rings
1¼ cups dry white wine
1 tsp. saffron threads, crushed
2 eggs
1 egg yolk
2 tbsp. crème fraîche (glossary) or sour cream
½ cup skim milk

Yogurt pastry

1 cup plus 2 tbsp. unbleached all-purpose flour
3 tbsp. polyunsaturated margarine, chilled
3 tbsp. sour cream
2 tbsp. plain low-fat yogurt

First prepare the pastry. Put the flour and margarine into a food processor, and process them until fine crumbs are formed. Add the sour cream and yogurt, and process again until the mixture forms a firm, slightly wet ball. Scrape down the sides of the bowl, and gather all the dough into a ball. Wrap the ball in plastic wrap and chill it in the refrigerator for one hour.

Lightly grease a 10-inch tart pan with a removable bottom. Place the ball of dough in the pan. Using a large spoon and your hands, gently flatten and spread the dough to line the pan, pressing it into a smooth, even layer over the bottom and sides. Place the pastry shell in the refrigerator until you are ready to fill it.

For the filling, place the mussels, leeks, and wine in a large, heavy-bottomed, nonreactive saucepan. Bring the liquid to a boil over high heat, then cover the pan and steam the mussels, shaking the pan occasionally, until the shells have opened—three to five minutes. Pour the contents of the pan into a cheesecloth-lined colander set over a bowl, and allow all the liquid to drain into the bowl. Pour the reserved liquid into a clean, nonreactive pan, and add the crushed saffron threads. Boil the liquid until it has reduced to 1 cup, then set it aside and allow it to cool. Remove the mussels from their shells, being sure to discard any that have not opened.

Preheat the oven to 350° F. Beat the eggs and egg yolk together, and then beat in the crème fraîche or sour cream. Add the cooled saffron liquid and the milk. Beat the mixture well.

Arrange the mussels and leeks evenly in the chilled pastry shell, and pour on the saffron custard. Place the quiche in the oven and immediately increase the heat to 400° F. Bake the quiche for 15 minutes, then lower the heat to 350° F. and cook the quiche for 25 to 35 minutes more, until the custard is set and the pastry golden brown. Remove the quiche from the oven and allow it to cool in its pan.

Transport the quiche, still in its pan and covered with foil, in a cooler. At the picnic, unmold it onto a flat platter and serve it cut into wedges.

EDITOR'S NOTE: *This recipe may be adapted to make six individual quiches, as shown on page 10. Use the same amount of pastry to line six 3¾-inch tart pans. For the filling, reduce the quantity of mussels to 2 pounds, and boil the cooking liquid down to ⅓ cup. Prepare the saffron custard in exactly the same way, but use only one egg and no additional yolk, 1 tablespoon of crème fraîche or sour cream, and sufficient skim milk to make ¾ cup of custard.*

Mushroom Strudel

Serves 6
Working time: about 40 minutes
Total time: about 1 hour and 30 minutes
(includes cooling)

Calories **130**
Protein **5g.**
Cholesterol **5mg.**
Total fat **5g.**
Saturated fat **2g.**
Sodium **130mg.**

2 tsp. virgin olive oil
1 large onion, finely chopped
2 garlic cloves, crushed
1 lb. mushrooms, wiped clean and finely chopped
2 tsp. chopped fresh marjoram, or ½ tsp. dried marjoram
1 tsp. Dijon mustard
¾ cup fresh whole-wheat breadcrumbs
½ tsp. salt
freshly grated nutmeg or ground nutmeg
freshly ground black pepper
4 sheets phyllo pastry, each about 18 by 12 inches
1 tbsp. unsalted butter, melted

Heat the oil in a heavy-bottomed saucepan over medium heat. Add the onion and garlic, and cook them until the onion has softened—about five minutes. Mix in the mushrooms, increase the heat to medium high, and cook, stirring, until the mushrooms give up their juices—about three to four minutes. Push the mushrooms to one side of the pan and boil the juices rapidly until they have evaporated—5 to 10 minutes. Stir the marjoram, mustard, breadcrumbs, salt, and some grated or ground nutmeg and black pepper into the mushrooms, and set the mixture aside to cool completely.

Preheat the oven to 400° F. Keeping the sheets you are not using covered with a damp cloth to prevent them from drying out, lay one sheet of phyllo pastry on the work surface, with a long side toward you, and brush it with a little of the melted butter. Lay a second sheet of pastry on top and brush it with a little more of the butter. Repeat the process with the third and fourth sheets of phyllo. Spoon the mushroom filling down the long side of pastry nearest to you, about 2 inches in from the edge, and pack it down lightly with the back of the spoon to form a sausage shape about 1 inch in diameter. Working away from you, roll up the filling inside the pastry. Using two metal spatulas, transfer the strudel to a large, lightly oiled baking sheet. Brush the strudel with the remaining butter and sprinkle it with a little nutmeg. Bake it in the oven until it is crisp and golden—20 to 25 minutes.

Let the strudel cool completely, then transfer it to a shallow, oblong container and cover it with a lid or a sheet of aluminum foil. Alternatively, wrap the strudel in a double thickness of foil. Cut the strudel into slices at the picnic site.

SUGGESTED ACCOMPANIMENT: *a salad of lettuce, tomato, black olives, and onion rings with a parsley and lemon dressing.*

Salmon Phyllo Parcels

Makes 6 parcels
Working time: about 45 minutes
Total time: about 1 hour and 20 minutes
(includes cooling)

Per parcel:
Calories **290**
Protein **27g.**
Cholesterol **70mg.**
Total fat **14g.**
Saturated fat **4g.**
Sodium **140mg.**

6 salmon steaks (about ¼ lb. each)
1 tsp. unsalted butter, melted
¼ tsp. salt
freshly ground black pepper
6 sheets phyllo pastry, each about 18 by 12 inches
12 long chives, 6 finely cut

Watercress dressing

1 oz. watercress, leaves only, finely chopped (about ½ cup)
¾ cup plain low-fat yogurt
1 tbsp. white wine vinegar
⅛ tsp. salt
2 tbsp. skim milk

Using a small, sharp knife, trim away the skin from the salmon steaks. Divide each steak into two boneless pieces by cutting down each side of the backbone and around the ribs. Preheat the broiler to hot. Roll up and tie the two pieces of each steak together with kitchen string to form six "noisettes" of salmon. Place the tied steaks in a broiler pan lined with foil. Brush each one lightly with a little of the melted butter, and season them with the salt and some black pepper. Broil the steaks for about two minutes on each side, or until the flesh is opaque. Drain the steaks thoroughly on paper towels and let them cool—about 30 minutes.

Meanwhile, prepare the watercress dressing. Put the chopped watercress into a mixing bowl, add the yogurt, vinegar, salt, and skim milk, and beat the ingredients together until they form a smooth sauce. Place the bowl in the refrigerator until you are ready to go to the picnic.

Preheat the oven to 400° F., and lightly grease a baking sheet. Using an 8½-inch plate as a guide, cut two large circles from each sheet of phyllo pastry. Keep the uncut sheets of pastry, and the circles as you cut them, covered by damp dishtowels to prevent them from drying out. Place one circle of pastry on the work surface and brush it with melted butter. Place another circle on top, then cover the two with a damp dishtowel. Sandwich the remaining phyllo pastry circles together in pairs in the same way, to give a total of six pairs of circles.

Remove the string from the salmon steaks. Place one steak in the center of each pair of pastry circles, and sprinkle the steaks with the cut chives. Gather the pastry edges up over the salmon steaks. Tie a chive firmly around the neck of each parcel, then carefully open out the pastry layers above the chive to create a decorative effect.

Place the parcels on the baking sheet and brush them with melted butter. Loosely cover the frilly top of each parcel with a piece of foil to prevent it from burning in the oven. Bake the parcels until they are golden brown—about 20 minutes. Cool them on a wire rack, then chill them until they are needed.

When you are ready to leave for the picnic, carefully pack the phyllo parcels in covered containers, surrounding them with crumpled paper towels or wax paper to keep them separate and upright. Place the containers in a cooler. Transfer the dressing to a container with a tightfitting lid, and put it into the cooler too. Serve each parcel with a little dressing.

Veal and Cashew-Nut Rolls

Makes 8 rolls
Working time: about 45 minutes
Total time: about 2 hours (includes cooling)

Per roll:
Calories **135**
Protein **16g.**
Cholesterol **40mg.**
Total fat **4g.**
Saturated fat **1g.**
Sodium **140mg.**

1 lb. lean veal, ground
½ lb. carrots, grated and placed in a sieve to drain
2 oz. cashew nuts (about ½ cup), coarsely chopped
2 oz. pickled gherkins, coarsely chopped (about ¼ cup)
½ lemon, grated zest and juice
1 tbsp. chopped fresh parsley
1 tbsp. chopped fresh sage, or 1 tsp. dried sage
¼ tsp. salt
freshly ground black pepper
4 sheets phyllo pastry, each about 18 by 12 inches
1 tbsp. safflower oil

Put the ground veal into a large mixing bowl. Add the carrots, nuts, gherkins, lemon zest and juice, parsley, sage, salt, and some black pepper. Using a fork or with your hands, combine the ingredients thoroughly. Turn the mixture onto a work surface and divide it into eight equal portions. Roll each portion into a sausage shape about 4½ inches long.

Preheat the oven to 350° F. Line a baking sheet with parchment paper.

Keeping the sheets you are not working with covered by a damp dishtowel to prevent them from drying out, lay one sheet of phyllo pastry on the work surface. Brush it with a little of the oil, and cover it with a second sheet of phyllo. Cut this double sheet of phyllo crosswise into four equal strips, each measuring 12 by 4½ inches. Cover the strips with a damp dishtowel. Repeat the procedure with the remaining two sheets of phyllo pastry.

Lay one of the prepared strips of phyllo on the work surface, and place a portion of veal and cashew-nut stuffing on the strip at one of the short ends. Roll up the pastry and filling tightly. Using a sharp knife, make three diagonal slashes across the top of the roll. Brush the roll with some of the oil and place it on the baking sheet. Use the remaining phyllo strips and stuffing to prepare another seven rolls.

Bake the filled rolls until they are golden brown—50 minutes to one hour. Cool them on a wire rack, then pack them, in a single layer, in a covered container lined with paper towels. Put the container into a cooler to transport to the picnic.

SUGGESTED ACCOMPANIMENT: *scallions and radishes.*

EDITOR'S NOTE: *In this recipe, lamb may be used in place of veal and hazelnuts in place of cashews, if preferred.*

Fresh Fruit in a Watermelon Bowl

Serves 8
Working time: about 45 minutes
Total time: about 2 hours (includes chilling)

Calories **80**
Protein **2g.**
Cholesterol **0mg.**
Total fat **0g.**
Saturated fat **0g.**
Sodium **10mg.**

1 watermelon (about 6½ lb.)
6 ripe figs, washed, stemmed, and cut lengthwise into eighths
½ lb. seedless red grapes, washed and stemmed
2 oranges, juice and grated zest
1 lemon, grated zest only
1 tbsp. ginger syrup, from a jar of preserved stem ginger
2 tbsp. honey

Slice off the top of the watermelon about one-fifth of the way down. Using a large tablespoon, scoop out the flesh from the lid. Remove the seeds and cut the flesh into 1-inch cubes and other similar-size chunks. Reserve the lid.

Run a long-bladed knife around the edge of the large piece of melon between the flesh and the skin, cutting down deeply and keeping as close as possible to the skin. Make a series of deep, parallel cuts, 1 inch apart, across the flesh, followed by a series of similar cuts at right angles to the first. Gently scoop out the long, square sections of flesh. Remove the seeds and chop the flesh into cubes. Use the large spoon to scrape the remaining flesh from the walls of the watermelon shell, and seed it and cut it into pieces in the same way as before. Reserve the watermelon shell. Put all the pieces of watermelon flesh into a large, flameproof bowl, and add the figs and grapes.

In a small, nonreactive saucepan, mix together the orange juice and zest, the lemon zest, the ginger syrup, and the honey. Bring the liquid slowly to a boil and pour it over the fruit. Stir the fruit and syrup together, then let the mixture cool for five minutes. Stir the fruit again, cover the bowl, and place it in the refrigerator for one hour. Turn the fruit over occasionally, to encourage it to absorb the syrup.

To pack the salad, transfer the chilled fruit to the watermelon shell, replace the lid, and wrap the whole assembly tightly in a double layer of plastic wrap. Wedge the filled watermelon upright in a cooler.

EDITOR'S NOTE: *If preferred, the watermelon flesh may be scooped from its shell with a melon baller.*

Goat-Cheese Cake with Fresh Figs

Serves 8
Working time: about 45 minutes
Total time: about 8 hours
(includes chilling)

Calories **165**
Protein **5g.**
Cholesterol **30mg.**
Total fat **8g.**
Saturated fat **3g.**
Sodium **140mg.**

5 oz. soft goat cheese
⅔ cup plain low-fat yogurt
3 tbsp. honey
1 tsp. fresh lemon juice
½ tsp. finely grated lemon zest
½ tsp. pure vanilla extract
⅛ tsp. pure almond extract
1 tbsp. cornstarch
1 tbsp. skim milk
1 egg, separated, yolk lightly beaten, white chilled
2 firm fresh figs, stemmed and quartered
½ oz. sliced almonds (3 tbsp.)

Hazelnut crumb crust

½ cup fresh whole-wheat breadcrumbs, toasted
1 oz. ground hazelnuts, toasted (¼ cup)
2 tbsp. sugar
¼ tsp. ground cinnamon
1 tbsp. apricot preserves without added sugar
1 tsp. polyunsaturated margarine
1 tsp. nut oil (walnut, hazelnut, or almond)

First prepare the hazelnut crumb crust. Line the bottom and sides of a 7-inch-square baking pan with parchment paper. In a mixing bowl, combine the toasted crumbs and hazelnuts with the sugar and cinnamon. Warm the apricot preserves in a small saucepan until they liquefy, whisking them to break up any lumps. Add the margarine and oil to the saucepan, and stir until the margarine melts. Pour the mixture into the dry ingredients and stir it in thoroughly with a wooden spoon. Turn the crumb mixture into the prepared pan and press it down firmly with the back of a spoon. Chill the crust in the refrigerator for at least one hour.

To make the filling, put the goat cheese, yogurt, honey, lemon juice, lemon zest, vanilla extract, and almond extract into a mixing bowl. Beat the mixture with a wooden spoon until it is smooth. Stir the cornstarch into the milk to form a smooth paste. Beat the paste into the cheese mixture, then beat in the egg yolk. Chill the filling in the refrigerator until it thickens—about one hour.

Preheat the oven to 325° F. Beat the egg white until it forms soft peaks, and use a rubber spatula to fold it gently into the chilled filling. Pour the filling over the chilled crust and level it with the back of a spoon. Press the fig quarters into the cheese filling, cut side upward, positioning them in two straight rows so that each serving will contain a fig quarter. Sprinkle the surface of the cheesecake with the sliced almonds.

Bake the cheesecake until the filling is just firm to the touch in the center—about 45 minutes. Leave it in the oven, with the door slightly ajar, to cool and set. Once the cake has reached room temperature, remove it from the oven and chill it for at least four hours.

Cover the cheesecake with plastic wrap or foil and carry it to the picnic site in its pan.

EDITOR'S NOTE: *The breadcrumbs and ground hazelnuts may be toasted at the same time. Spread out the crumbs on one end of a baking sheet and the hazelnuts on the other. Place the baking sheet in a preheated 350° F. oven. Stir the crumbs and hazelnuts occasionally, but keep them separate. Remove the hazelnuts after 10 minutes and the crumbs after 15 minutes. Allow both to cool.*

Mixed-Berry Yogurt Ice

Serves 10
Working time: about 40 minutes
Total time: about 11 hours
(includes freezing)

Calories **200**
Protein **5g.**
Cholesterol **0mg.**
Total fat **1g.**
Saturated fat **trace**
Sodium **65mg.**

1½ lb. mixed berries (blackberries, strawberries, blueberries, raspberries, black currants, red currants, or a combination of any of these), hulled, and stemmed or picked over, as appropriate
1½ cups sugar
3 egg whites
2½ cups plain low-fat yogurt
2 tbsp. Kirsch

Purée the berries in a food processor. Press the purée through a fine sieve and set it aside.

Put ½ cup of water and the sugar into a heavy-bottomed saucepan. Set the pan over medium heat and stir the mixture gently with a wooden spoon to dissolve the sugar; brush down any sugar crystals stuck to the sides of the pan with a pastry brush dipped in hot water.

Warm a candy thermometer in a cup of hot water and place it in the pan. Increase the heat, bring the syrup to a boil, and continue to boil it rapidly until the temperature on the thermometer reaches the hard-ball stage—250° to 266° F.

While the sugar syrup is cooking, beat the egg whites in a large bowl until they form stiff peaks. Beating all the time, pour the boiling sugar syrup into the egg whites in a thin, steady stream, to make a meringue. Continue to beat the meringue mixture vigorously until it is cool—about 10 minutes—then let it stand for five minutes to cool completely.

Measure 1½ cups of the fruit purée and transfer the remainder to a container with a tightfitting lid. Using a rubber spatula, carefully fold the 1½ cups of fruit purée into the cooled meringue, then fold in the yogurt and the Kirsch.

Transfer the mixture to a 1½-quart covered container, smooth it level, and cover it with the lid. Place the container in the freezer, which should be set as low as possible, and allow it to set—10 to 12 hours. Do not remove the yogurt ice from the freezer until you are ready to leave for the picnic.

Transport the yogurt ice and the reserved fruit purée in a cooler lined with ice packs. Serve the ice with the fruit purée.

SUGGESTED ACCOMPANIMENT: *extra berries, carried in a covered, rigid container to prevent crushing.*

Pear and Banana Bread

Serves 8
Working time: about 30 minutes
Total time: about 4 hours (includes cooling)

Calories **300**
Protein **6g.**
Cholesterol **30mg.**
Total fat **8g.**
Saturated fat **2g.**
Sodium **160mg.**

¼ lb. dried bananas, finely chopped
4 tbsp. polyunsaturated margarine
6 tbsp. dark brown sugar
2 cups whole-wheat flour
2 tsp. baking powder
⅛ tsp. salt
1 egg, beaten
1 pear, peeled, cored, and finely chopped

Pear or apple glaze

2 tbsp. honey
2 tbsp. pear or apple butter without added sugar

Put the dried bananas into a saucepan with 1 cup of water. Bring the liquid to a boil, then lower the heat, cover the pan, and simmer the bananas until they are soft—30 to 35 minutes. Using a slotted spoon, transfer the bananas to a plate and allow them to cool for 10 minutes. Strain and reserve the cooking liquid.

Preheat the oven to 350° F. Lightly grease a loaf pan 7½ by 3¾ by 2 inches.

Purée the bananas in a food processor, then add the margarine and sugar, and process again until the mixture is light and fluffy. Transfer this mixture to a mixing bowl and sift in the flour, baking powder, and salt. Add the egg and the pear to the bowl, and mix all the ingredients together thoroughly with a wooden spoon. The batter should be of a soft, dropping consistency; if it is too dry, add a tablespoon or two of the reserved banana-cooking liquid.

Pour the mixture into the prepared pan, level it with the back of a spoon, and bake it until a thin skewer inserted in the center comes out clean—50 minutes to one hour. (If the top of the loaf appears too brown toward the end of the cooking time, cover it with foil or wax paper.) Invert the loaf onto a wire rack and let it cool for about one hour.

To make the glaze, stir together the honey and the apple or pear butter in a small saucepan. Bring the mixture to a boil, lower the heat, and simmer it until it is thick and syrupy—three to four minutes. Allow the glaze to cool for five minutes. Using a pastry brush, paint the glaze lightly over the top of the bread. Let the glazed loaf cool for another hour before wrapping it in foil and packing it in a covered container.

EDITOR'S NOTE: *Dried bananas and pear and apple butters are available from most health-food stores.*

2 *Cornish hens, halved and then marinated in rum, honey, and lime juice and coated in crushed coriander seeds and pepper, cook over hot coals (recipe, page 83).*

New Ways with an Ancient Art

Barbecues not only greatly extend the range of foods that can be enjoyed outdoors, they also make the cooking of the food an integral feature of the meal in which all the guests can share. The 45 recipes in this chapter confirm that 20th-century tastes and innovations, allied with time-honored culinary knowledge, have reestablished this traditional technique as one of the most rewarding means of preparing food.

Ever since food was first cooked on open fires, the mainstay of outdoor cooking has been meat. The lean, prime cuts used in the recipes in this chapter are naturally tender, but even the best steaks or chops, when trimmed of fat and grilled without oily basting liquids, can dry out and become tough over a barbecue's searing heat. For this reason, most of the recipes here call for the meat to be marinated for several hours beforehand. Acidic marinades tenderize the meat, reducing cooking time to a minimum. Yogurt-based marinades are especially useful for low-calorie cooking. Not only does yogurt help tenderize the meat, it also can form a protective coating, allowing thick or unevenly shaped cuts, such as the butterflied leg of lamb on page 67, to cook without drying out.

Even sausages, those frequently fatty and salty standbys of outdoor cooking, can remain part of a nutritious barbecue when made at home. Use only lean meat and keep the texture slightly coarse; too smooth a consistency can cause a lean sausage to dry out when cooking.

Poultry is another staple of the barbecue menu. Threaded on skewers, marinated cubes of chicken cook to perfection over white-hot coals. For even cooking on a grill, a whole bird can be split and flattened *(page 84)*. Alternatively, roast a whole chicken on a spit *(page 82)*, a task made immeasurably easier by the electric rotisserie. Make room for a drip pan under the spit by raking the hot coals to the sides of the barbecue firebox.

Seafood is particularly delicious when cooked over coals. Firm-fleshed fish or shellfish, such as the monkfish, scallops, and shrimp on page 92, can be skewered and cooked as kabobs. More delicately textured fish can be wrapped in foil or lettuce leaves *(pages 90 and 95)* or grilled whole in an enclosed fish basket *(page 96)*. Most seafood cooks quickly over medium-hot coals; the higher temperature required to sear meat will dry out a fish's naturally tender flesh.

Vegetarians will find recipes here too. Kabobs of cheese, fruit, and vegetables *(page 98)* or marinated mixed vegetables baked in foil *(page 100)* make a delicious alternative to a main dish of meat or fish. Round off an outdoor meal with baked apples and chestnuts *(page 102)* before extinguishing the fire.

Mexican Beef Brochettes

Serves 4
Working time: about 25 minutes
Total time: about 5 hours
(includes marinating)

Calories **250**
Protein **27g.**
Cholesterol **55mg.**
Total fat **15g.**
Saturated fat **4g.**
Sodium **155mg.**

1¼ lb. round steak, in 1 or 2 slices about ½ inch thick, trimmed of fat
2 bay leaves
dried bamboo leaves for garnish (optional)
¼ tsp. salt
lime slices for garnish

Cilantro marinade

¼ cup finely chopped onion
1 garlic clove, crushed
1 to 2 red chili peppers, seeded and finely chopped (cautionary note, opposite)
½ tsp. ground cumin
½ tbsp. chopped fresh oregano, or ½ tsp. dried oregano
½ tsp. paprika
½ tsp. ground cinnamon
6 cloves
1 tbsp. sesame seeds
2 tbsp. finely chopped cilantro
1½ tbsp. safflower oil
1 tbsp. fresh lime juice

In a shallow, nonreactive dish, combine all the marinade ingredients. Cut the steak into strips about 6 inches long and ¼ inch wide, and stir them into the marinade together with the bay leaves. Cover the dish and let the meat marinate in the refrigerator for at least four hours, or overnight, turning it once or twice during this time. Remove the steak from the refrigerator at least 30 minutes before cooking.

Soak eight wooden skewers in water for 10 minutes. Thread the strips of marinated meat onto the skewers, sprinkling them with any remaining marinade. Cook the brochettes over hot coals for five to eight minutes, turning them frequently.

Transfer the brochettes to a serving plate, lined with dried bamboo leaves, if you have them, and sprinkle them with the salt. Serve the brochettes garnished with the lime slices.

SUGGESTED ACCOMPANIMENT: *mixed bean and corn salad.*

Steakburgers with Parsnips and Dark Beer

Serves 12
Working (and total) time: about 50 minutes

Calories **130**
Protein **17g.**
Cholesterol **35mg.**
Total fat **5g.**
Saturated fat **2g.**
Sodium **125mg.**

1 cup dark beer
1½ lb. lean steak, trimmed of fat and ground
1 onion, finely chopped
10 oz. parsnips, peeled and finely grated
2 tsp. chopped fresh thyme
2 tbsp. chopped fresh parsley
⅓ cup fresh whole-wheat breadcrumbs
1 tbsp. grainy mustard
½ tsp. salt
freshly ground black pepper

Put the beer into a small, heavy-bottomed, nonreactive saucepan. Bring the beer to a boil, then lower the heat and simmer it until it has reduced to 4 tablespoons—about five minutes. Place the ground steak in a large bowl, and add the onion, parsnips, thyme, parsley, breadcrumbs, mustard, salt, and some pepper. Pour in the beer. Using a wooden spoon, work the ingredients together until they are thoroughly combined.

Divide the mixture into 12 equal portions. Shape each portion into a ball, and flatten each ball into a patty. Lightly oil the rack, and cook the steakburgers over medium-hot coals for seven to eight minutes on each side, until they are just cooked through.

SUGGESTED ACCOMPANIMENT: *grilled sliced red onions and wild mushrooms.*

Chilies—A Cautionary Note

Both dried and fresh hot chilies should be handled with care; their flesh and seeds contain volatile oils that can make skin tingle and cause eyes to burn. Rubber gloves offer protection—but the cook should still be careful not to touch the face, lips, or eyes when working with chilies.

Soaking fresh chilies in cold, salted water for an hour will remove some of their fire. If canned chilies are substituted for fresh ones, they should be rinsed in cold water in order to eliminate as much of the brine used to preserve them as possible.

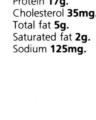

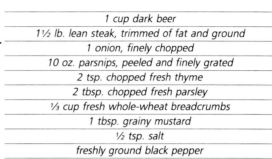

Mustard Steaks with Yogurt Sauce and Belgian Endive Salad

Serves 4
Working time: about 20 minutes
Total time: about 45 minutes

Calories **325**
Protein **45g.**
Cholesterol **100mg.**
Total fat **14g.**
Saturated fat **6g.**
Sodium **125mg.**

4 sirloin steaks (about 5 oz. each), trimmed of fat
2 tbsp. grainy mustard, tarragon flavored if possible
2 garlic cloves, crushed
⅔ cup plain low-fat yogurt
freshly ground black pepper

Belgian endive salad

3 oz. mushrooms, wiped clean and trimmed
2 tbsp. fresh lemon juice
6 oz. Belgian endive, trimmed and thinly sliced
¼ cup radish sprouts (glossary)
4 scallions, trimmed and sliced
½ sweet red or orange pepper, sliced and blanched

Starting at the untrimmed side of each steak, cut a pocket almost through to the opposite side. Coat the insides of the pockets with half of the grainy mustard, then rub the steaks all over with half of the crushed garlic. Place the steaks in a dish and set them aside, covered, in a cool place for 30 minutes to marinate.

Meanwhile, make the sauce. Put the yogurt, the remaining mustard and garlic, and plenty of freshly ground black pepper into a bowl, and mix them together thoroughly.

For the salad, slice the mushrooms and put them into a bowl with the lemon juice. Toss the mushrooms well and let them stand for 10 minutes. Add the Belgian endive, radish sprouts, scallions, and sweet pepper, and mix the ingredients together well. Cover the salad and chill it until it is needed.

Brush the rack with oil and cook the steaks over hot coals for three to five minutes on each side. Serve the steaks with the salad and sauce.

Grilled Veal Cutlets

Serves 4
Working time: about 25 minutes
Total time: about 4 hours and 25 minutes
(includes marinating)

Calories **150**
Protein **53g.**
Cholesterol **30mg.**
Total fat **7g.**
Saturated fat **5g.**
Sodium **220mg.**

8 small thick-cut veal cutlets (about 1½ oz. each), trimmed of fat
¼ cup plain low-fat yogurt
1 tbsp. virgin olive oil
1 tbsp. balsamic vinegar
1 tbsp. grainy mustard
ground white pepper
8 fresh sage leaves, finely chopped
¼ tsp. salt
coarsely crushed white peppercorns (optional)

Lay a cutlet on the work surface between two sheets of plastic wrap. Using the smooth side of a meat mallet or a rolling pin, pound it until it is about 1/16 inch thick. Repeat this process with the other cutlets. In a small bowl, whisk together the yogurt, oil, vinegar, mustard, pepper, and chopped sage leaves. Brush the cutlets with the marinade and place them in a shallow, nonreactive dish; reserve any remaining marinade. Cover the dish, and let the cutlets marinate for four to six hours at room temperature, or for 12 to 24 hours in the refrigerator. (Remove the chilled cutlets from the refrigerator about one hour before cooking to allow them to reach room temperature.)

Cook the veal cutlets over hot coals for 45 seconds on each side, basting them with any remaining marinade. Sprinkle the cooked cutlets with the salt and, if you like, with crushed white peppercorns. Serve the cutlets immediately.

SUGGESTED ACCOMPANIMENTS: *a salad of pink grapefruit and young spinach leaves; radicchio hearts dressed with a balsamic vinaigrette; crusty rolls.*

Peppercorn-Crusted Tenderloin with Three Sauces

Serves 16
Working time: about 1 hour and 30 minutes
Total time: about 2 hours and 15 minutes

Calories **290**
Protein **33g.**
Cholesterol **72mg.**
Total fat **16g.**
Saturated fat **6g.**
Sodium **480mg.**

3 garlic cloves, crushed
4½ lb. beef tenderloin in one piece, trimmed of fat
½ cup black peppercorns, crushed
2 tbsp. virgin olive oil

Spinach sauce

1 tbsp. polyunsaturated margarine
1 leek, trimmed, washed thoroughly, and sliced
1 shallot, chopped
2 garlic cloves, coarsely chopped
1 lb. fresh spinach, washed and stemmed
1 tbsp. fresh lemon juice
½ tsp. salt
3 tbsp. crème fraîche (glossary) or sour cream

Pumpkin sauce

1 lb. pumpkin, peeled, seeds removed, flesh cubed
1¼ cups unsalted chicken stock (recipe, page 139)
1 tsp. molasses
¾ oz. Parmesan cheese, grated
1 tbsp. cut chives
¼ small nutmeg, grated, or ¼ tsp. ground nutmeg
1 tsp. salt
¼ cup sour cream

Parsnip and apple sauce

14 oz. parsnips, trimmed and cubed
3 baking apples, peeled, cored, and coarsely chopped, placed in acidulated water
1 cinnamon stick
½ lemon, peel only, cut into wide strips
2 tbsp. polyunsaturated margarine
1 tsp. salt
1 tbsp. finely chopped fresh chervil

Rub the garlic all over the beef tenderloin. Put the peppercorns on a plate and roll the beef in them, pressing them firmly and evenly into the surface to form a compact crust. Place the meat on a platter, then cover it and set it aside while you prepare the sauces.

For the spinach sauce, melt the margarine in a large saucepan over medium heat. Add the leek, shallot, and garlic, and cook the vegetables until they are just softened—about five minutes. Add the spinach with water still clinging to its leaves, then cook the vegetables for one minute more, turning the spinach continuously to prevent it from sticking and to coat it in the cooking juices. Cover the saucepan and cook the vegetables gently, stirring occcasionally, until they are tender—about five minutes. Remove the pan from the heat and let the spinach mixture cool slightly, then transfer it to a food processor or blender with all the cooking juices, and process it to a purée. Add the lemon juice and the salt, and process the sauce for 10 seconds before adding the crème fraîche or sour cream. Process the sauce very briefly, then pour it into a small, nonreactive saucepan, ready to be reheated before serving.

For the pumpkin sauce, put the pumpkin into a large saucepan and add the chicken stock. Bring the stock to the simmering point, then simmer the pumpkin until it is soft—15 to 20 minutes. Remove the pan from the heat, allow the pumpkin to cool slightly, then transfer it to a food processor or blender, pouring in all the cooking liquid. Add the molasses, Parmesan cheese, chives, nutmeg, and salt, and process the mixture until it forms a smooth purée. Add the sour cream to the sauce and process it for a few seconds more. Press the sauce through a fine sieve into a small saucepan, then set it aside, ready to be reheated.

To make the third sauce, place the parsnips and apples in a large saucepan. Add the cinnamon stick and lemon peel. Pour in 1 cup of water, and bring it to a simmer over medium heat. Simmer the parsnips and apples for 10 to 15 minutes, or until they are soft. Discard the cinnamon stick and all but a 1-inch strip of the lemon peel. Transfer the parsnips and apples and the reserved lemon peel with all the cooking liquid to a food processor or blender. Add the margarine and salt, then process the mixture until it forms a smooth purée. Press the sauce through a fine sieve into a saucepan. Stir in the chervil and set the sauce aside.

Brush the olive oil over the beef's peppercorn crust, reserving any excess to baste the meat as it cooks. Set the rack close to medium-hot coals, and cook the meat for 15 minutes to seal it, turning it frequently and basting it with any remaining oil. Raise the rack and continue to cook the meat for 15 minutes more for rare beef, or 20 minutes for rare to medium meat. During the latter stage of the cooking, keep the thin end of the tenderloin away from the hottest part of the fire to prevent it from overcooking.

While the beef is cooking, gently reheat the sauces without letting them boil. Transfer the peppercorn-crusted tenderloin to a board or serving platter, and carve it into thick slices. Serve the sauces separately.

Aromatic Leg of Lamb

TURNING THE LAMB AND BASTING IT AT REGULAR INTERVALS DURING COOKING KEEPS THE JUICES WITHIN THE MEAT AND ENSURES SUCCULENCE.

Serves 12
Working time: about 1 hour
Total time: about 27 hours (includes marinating)

Calories **250**
Protein **31g.**
Cholesterol **80mg.**
Total fat **12g.**
Saturated fat **5g.**
Sodium **170mg.**

⅔ cup plain low-fat yogurt
1 tbsp. fresh lemon juice
1 tbsp. ground coriander
2 tsp. ground cinnamon
1 tsp. ground cardamom
1 tsp. ground ginger
½ tsp. ground cloves
freshly ground black pepper
1 tbsp. virgin olive oil
5 lb. leg of lamb, boned, trimmed of fat, and opened out flat
½ tsp. salt
1 tbsp. poppy seeds
1 tbsp. sesame seeds
1 large pita bread (optional)

Citrus-yogurt sauce

1 lemon, finely grated zest only
1 cup sour cream
½ cup plain low-fat yogurt
2 tbsp. fresh lemon balm (glossary), finely chopped

In a small bowl, stir together ⅔ cup yogurt, lemon juice, coriander, cinnamon, cardamom, ginger, cloves, and some black pepper to form a light paste. Spread the paste all over the lamb. Place the lamb in a large, flat dish, cover it, and let the meat marinate in the refrigerator for at least 24 hours, or up to three days. Remove the meat from the refrigerator at least two hours before you plan to cook it.

Open up the meat to form a rough rectangle. Thread two metal skewers through the meat, each about 3 inches from the edge of a long side; this will keep the meat flat while it is cooking. Set the rack at its lowest position and brush it lightly with oil. Sear each side of the lamb over hot coals for five to eight minutes, or until the surface is caramelized and lightly charred. Remove the meat from the rack and adjust the rack to its highest position. Return the meat to the rack. Brush one side with a little oil, sprinkle on ¼ teaspoon of the salt and 1½ teaspoons each of the poppy and sesame seeds, and cook the lamb for three minutes more. Turn the meat over, brush it with oil, sprinkle on the remaining salt and poppy and sesame seeds, and grill it for three minutes. Turn the lamb four more times, brushing it each time with any remaining marinade or with a little oil and grilling it for three minutes after each turn. The meat should be crisp and dark on the outside but still tender and pink inside. For meat that is more well done, cook it for four to six minutes more, turning it once and brushing on more oil as necessary to prevent it from drying out. If you like, place the cooked leg on a round of pita bread set on a carving surface: The bread will catch the meat juices and may be served in chunks with the meat. Remove the skewers, cover the meat lightly with foil, and allow it to rest for 5 to 10 minutes before carving.

Meanwhile, prepare the sauce. Set 1 teaspoon of the lemon zest aside. Mix together the remaining lemon zest, the sour cream, the yogurt, and, the lemon balm. Sprinkle the reserved lemon zest over the sauce. Serve the meat accompanied by the sauce.

SUGGESTED ACCOMPANIMENT: *a salad of crisp mixed lettuce leaves with blanched sliced zucchini and snow peas.*

EDITOR'S NOTE: *Throwing cinnamon sticks and bay leaves onto the coals for the last 5 to 10 minutes of grilling will enhance the flavor of the meat.*

Caucasian Lamb Kabobs with Fruit Pilaf

Serves 6
Working time: about 1 hour and 15 minutes
Total time: about 25 hours (includes marinating)

Calories **390**
Protein **29g.**
Cholesterol **65mg.**
Total fat **12g.**
Saturated fat **4g.**
Sodium **150mg.**

2 tsp. safflower oil
1 small onion, finely chopped
1 lb. red plums, pitted and chopped
1 tbsp. red wine vinegar
1 tbsp. honey
1 tsp. ground cinnamon
¼ tsp. ground allspice
freshly ground black pepper
1¼ lb. lean loin of lamb, trimmed of fat and cut into ½-inch cubes
1 tbsp. chopped fresh basil
½ cup sour cream

Fruit pilaf

¾ cup long-grain rice
6 tbsp. raisins
6 tbsp. chopped dried pears
6 tbsp. chopped dried apricots
½ cup unsweetened white grape or apple juice
1 tsp. safflower oil
¼ tsp. salt
¼ tsp. powdered saffron
1 cinnamon stick
1 tsp. honey
1 fresh peach or nectarine, peeled, pitted, and diced
½ oz. whole blanched almonds (1½ tbsp.), toasted
¼ cup loosely packed fresh mint, chopped

Heat the oil in a heavy-bottomed, nonreactive skillet, add the onion, and cook it over medium heat for five minutes, or until it is soft. Add the plums, vinegar, honey, cinnamon, allspice, and some black pepper, and simmer the plums until they are very soft—about 20 minutes. Purée the contents of the pan in a food processor or blender.

Place the lamb cubes in a shallow, nonreactive dish. Reserve 6 tablespoons of the plum purée; stir the basil into the remaining purée and pour it over the lamb, turning the cubes of meat to coat them evenly. Put the lamb, loosely covered, in the refrigerator to marinate for about 24 hours.

Two hours before cooking the dish, rinse the rice, then pour ⅔ cup of cold water over it and set it aside to soak. Remove the lamb from the refrigerator to allow it to reach room temperature. At the same time, place the raisins, dried pears, and dried apricots in a bowl, and pour in the grape or apple juice.

When you are ready to cook the rice, drain it and place it in a large saucepan with an equal volume of cold water. Add the oil, salt, and saffron, and bring the liquid to a boil. Stir the rice, lower the heat, and simmer the rice gently, tightly covered, for about 20 minutes, or until the grains have absorbed all the liquid; do not stir the rice while it is cooking.

Meanwhile, transfer the dried fruit and juice to a nonreactive saucepan. Add the cinnamon stick and honey, cover the pan, and simmer the dried fruit until it is soft—about 10 minutes. Remove the lid and reduce the liquid until only a small amount of fruit syrup remains. Discard the cinnamon stick.

Stir the cooked dried fruit and its syrup into the rice, together with the diced peach or nectarine. Allow the rice to cool a little, then stir in the toasted almonds and the chopped mint. Cover the pan loosely and set it aside in a warm place until it is needed.

Lightly oil six long metal skewers. Thread the lamb cubes onto the skewers, reserving any excess marinade. Oil the rack lightly, and cook the kabobs over medium-hot coals for about 15 minutes, turning them frequently and occasionally basting them with any remaining marinade. Rest the cooked kabobs on a warmed serving platter for five minutes. Meanwhile, place the sour cream in a serving bowl and gently drop the reserved plum purée onto the surface.

To serve, spoon some fruit pilaf onto a plate. Arrange the lamb cubes from one skewer on the pilaf, and dribble some of the sour cream over the meat.

EDITOR'S NOTE: *Pilaf is traditionally served warm, rather than hot or cold. It may be prepared in advance and gently reheated in a shallow foil tray set over the rack, provided it is stirred frequently. To toast almonds, put them under the broiler for two minutes or until they are golden; turn or shake them constantly.*

Spit-Roasted Moroccan Lamb

Serves 12
Working time: about 30 minutes
Total time: about 6 hours and 30 minutes
(includes marinating)

Calories **275**
Protein **37g.**
Cholesterol **100mg.**
Total fat **14g.**
Saturated fat **5g.**
Sodium **85mg.**

4 lb. lean leg of lamb, skin and all visible fat removed
4 garlic cloves, each cut lengthwise into 8 slivers
3 tbsp. safflower oil
1 tbsp. ground cumin
2 tbsp. ground coriander
2 tsp. ground cinnamon
2 tbsp. chopped fresh mint

Cut off and discard the knuckle from the leg of lamb. Make deep incisions about 2 inches apart all over the leg, and insert the garlic slivers in the cuts. Mix together the oil, cumin, coriander, cinnamon, and chopped mint, and rub half of the mixture over the lamb, coating it completely. Set the remaining spice and mint mixture aside. Cover the meat and let it marinate in the refrigerator for at least four hours, or overnight. Remove the meat from the refrigerator about two hours before you plan to cook it, to allow it to reach room temperature.

Place the leg diagonally on a rotating spit so that the weight is evenly distributed and the spit will turn easily. Roast the meat, rotating it, over very hot coals. Start carving the lamb after 15 to 20 minutes, leaving the rest of the leg on the spit to continue cooking. Baste the area from which you have carved the slices with the reserved spice marinade. Continue to carve slices from the lamb as it cooks—about every 10 minutes.

SUGGESTED ACCOMPANIMENTS: *warmed pita bread in which to serve the slices of meat; a cucumber, mint, and yogurt salad.*

Lamb Skewers with Plantain

Serves 4
Working time: about 30 minutes
Total time: about 1 hour

Calories **425**
Protein **31g.**
Cholesterol **80mg.**
Total fat **16g.**
Saturated fat **5g.**
Sodium **160mg.**

1 lb. lean loin of lamb, trimmed of fat
1 tbsp. virgin olive oil
3 drops bitters
1 garlic clove, finely chopped
1 tsp. coarsely chopped fresh thyme
¼ tsp. salt
freshly ground black pepper
2 ripe plantains (about 11 oz. each)

Cut the trimmed lamb into disk-shaped slices about ½ inch thick. Squeeze each disk of lamb into a crescent shape and skewer it lengthwise so that the skewer maintains the crescent form; divide the crescents among four skewers. Place the skewers on a tray or a large, flat plate while you prepare the marinade.

In a small bowl, combine the olive oil, bitters, garlic, thyme, salt, and some pepper. Brush the lamb skewers with this marinade and set them aside, covered, in a cool place for 30 minutes, or up to three hours.

Meanwhile, prepare the plantains. Remove the ends and put them into a large saucepan of boiling water. Boil the plantains, uncovered, foı 20 minutes, then drain them and allow them to cool. When they are cool enough to handle, peel them and cut each one lengthwise into four slices. Cut each slice of plantain into 2-inch-long pieces. Thread the plantain onto four skewers, folding each piece once crosswise: Double over each piece of plantain so that its ends almost meet, and skewer it to hold this form. Brush the plantain skewers lightly with oil.

Place the lamb and plantain skewers on the rack over hot coals, and cook them for six minutes, turning them once as they cook.

SUGGESTED ACCOMPANIMENT: *radicchio salad.*

Lamb Burgers with Basil and Parmesan Sauce

Serves 8
Working time: about 40 minutes
Total time: about 1 hour

Calories **215**
Protein **28g.**
Cholesterol **75mg.**
Total fat **9g.**
Saturated fat **4g.**
Sodium **95mg.**

1½ lb. lean leg of lamb, trimmed of fat and ground
3 onions, chopped
½ lb. zucchini (2 small), coarsely grated
⅔ cup fresh whole-wheat breadcrumbs
¼ tsp. salt
freshly ground black pepper
½ tsp. virgin olive oil
⅔ cup unsalted vegetable stock (recipe, page 139)
½ cup loosely packed fresh basil leaves, coarsely chopped
¼ cup freshly grated Parmesan cheese

Put the ground lamb into a bowl. Add a third of the chopped onion, all of the zucchini, the breadcrumbs, the salt, and some pepper. Using a wooden spoon or your hands, work the ingredients together until they are thoroughly combined. Divide the mixture into 16 equal portions, then shape each portion into a patty about 2½ inches in diameter and ½ inch thick. Place the burgers on a baking sheet and set them aside.

Heat the oil in a small saucepan over medium heat. Add the remaining chopped onions and cook them gently until they begin to soften—about three minutes. Pour the vegetable stock into the pan and bring it to a boil, then cover the pan and lower the heat. Simmer the sauce until the onion is tender—four to five minutes. Stir in the basil and cheese, and add some pepper. Cook the sauce for one minute more, then transfer it to a food processor or blender and process it until it is smooth. Pour the sauce back into the saucepan, and set it aside, ready to be reheated very gently just before serving.

Lightly oil the rack, and cook the burgers over hot coals for seven to eight minutes on each side. Serve them at once, with a little of the reheated sauce.

SUGGESTED ACCOMPANIMENT: *yellow pepper and pasta salad, sprinkled with toasted pine nuts.*

Shoulder of Lamb with Anchovy Stuffing

Serves 10
Working time: about 45 minutes
Total time: about 12 hours (includes marinating)

Calories **185**
Protein **24g.**
Cholesterol **65mg.**
Total fat **9g.**
Saturated fat **3g.**
Sodium **290mg.**

½ oz. rosemary sprigs, woody stems trimmed
½ cup loosely packed fresh parsley
3 garlic cloves
½ lemon, grated zest and juice
2 oz. canned anchovy fillets in oil
freshly ground black pepper
one 2½-lb. shoulder of lamb, skinned and boned, trimmed of all fat

Lemon sauce

1 tbsp. virgin olive oil
1 small onion, finely chopped
1 tbsp. unbleached all-purpose flour
2 cups unsalted chicken or vegetable stock (recipes, page 139)
1 lemon, finely grated zest and juice
2 tbsp. chopped fresh parsley

Place the rosemary sprigs in a food processor with the parsley, garlic, lemon zest and juice, anchovies with their oil, and some freshly ground black pepper. Process the ingredients until they form a smooth paste.

Wipe the lamb with paper towels to remove any watery juices. Lay the meat out flat on the work surface, boned side up, and spread the herb and anchovy paste over the meat as evenly as possible. Fold the two opposite sides of the meat over the filling so that they meet in the center; secure them in place with long metal skewers to prevent the paste from running out of the cavity. Cover the lamb and let it marinate in the refrigerator for at least eight hours, or up to 24 hours. Remove the meat from the refrigerator about two hours before you plan to cook it, to allow it to reach room temperature.

Lightly oil the rack, and cook the stuffed lamb over medium-hot coals for about two hours, turning it frequently. Test the meat by inserting a skewer in the center—the juices will run clear when the lamb is well cooked. (For meat that is slightly pink in the middle, reduce the cooking time to one and a quarter to one and a half hours.)

About 20 minutes before the lamb is ready, prepare the sauce. Heat the oil in a small, heavy-bottomed, nonreactive saucepan. Add the onion and cook it over medium heat until it is transparent—about five minutes. Stir in the flour and cook for one minute, stirring constantly. Gradually pour in the stock, stirring continuously, and bring the sauce to a boil. Lower the heat and simmer the sauce for 10 minutes, then stir in the lemon zest and juice, and simmer the sauce for five minutes more. Remove the pan from the heat. Stir the parsley into the sauce just before serving.

Carve the lamb into thick slices, and pour a little of the sauce over each serving.

SUGGESTED ACCOMPANIMENTS: *small new potatoes, parboiled for 10 to 15 minutes until they are just tender, then skewered, brushed with honey, and heated on the grill for three to four minutes; oakleaf lettuce.*

Lamb Noisettes with Tomato and Olive Relish

Serves 4
Working time: about 30 minutes
Total time: about 5 hours and 30 minutes
(includes marinating)

Calories **225**
Protein **28g.**
Cholesterol **70mg.**
Total fat **10g.**
Saturated fat **4g.**
Sodium **180mg.**

4 long, thick rosemary sprigs, plus rosemary sprigs for garnish (optional)
4 lean noisettes of lamb (glossary), trimmed of fat (about 3½ oz. each)
1 onion, thinly sliced
2 garlic cloves, chopped
1 tsp. chopped fresh oregano, or ¼ tsp. dried oregano
¼ tsp. salt
freshly ground black pepper
⅔ cup dry white wine

Tomato and olive relish

1 tsp. virgin olive oil
1 small onion, finely chopped
8 black olives, pitted and finely chopped
2 tsp. white wine vinegar
½ tsp. sugar
2 tsp. chopped fresh thyme, or ½ tsp. dried thyme leaves
2 tbsp. dry white wine or water
5 tomatoes, peeled, seeded (technique, page 138), coarsely chopped, and strained

Push a rosemary sprig through each noisette, then place the noisettes in a shallow, nonreactive dish large enough to hold them in a single layer. Sprinkle the onion, garlic, oregano, salt, and some pepper evenly over the lamb, then pour on the wine. Cover the dish and put the lamb in the refrigerator to marinate for about four hours; turn the noisettes several times during this period. Remove the lamb from the refrigerator about one hour before cooking, to allow it to reach room temperature.

To make the tomato and olive relish, heat the oil in a small, nonreactive saucepan. Add the onion and cook it over very low heat for about eight minutes, stirring occasionally, until it is softened but not browned. Stir in the olives, vinegar, sugar, thyme, wine or water, and tomatoes. Remove the pan from the heat and set it aside.

Lightly oil the rack, and cook the noisettes over hot coals for six to eight minutes on each side, until they are firm to the touch and browned. Meanwhile, reheat the relish for about two minutes, and transfer it to a serving bowl. Remove the strings from the noisettes, and serve them accompanied by the relish and, if you wish, garnished with rosemary.

EDITOR'S NOTE: *If the rosemary sprigs are too soft to push through the noisettes, make a hole in the noisettes first with a metal skewer.*

Pork and Apple Kabobs

Serves 4
Working time: about 45 minutes
Total time: about 2 hours and 45 minutes
(includes marinating)

Calories **300**
Protein **35g.**
Cholesterol **80mg.**
Total fat **12g.**
Saturated fat **4g.**
Sodium **100mg.**

1¼ cups beer
6 black peppercorns, crushed
½ tsp. ground cloves
2 tsp. finely chopped fresh sage
2 tsp. chopped fresh rosemary
1 lb. pork tenderloin, trimmed of fat, cut into 1-inch cubes
2 crisp tart apples
1 tbsp. safflower oil

Pour the beer into a large bowl. Add the peppercorns, cloves, sage, and rosemary, and stir well. Add the pork cubes, turning them to coat them evenly. Cover the pork and set it aside to marinate for at least two hours at room temperature.

Remove the cubes of pork from the marinade and reserve the marinade. Lightly oil four skewers. Core the apples and cut each one into six wedges; dip each piece of apple in the reserved marinade. Thread pieces of pork and apple alternately onto each of the four skewers, starting and ending with a cube of pork. Stir the oil into the remaining marinade and baste the kabobs with this mixture.

Place the kabobs on the grill and cook them, over hot coals, for 15 to 20 minutes, until they are cooked through; turn the kabobs and baste them with marinade several times during cooking.

SUGGESTED ACCOMPANIMENT: *celery, nut, and raisin salad with a yogurt and parsley dressing.*

Skewers of Spiced Pork, Eggplant, and Pepper

Serves 12
Working time: about 30 minutes
Total time: about 2 hours and 30 minutes
(includes marinating)

Calories **155**
Protein **22g.**
Cholesterol **50mg.**
Total fat **6g.**
Saturated fat **2g.**
Sodium **100mg.**

2 lb. lean pork loin, trimmed of all fat, cut into ½-inch slices
3 medium eggplants, quartered and cut into 1-inch slices
3 sweet green peppers, seeded, deribbed, and cut into 1-inch squares
1 tbsp. safflower oil

Garlic and cumin marinade

2 green chili peppers, seeded and finely chopped (cautionary note, page 63)
1 small onion, thinly sliced
1-inch piece fresh ginger, finely chopped
4 garlic cloves, crushed
3 bay leaves
1 lime, grated zest and juice
2 cinnamon sticks, halved
1 tbsp. whole cloves
2 tsp. ground cumin
¼ tsp. ground turmeric
1 tbsp. garam masala (glossary)
½ tsp. salt
freshly ground black pepper
⅔ cup plain low-fat yogurt

In a bowl, mix together the marinade ingredients. Add the pork slices, tossing them in the marinade to coat them well. Cover the bowl and let the meat chill in the refrigerator for two to four hours.

Remove the pork from the marinade and discard the bay leaves, cloves, and pieces of cinnamon stick. Thread the pork onto 12 metal skewers, pushing the skewers through the circumference of each slice. Thread the pieces of eggplant and sweet green pepper alternately onto 12 more skewers. Brush the vegetable kabobs with the safflower oil.

Oil the rack lightly and cook the pork and vegetable kabobs over hot coals for three to four minutes on each side, until the meat is lightly browned and cooked through and the peppers and eggplant are tender. Serve the kabobs immediately.

Piquant Pork Chops

Serves 4
Working time: about 15 minutes
Total time: about 9 hours (includes marinating)

Calories **205**
Protein **30g.**
Cholesterol **70mg.**
Total fat **7g.**
Saturated fat **3g.**
Sodium **85mg.**

1 lime, juice only
2 tsp. honey
1 tsp. hot red-pepper sauce
1 tbsp. red wine vinegar
¼ cup unsalted tomato paste
1 tsp. allspice
freshly ground black pepper
4 pork loin chops (about 6 oz. each), trimmed of fat

Mix the lime juice, honey, hot red-pepper sauce, red wine vinegar, tomato paste, allspice, and freshly ground black pepper together in a large bowl. Put the pork chops into the bowl and turn them so that they are evenly coated with the marinade. Let the chops marinate in the refrigerator for eight hours, or overnight. Remove them from the refrigerator about an hour before you plan to cook them.

Lightly oil the rack, and cook the chops over hot coals for about six minutes on each side, basting them with any remaining marinade.

SUGGESTED ACCOMPANIMENT: *pineapple, cucumber, and fennel salad with chopped mint.*

Pork Sheftalias with Oregano

SHEFTALIAS, MEATBALLS WRAPPED IN CAUL FAT, ARE A POPULAR GREEK AND CYPRIOT BARBECUE TREAT.

Serves 6
Working time: about 25 minutes
Total time: about 4 hours and 45 minutes
(includes marinating)

Calories **190**
Protein **25g.**
Cholesterol **55mg.**
Total fat **5g.**
Saturated fat **2g.**
Sodium **220mg.**

1 lb. lean pork, trimmed of fat and ground
1 large onion
4 tsp. chopped fresh oregano, or 1 tsp. dried oregano
2 tbsp. chopped flat-leaf parsley, plus flat-leaf parsley sprigs for garnish
3 tbsp. red wine
freshly ground black pepper
⅔ cup fresh breadcrumbs
¼ tsp. salt
1 egg white
6 oz. caul fat

Put the ground pork into a bowl and coarsely grate the onion over it. Mix in the oregano, chopped parsley, wine, and a few generous grindings of black pepper. Cover the bowl, place it in the refrigerator, and let the meat marinate for at least four hours, or overnight.

Add the breadcrumbs and salt to the marinated pork, and mix them in well. In a separate bowl, beat the egg white until it is fluffy but not stiff, then fold it into the pork and breadcrumb mixture. Shape the mixture into 18 balls. Cut the caul fat into 18 pieces, each about 5 inches in diameter. Loosely wrap a piece of caul fat around each ball. Lightly oil the rack, and cook the *sheftalias* over hot coals for about 20 minutes, or until they are cooked inside and firm but slightly spongy when pressed; turn the balls every three to four minutes during cooking. Serve the *sheftalias* garnished with sprigs of flat-leaf parsley.

SUGGESTED ACCOMPANIMENTS: *a salad of cucumber, tomato, lettuce, and flat-leaf parsley; hot pita bread.*

EDITOR'S NOTE: *Caul fat is the weblike fatty membrane that surrounds a pig's stomach.*

Pork Rolls with Fennel

Serves 4
Working time: about 1 hour and 30 minutes
Total time: about 10 hours
(includes marinating)

Calories **310**
Protein **38g.**
Cholesterol **85mg.**
Total fat **16g.**
Saturated fat **4g.**
Sodium **150mg.**

2 pork tenderloins (about 9 oz. each), trimmed of fat
2 tbsp. virgin olive oil
1 tsp. fennel seeds, crushed
1 garlic clove, crushed
2 lemons, finely grated zest and juice
freshly ground black pepper
1 large bulb fennel (about ½ lb.), finely chopped, feathery leaves reserved
⅛ tsp. salt
1 tsp. honey

Make a slit down the length of each pork tenderloin, slicing three-quarters of the way through the middle of the meat. Open out each tenderloin into a rectangular shape and lay it flat on a piece of plastic wrap; cover each tenderloin with a second piece of plastic wrap. Using a meat mallet or a rolling pin, pound the tenderloins into oblongs about ¼ inch thick. Lay both pieces of meat in a large, rectangular dish. In a small bowl, mix the oil with the fennel seeds, garlic, lemon zest, and 4 tablespoons of water. Add some black pepper and mix in the chopped fennel. Spread this mixture evenly over the pork, cover the dish, and let the meat marinate in the refrigerator for at least eight hours, or overnight.

Remove the pieces of pork from the dish, scrape off all the marinade ingredients into a bowl, and set the bowl aside. Lay the tenderloins on a work surface and arrange the reserved fennel leaves evenly over them, setting aside a few for garnish. Sprinkle the salt over the chopped fennel mixture in the bowl, then use a slotted spoon to drain the chopped fennel and spread it evenly over the pork; keep the marinade juices that are left in the bowl. Roll up each tenderloin to enclose the fennel, and tie it with string. Lay the rolls, end to end, on a 16-by-12-inch double-thickness sheet of foil. Wrap the foil around the pork rolls, folding the edges together to seal the packages.

Place the foil-wrapped pork rolls on a rack over hot coals and cook them for 40 minutes, turning them over every 10 minutes; take care not to split the foil as you turn the packages. Remove the cooked pork from the foil, and transfer the cooking juices in the foil to a small bowl. Stir in the lemon juice, the honey, and the reserved marinade juices, then brush a little of this mixture over each roll. Return the pork rolls to the grill, without the foil, and cook them for 10 minutes more, basting them frequently with the juices and turning them until they are golden brown all over. Cut each pork roll into four thick slices. Serve the slices garnished with the remaining fennel leaves.

SUGGESTED ACCOMPANIMENTS: *a selection of grilled summer vegetables; corn relish.*

EDITOR'S NOTE: *If there are no feathery leaves on the fennel bulbs, spread about 1 cup of watercress leaves over the pork tenderloins instead; garnish the sliced pork rolls with sprigs of watercress.*

Mustard-Marinated Rabbit with Brandied Peaches

Serves 6
Working time: about 35 minutes
Total time: about 7 hours (includes marinating)

Calories **470**
Protein **24g.**
Cholesterol **75mg.**
Total fat **10g.**
Saturated fat **4g.**
Sodium **35mg.**

2 garlic cloves, crushed
1 rabbit (about 2 lbs.), cut into 6 pieces, trimmed of fat and membrane
6 juniper berries
1¼ cups red wine
1 tbsp. virgin olive oil
1 tbsp. grainy mustard
1 tsp. light brown sugar
2 tbsp. sour cream

Spiced brandied peaches

¾ cup light brown sugar
1¼ cups brandy
1¼ cups fruity white wine
½ large lemon, juice and pared zest
2 tbsp. pumpkin-pie spice
1 cinnamon stick
1 tsp. freshly grated nutmeg or ground nutmeg
6 firm peaches, halved and pitted

Spread the crushed garlic evenly over the rabbit pieces and place them in a nonreactive dish. Toast the juniper berries in a heavy-bottomed skillet over high heat until they release their aroma—about two minutes. Add the juniper berries to the wine together with the oil, mustard, sugar, and sour cream, and whisk the ingredients together with a fork. Pour the marinade over the rabbit pieces and set the rabbit aside to marinate for six to eight hours, turning the meat every hour.

About an hour before you plan to cook the rabbit, poach the peaches. Place the sugar, brandy, white wine, lemon juice and zest, pumpkin-pie spice, cinnamon stick, and nutmeg in a nonreactive saucepan just large enough to comfortably hold the 12 peach halves. Bring the liquid to a boil and add the halved peaches, skin side down. Lower the heat, cover the pan, and simmer the peaches gently for 15 minutes, turning them once. Remove the pan from the heat and set the peaches aside in a warm place.

Remove the rabbit pieces from their dish and reserve the marinade. Cook the rabbit over hot coals for 25 to 30 minutes, turning several times and basting them with the marinade.

Just before serving, remove the peaches from their pan with a slotted spoon. Place two peach halves, skin side down, on each of six serving plates. Strain the syrup into a bowl and pour 1 tablespoon over each peach half. Serve the rabbit with the peaches.

SUGGESTED ACCOMPANIMENT: *mixed wild and long-grain rice.*

Bittersweet Duck-Breast Salad

Serves 6
Working time: about 30 minutes
Total time: about 8 hours and 30 minutes
(includes marinating)

alories **145**
otein **14g.**
nolesterol **75mg.**
otal fat **9g.**
aturated fat **2g.**
odium **215mg.**

4 dried bay leaves
½ tsp. salt
12 juniper berries
1 tsp. black peppercorns
2 tsp. coriander seeds
1 lb. duck-breast fillets, skinned, all visible fat removed
4 tsp. virgin olive oil
½ lb. Belgian endive, separated into leaves, leaves washed and dried
2½ cups loosely packed watercress, trimmed, washed, and dried
2 small oranges, zest finely shredded, flesh segmented
½ oz. walnuts (2 tbsp.)
2 tsp. walnut oil
2½ tbsp. fresh orange juice

Using a mortar and pestle, pound the bay leaves to a powder with the salt. Add the juniper berries, peppercorns, and coriander seeds, and crush the spices to a fine powder. Rub this mixture over the duck breasts, then place them in a dish. Cover the dish and let the duck marinate in the refrigerator for at least eight hours, or up to 24 hours.

Remove the duck from the refrigerator at least one hour before cooking. Wipe the meat with paper towels to remove any liquid, any excess salt, and most of the spices. Brush the duck with 1 teaspoon of the olive oil, and lightly oil the grill rack.

Place the Belgian endive in a large salad bowl with the watercress, orange segments, and walnuts. In a small screw-top jar, combine the walnut oil with 2 teaspoons of the olive oil and 1½ tablespoons of the orange juice, then set the salad and dressing aside.

Mix the remaining olive oil and orange juice together, and brush a little of this mixture over the duck breasts. Cook the duck over medium-hot coals for two minutes, then turn the breasts and continue to cook them for three to four minutes more, until the meat is lightly browned on the outside but still slightly pink in the middle. Turn the duck breasts every one to two minutes during cooking, brushing them lightly with the orange juice and olive oil mixture.

Let the cooked duck rest for two to three minutes, then slice the meat into strips and add them to the salad bowl. Add the finely shredded orange zest. Shake the jar of dressing, pour it over the salad, and toss all of the ingredients together.

EDITOR'S NOTE: *To segment an orange, first cut off all the peel and pith. Hold the fruit over a bowl to catch the juice, then use a serrated knife to cut between the membranes that divide the segments. Cut in toward the center of the fruit, removing each segment in turn. (Squeeze all the juice from the remaining core and membranes before discarding them.)*

Spit-Roasted Savory Chicken

Serves 8
Working time: about 35 minutes
Total time: about 7 hours (includes marinating)

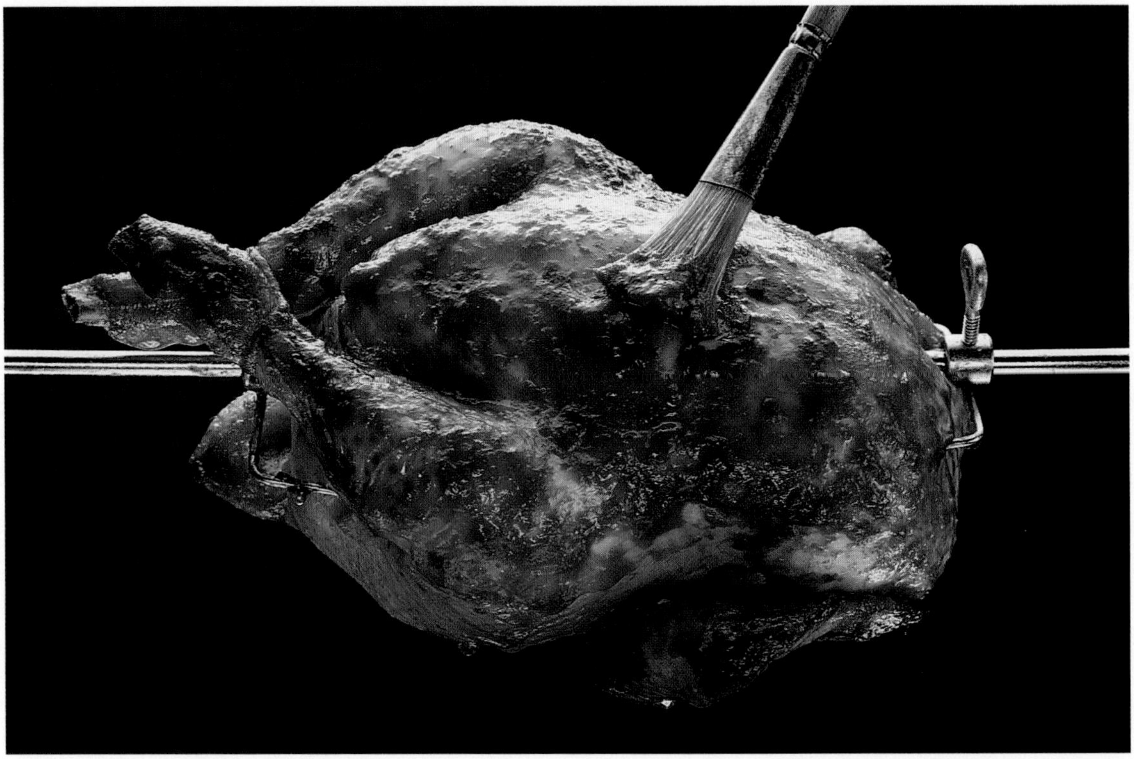

Calories **195**
Protein **24g.**
Cholesterol **90mg.**
Total fat **9g.**
Saturated fat **2g.**
Sodium **85mg.**

2 tbsp. safflower oil
1 small onion, grated
1 lb. tomatoes (3 medium), peeled, seeded, (technique, page 138), and chopped
½ lemon, strained juice only
2 tbsp. Worcestershire sauce
1 tsp. hot red-pepper sauce
1 tsp. dry mustard
2 tbsp. dark brown sugar
one 3½-lb. roasting chicken, giblets reserved for another use, rinsed and patted dry

First make the marinade. Heat the oil in a heavy, nonreactive saucepan over low heat. Add the onion and cook for two minutes, or until it is softened but not browned. Stir in the tomatoes, lemon juice, Worcestershire sauce, hot red-pepper sauce, mustard, and sugar. Cover the pan and simmer the ingredients for 15 minutes, stirring occasionally, until the tomatoes are reduced to a purée. Remove the pan from the heat and pour the marinade into a bowl, then set it aside until it is cool—about one hour.

Put the chicken in a large bowl and pour the cooled marinade over it. Cover the bowl and let the chicken marinate for at least four hours at room temperature, turning it several times.

Insert a rotisserie spit in the chicken by pushing it through the neck flap just above the breastbone and out just above the tail. Secure the spit with the holding forks, and attach the spit to the turning mechanism. Following the manufacturer's instructions, insert the drip tray immediately below the chicken to catch the cooking juices.

Cook the chicken until it is tender and the juices run clear when a thigh is pierced with a skewer—one and a quarter to one and a half hours. Baste the chicken frequently while it is cooking, first with the marinade, then with the cooking juices from the tray.

Cornish Hens with Rum

Serves 4
Working time: about 30 minutes
Total time: about 1 hour and 20 minutes
(includes marinating)

:alories **190**
'rotein **27g.**
:holesterol **90mg.**
;aturated fat **4g.**
'otal fat **1g.**
;odium **120mg.**

2 Cornish hens (about ¾ lb. each)
2 tbsp. dark rum
1 lime, juice only
1½ tbsp. honey
1 garlic clove, crushed
⅛ tsp. salt
1 tbsp. coriander seeds
½ tsp. black peppercorns

Using a pair of poultry shears or strong kitchen scissors, halve each Cornish hen lengthwise by cutting through the backbone and breastbone. Cut off and discard the leg tips and the tail. Wash the halves under running water and pat them dry.

In a small bowl, mix together the rum, lime juice, honey, garlic, and salt. Place the Cornish-hen halves in a shallow, nonreactive dish just large enough to accommodate them. Rub the rum mixture all over the Cornish hens, then set them aside in a cool place, covered, to marinate for 30 minutes.

Using a mortar and pestle or a coffee grinder, coarsely crush the coriander seeds and peppercorns. Remove the Cornish-hen halves from the marinade, and reserve the marinade.

Piercing the legs and wings as shown in the photograph below, thread two hen halves onto each of two long metal skewers. Brush the skewered Cornish hens with a little of the remaining marinade, then press the crushed coriander seeds and peppercorns all over the skin side of the birds.

Lightly oil the rack. Cook the Cornish-hen halves over hot coals for 20 to 25 minutes, turning them every five minutes, until the juices run clear when a skewer is inserted in a thigh.

SUGGESTED ACCOMPANIMENT: *a salad of mixed blanched vegetables, dressed with a vinaigrette.*

Yogurt Chicken Drumsticks

Serves 8
Working time: about 30 minutes
Total time: about 3 hours and 30 minutes
(includes marinating)

Calories **160**
Protein **26g.**
Cholesterol **90mg.**
Total fat **6g.**
Saturated fat **2g.**
Sodium **190mg.**

16 chicken drumsticks (about 3 lb.), skinned
½ tsp. salt
1 lemon, grated zest and juice
3 tbsp. paprika
½ tsp. hot red-pepper sauce
⅔ cup plain low-fat yogurt
freshly ground black pepper
crisp salad leaves for garnish

Cut two deep, diagonal slits in opposite sides of each drumstick. In a small bowl, stir the salt and the grated lemon zest into the lemon juice, then rub the mixture over each drumstick and into the slits. Lay the drumsticks on a wire rack set over a sheet pan, and sieve 1 tablespoon of the paprika evenly over the upper side of the drumsticks.

In another bowl, mix together the hot red-pepper sauce, the yogurt, and some black pepper. Using a brush, coat the paprika-sprinkled side of each drumstick with the yogurt mixture. Turn the drumsticks over, sieve another tablespoon of paprika over them, and coat them with the remaining yogurt mixture. Set the drumsticks aside in a cool place for three hours, or until the yogurt begins to dry.

Lightly oil the rack, and cook the drumsticks over hot coals for 15 to 20 minutes, turning them every five minutes. After the last turn, sprinkle the remaining paprika over the drumsticks. Serve the drumsticks immediately, garnished with crisp salad leaves.

SUGGESTED ACCOMPANIMENT: *sliced mushroom and sweet red-pepper salad.*

Grilled Cornish Hens with Peppered Fruit

Serves 4
Working time: about 1 hour and 15 minutes
Total time: about 15 hours (includes marinating)

Calories **450**
Protein **33g.**
Cholesterol **90mg.**
Total fat **13g.**
Saturated fat **3g.**
Sodium **105mg.**

2 Cornish hens (about ¾ lb. each)
¼ cup sweet white wine
1 tbsp. honey
1 tsp. Sichuan peppercorns
2 tsp. five-spice powder (glossary)
1 tsp. dry mustard
2 garlic cloves
1-inch piece fresh ginger, peeled
½ lime, juice only
1 tbsp. grape-seed or safflower oil
lime wedges for garnish

Peppered fruit

½ cup light brown sugar
1 lime, peel of whole cut into fine strips, and juice of half
2-inch piece fresh ginger, cut in half
½ tsp. green peppercorns, rinsed and crushed
1 chili pepper, seeded and cut into strips (cautionary note, page 63)
½ small pineapple, peeled, cored, and cut into 8 chunks
1 small mango, peeled, pitted, and cut into 8 chunks
1 small banana, cut into 8 pieces
½ avocado, peeled, pitted, and cut into 12 pieces

Lay one Cornish hen on the work surface, brea down. Using a sharp knife, cut through the cartilag on each side of the backbone from the tail toward th neck; use a sawing motion to cut through the rib cag Pull the backbone free and discard it. Turn the bird ov and position it with its legs toward you. Place the he of your hand on the breast and press down hard t break the breastbone, rib cage, collarbones, and wish bone, so that the bird lies flat. Slip your fingers und the skin at the neck and loosen the skin all over th bird, including the thigh. Repeat with the other bir

In a small, nonreactive saucepan, warm the wir with the honey and the Sichuan peppercorns until th honey has dissolved. Stir in the five-spice powder ar mustard, then remove the pan from the heat. Place th garlic in a press, and squeeze out the juice and minimum of pulp into the wine mixture. Put the ging into the garlic press, and squeeze as much ginger juic as possible into the saucepan. Add the lime juice ar stir well. Place the birds in a large, shallow, nonreacti dish and pour the prepared wine marinade over ther Cover the dish and put the Cornish hens in the r frigerator to marinate for at least 12 hours, or up to 2 hours, turning them from time to time to coat the evenly in the marinade.

About one and a half hours before grilling the Cornish hens, remove the birds from the refrigerator and start preparing the peppered fruit. In a saucepan, dissolve the sugar in 1 cup of water. Add the strips of lime peel and the ginger. Bring the liquid to a boil and boil it for five minutes. Remove the pan from the heat, add the peppercorns and chili pepper, and let the syrup cool. Strain the cooled syrup into a dish. Add the lime juice and the pineapple and mango chunks, turning them to coat them with syrup. After 30 minutes, submerge the banana and avocado in the syrup, and set the fruit aside.

About 10 minutes before grilling the Cornish hens, put four wooden or bamboo skewers to soak in cold water. Pat the Cornish hens dry with paper towels and thread two lightly oiled metal skewers through each bird: one skewer through both wings and the second through both thighs. Drain the fruit and thread the pieces onto the soaked skewers. Boil the syrup rapidly until it is reduced to 2 to 3 tablespoons, and brush a little of the reduced syrup over the skewered fruit; reserve the remaining syrup.

Lightly oil the rack. Cook the Cornish hens for 20 minutes over medium-hot coals; start with the skin side down, and turn the birds once or twice during cooking. Brush the underside of the Cornish hens with a little of the grape-seed or safflower oil and the leftover marinade, as necessary, to keep them from drying out. About two minutes before the Cornish hens are cooked, glaze the skin side of each bird with the remaining reduced fruit syrup. Remove the Cornish hens from the heat and let them stand for three to five minutes before removing the skewers.

Meanwhile, grill the skewered fruit until the pieces are lightly caramelized—five to six minutes. Glaze the cooked fruit with a little more of the reduced syrup just before serving.

Serve the Cornish hens and peppered fruit hot, garnished with lime wedges.

SUGGESTED ACCOMPANIMENT: *brown rice.*

EDITOR'S NOTE: *For a slightly less spicy syrup in which to marinate the fruit, remove the strips of chili 10 minutes after the syrup has been set aside to cool.*

Thai-Style Chicken Satay

SATAY, SKEWERS OF MEAT GRILLED OVER CHARCOAL, ARE ENJOYED ALL OVER SOUTHEAST ASIA. THIS CHICKEN VERSION IS DISTINGUISHED BY THE TYPICALLY THAI SPICES GINGER, LEMON GRASS, AND CILANTRO.

Serves 6
Working time: about 1 hour
Total time: about 2 hours and 30 minutes
(includes marinating)

Calories **260**
Protein **22g.**
Cholesterol **80mg.**
Total fat **14g.**
Saturated fat **4g.**
Sodium **95mg.**

2 lb. chicken thighs, skinned and boned
1 tsp. tamarind concentrate (glossary), optional
2 garlic cloves, chopped
6 shallots, chopped
1-inch piece fresh ginger
1 tbsp. dark brown sugar
1 lime, juice only
1 tbsp. safflower oil
4 tsp. Asian fish sauce (glossary)

Pineapple and cucumber relish

½ slightly underripe pineapple
½ cucumber, peeled
¼ tsp. salt
¼ to ½ tsp. sugar
2 limes, juice only
2 small red onions, sliced into rings
1 red chili pepper, seeded and thinly sliced into rings (cautionary note, page 63)

Peanut and coconut dipping sauce

6 tbsp. unsalted dry-roasted peanuts, coarsely crushed
1 garlic clove, chopped
1 medium red onion, chopped
2 lemon grass bulbs, chopped
2 tbsp. cilantro
1 red chili pepper, seeded and chopped (cautionary note, page 63)
1 tsp. safflower oil
1 cup unsweetened coconut milk
1 tbsp. Asian fish sauce (glossary)
1 tsp. dark soy sauce
2 tsp. dark brown sugar
½ tsp. shrimp paste (optional)

Cut the chicken across the grain into long ribbons about ¼ inch thick and ¾ inch wide. Place the strips in a large, shallow, nonreactive dish.

Pound the tamarind concentrate, if you are using it, the garlic, the shallots, the ginger, and the sugar to a thick paste using a mortar and pestle. Add the lime juice, oil, and fish sauce, and stir them in. Pour this mixture over the chicken strips and turn them over to coat them thoroughly. Cover the dish and let the chicken marinate in the refrigerator for at least one hour, or overnight, stirring occasionally.

For the relish, remove the flesh from the pineapple half with a grapefruit knife, leaving a ½-inch-thick shell. Cover the shell with plastic wrap and put it into the refrigerator until it is needed. Remove any brown eyes from the flesh, and discard the central core if it is fibrous. Cut the flesh into ¾-inch chunks. Halve the cucumber lengthwise; remove the seeds with a spoon and discard them. Cut the cucumber into chunks. Mix the salt, ¼ teaspoon of the sugar, and the lime juice in a bowl. Add the pineapple, cucumber, red onion, and chili, and toss these ingredients well; add the remaining sugar if the pineapple is too sharp for your taste. Cover the dish with plastic wrap and place it in the refrigerator for at least one hour, or overnight, stirring the contents several times.

Soak twenty-four 10-inch bamboo skewers in water for 10 minutes. Remove the chicken strips from the marinade and thread each strip onto a skewer as if you were sewing with a needle, then gather up the strip slightly so that the meat on each skewer measures about 5 inches in length. Reserve the marinade.

Next, make the peanut and coconut sauce. Pound the peanuts, garlic, red onion, lemon grass, cilantro, and chili to a smooth paste using the mortar and pestle. Heat the oil in a wok or heavy-bottomed skillet and gently sauté the paste until it is light brown. Add the coconut milk, fish sauce, soy sauce, sugar, and shrimp paste, if you are using it, and bring the ingredients to a boil. Remove the pan from the heat and cover it with a lid.

Lightly oil the rack, and cook the satay over hot coals for 8 to 10 minutes, turning them once and brushing them several times with the marinade. Spoon the pineapple and cucumber relish into the chilled pineapple shell. Transfer the peanut and coconut sauce to serving bowls. Serve the satay immediately, with the dipping sauce and the relish.

SUGGESTED ACCOMPANIMENT: *triangles of toasted thin bread.*

AN ARRAY OF HOMEMADE SAUSAGES

Prepared sausages, a barbecue favorite, often contain a high percentage of fat, salt, preservatives, and other undesirable ingredients. By making sausages yourself, however, you can choose the cut of meat and trim it of all fat, vary the ingredients, and experiment with interesting combinations of herbs and spices. Meat may even be omitted entirely. Do not overchop or overgrind sausage meat, as too smooth a texture will cause the sausage to dry out during cooking. Aim for a coarse texture, achieved either by patient hand-chopping using two sharp, heavy knives or by using a meat grinder. Good results can also be achieved with a food processor, but be sure to chill the container and blade for at least 30 minutes, and hand-chop the meat into ¾-inch cubes before processing it; never put more than 1 pound at a time into the processor bowl and stop the machine as soon as the meat is chopped, just before it forms a ball.

Use natural lamb sausage casings, which are obtainable from good butchers. Before filling them, soak the casings in acidulated water for about one hour, until they are soft and elastic, then cut them into them into lengths of about 3½ feet. Rinse each length of casing by rolling one end over a sink faucet or funnel and running cold water through it. Discard any punctured casings and lay out the rest to drain.

To fill the casings, roll one length onto the tube of the sausage-making attachment of a meat grinder. Leave about 4 inches hanging loose and tie a knot in the end. Fill the grinder's bowl with the stuffing and turn the handle. As the casing fills, gradually slip it off the tube; make sure the stuffing is loosely packed. Alternatively, use a food processor with a sausage-making attachment, or gather the casing around the neck of a funnel and press the filling through the funnel with a pestle.

When only about 4 inches of casing remains unfilled, slip it off the tube or funnel and knot it. Roll the casing on a work surface to even out the stuffing. To form links, twist the casing three or four times every 5 inches.

Chicken Sausages with Ricotta and Spinach

Makes 12 sausages
Working time: about 1 hour
Total time: about 1 hour and 15 minutes

¼ lb. spinach, washed, center stems removed
2 cups loosely packed sorrel, washed, center stems removed
1 lb. 6 oz. chicken (leg or thigh), ground
⅔ cup low-fat ricotta cheese
4 shallots, finely chopped
1 tbsp. chopped fresh parsley
1 tbsp. chopped fresh tarragon
¾ tsp. salt
freshly ground black pepper
⅓ cup plain low-fat yogurt
7 feet lamb sausage casings, soaked

Per sausage:
Calories **105**
Protein **16g.**
Cholesterol **45mg.**
Total fat **3g.**
Saturated fat **1g.**
Sodium **160mg.**

Blanch the spinach and sorrel, and refresh them under cold water; drain and chop them. Wrap them in a piece of cheesecloth or in paper towels, squeeze them dry, and place them in a bowl. Mix in the chicken, ricotta, shallots, parsley, tarragon, salt, some pepper, and half of the yogurt. Add more yogurt until the mixture is loose enough to be squeezed through a pastry bag but stiff enough to be molded into a walnut-size ball.

Following the instructions *(box, left),* fill the casings with the mixture and form links. Cut between the links to separate the sausages. Prick each sausage several times. Oil the rack lightly and cook the sausages over medium-hot coals, turning them often, until they are golden brown—10 to 15 minutes.

SUGGESTED ACCOMPANIMENT: *a salad of radicchio, red onion, and daikon radishes.*

Lamb Sausages with Yogurt and Thyme

Makes 12 sausages
Working time: about 1 hour
Total time: about 1 hour and 15 minutes

⅓ cup couscous
1 lb. 6 oz. lean leg of lamb, trimmed of fat and ground
¼ cup plain low-fat yogurt
¼ cup sour cream
1 tbsp. virgin olive oil
1 large sweet red or orange pepper, peeled (technique, page 138), seeded, and finely diced
1½ tbsp. fresh thyme
1 onion, finely chopped
2 cloves garlic, finely chopped
4 black olives, pitted and finely diced
¾ tsp. salt
freshly ground black pepper
7 feet lamb sausage casings, soaked

Per sausage:
Calories **135**
Protein **16g.**
Cholesterol **40mg.**
Total fat **6g.**
Saturated fat **5g.**
Sodium **175mg.**

Soak the couscous in ½ cup of water for 10 to 15 minutes, until it has absorbed all the water. Place the soaked couscous on a piece of cheesecloth or a paper towel, and squeeze out as much water as possible. Put the couscous in a large bowl. Add the lamb, yogurt, sour cream, olive oil, sweet pepper, thyme, onion, garlic, olives, salt, and some black pepper, and mix the ingredients well.

Following the instructions *(box, left),* fill the casings with the mixture and form links. Cut between the links to separate the sausages. Prick each sausage several times. Oil the rack lightly and cook the sausages over medium-hot coals, turning them often, until they are golden brown—10 to 15 minutes.

SUGGESTED ACCOMPANIMENT: *a salad of oakleaf lettuce.*

Pork Sausages with Orange and Sage

Makes 12 sausages
Working time: about 1 hour
Total time: about 1 hour and 15 minutes

1½ lb. pork loin, trimmed of excess fat, coarsely chopped
¼ lb. lean bacon, trimmed of fat and finely diced
4 tsp. grated orange zest
2 tbsp. shredded fresh sage leaves
1 onion, finely chopped
1 garlic clove, finely chopped
1 tsp. ground ginger
¾ tsp. salt
ground white pepper
2 tbsp. sweet vermouth or sherry
1½ tsp. orange-flavored liqueur or brandy
2 tbsp. fresh orange juice
¾ cup fresh breadcrumbs
7 feet lamb sausage casings, soaked
¼ cup unsalted chicken stock (recipe, page 139), reduced by boiling to 2 tbsp.

Per sausage:
Calories **170**
Protein **20g.**
Cholesterol **45mg.**
Total fat **8g.**
Saturated fat **4g.**
Sodium **325mg.**

In a large bowl, blend together all the ingredients except for the casings and 1 tablespoon of the reduced stock. Gradually blend in some or all of the remaining stock until the mixture is loose enough to be squeezed through a pastry bag but stiff enough to be molded into a walnut-size ball.

Following the instructions *(box, left),* fill the casings with the stuffing and form links. Cut between the links to separate the sausages. Prick each sausage several times. Oil the rack lightly and cook the sausages over medium-hot coals, turning them often, until they are golden brown—10 to 15 minutes.

SUGGESTED ACCOMPANIMENT: *orange and watercress salad.*

Beef Sausages with Five-Spice Powder

Makes 12 sausages
Working time: about 1 hour
Total time: about 1 hour and 15 minutes

1¼ lb. lean beef round, trimmed of fat and ground
½ cup rolled oats
2 garlic cloves, finely chopped
1-inch piece fresh ginger, finely chopped
5 scallions, finely chopped
1½ tbsp. low-sodium light soy sauce
1½ tbsp. low-sodium dark soy sauce
3 tbsp. rice wine or dry sherry
1 tsp. honey
2 tsp. five-spice powder (glossary)
¼ tsp. cayenne pepper
7 feet lamb sausage casings, soaked
⅓ cup unsalted veal stock (recipe, page 139) or water

Per sausage:
Calories **155**
Protein **16g.**
Cholesterol **40mg.**
Total fat **5g.**
Saturated fat **3g.**
Sodium **50mg.**

In a bowl, blend together all the ingredients except for the casings and half of the stock or water. Mix in some or all of the remaining stock or water until the mixture is loose enough to be squeezed through a pastry bag but stiff enough to be shaped into a walnut-size ball.

Following the instructions, *(box, left),* fill the casings with the stuffing and form links. Cut between the links to separate the sausages. Prick each sausage several times. Oil the rack lightly and grill the sausages over medium-hot coals, turning them often, until they are golden brown—10 to 15 minutes.

SUGGESTED ACCOMPANIMENTS: *wild rice; oyster mushroom salad.*

Spicy Potato Sausages with Cilantro

Makes 12 sausages
Working time: about 1 hour
Total time: about 2 hours

1 tbsp. unsalted butter
1 large onion, finely chopped
10 oz. mushrooms, finely chopped
1 or 2 garlic cloves, finely chopped
1-inch piece fresh ginger, finely chopped
1½ lb. potatoes, boiled and mashed
1 egg, plus 1 egg white
1 tsp. poppy seeds
1 tsp. mustard seeds, toasted
1½ tbsp. cut chives
1½ tbsp. chopped cilantro
¾ tsp. salt
¼ tsp. cayenne pepper
freshly ground black pepper
¼ cup plain low-fat yogurt
7 feet lamb sausage casings, soaked

Per sausage:
Calories **75**
Protein **3g.**
Cholesterol **20mg.**
Total fat **2g.**
Saturated fat **1g.**
Sodium **140mg.**

Melt the butter in a pan, and sauté the onion over medium heat until it is soft—about five minutes. Increase the heat, add the mushrooms, garlic, and ginger, and sauté until the mixture is quite dry—about three minutes.

Place the potatoes in a bowl over a pan of simmering water. Add the egg and egg white, and stir until the egg thickens. Remove the bowl from the heat, and stir in the onion mixture and all the ingredients except for the casings. Cool the filling, then chill it.

Following the instructions *(box, left),* fill the casings with the mixture and form links. Cut between the links to separate the sausages. Prick each sausage several times. Oil the rack lightly and cook the sausages over medium-hot coals, turning them often, until they are golden brown—15 to 20 minutes.

SUGGESTED ACCOMPANIMENT: *a mixed salad.*

Cod Steaks Topped with Tomato and Basil

Serves 4
Working time: about 20 minutes
Total time: about 30 minutes

Calories **170**
Protein **27g.**
Cholesterol **75mg.**
Total fat **4g.**
Saturated fat **1g.**
Sodium **120mg.**

1 lb. tomatoes (about 3 medium), peeled, seeded (technique, page 138), and chopped
¾ cup loosely packed basil leaves, chopped
3 tbsp. medium-dry sherry
⅛ tsp. salt
freshly ground black pepper
2 tsp. virgin olive oil
4 cod steaks (about 5 oz. each), central bones removed

In a bowl, mix the tomatoes with the basil and sherry, and season the mixture with the salt and some pepper. Brush the olive oil over four double-thickness rectangles of foil, each one measuring about 13 by 8 inches. Lay a cod steak on each piece of foil and top it with a quarter of the tomato mixture. Wrap the foil around the fish steaks, sealing the edges securely to keep all the cooking juices in the packets.

Cook the cod steaks over hot coals for three to five minutes on each side, taking care not to split the foil when turning the packets over. Unwrap the packets with the tomato side up and slide the contents of each one onto an individual plate. Remove and discard the thin strips of cod skin and serve the steaks at once.

SUGGESTED ACCOMPANIMENT: *parslied new potatoes.*

Grilled Fish Steaks with Red Peppers

Serves 4
Working time: about 45 minutes
Total time: about 1 hour

Calories **215**
Protein **27g.**
Cholesterol **75mg.**
Total fat **12g.**
Saturated fat **2g.**
Sodium **215mg.**

1¼ lb. grouper or cod fillets, skin left on, cut into 4 pieces
1½ tbsp. virgin olive oil
2 limes, juice of one, the other cut into wedges for garnish
½ tsp. salt
freshly ground black pepper
2 large sweet red peppers

Put the fish pieces, skin side down, in a shallow, nonreactive dish. In a small bowl, combine the olive oil, lime juice, salt, and some black pepper. Reserve 1 tablespoon of this marinade, and brush the remainder on the exposed side of the steaks. Set the fish aside, covered, to marinate for 30 minutes.

Meanwhile, place the sweet red peppers on the rack over hot coals. Cook them for 10 to 15 minutes, turning them frequently, until their skins blacken. Remove the peppers from the grill and allow them to cool.

When the peppers are cool enough to handle, peel off their skins. Slice the skinned peppers thinly and evenly. Toss the slices in the reserved marinade, and set them aside until they are needed.

Place the fish in an oiled grilling basket and grill it, skin side down, over low coals, for 10 to 15 minutes. Turn the fish over and cook it for 5 minutes more. Serve the fish immediately, accompanied by the red-pepper strips and garnished with the lime wedges.

SUGGESTED ACCOMPANIMENT: *potato and watercress salad.*

Sesame Seafood Kabobs

Serves 4
Working time: about 30 minutes
Total time: about 1 hour and 30 minutes

Calories **195**
Protein **21g.**
Cholesterol **85mg.**
Total fat **7g.**
Saturated fat **3g.**
Sodium **130mg.**

1 cup dry white wine
1 tbsp. safflower oil
1 garlic clove, crushed
½ lemon, grated zest, plus 1 tbsp. juice
⅛ tsp. salt
freshly ground black pepper
¾ lb. monkfish fillets
1 tsp. cornstarch
1 tbsp. chopped mixed fresh herbs, such as basil, parsley, and chives
1 tbsp. toasted sesame seeds
4 large raw shrimp (with the heads on, if possible)
8 scallops, bright white connective tissue removed
shredded lettuce for garnish

In a bowl, mix ½ cup of the wine with the oil, garlic, lemon zest and juice, salt, and some pepper. Pour half of the mixture into a small, nonreactive saucepan and set it aside. Cut the monkfish into 12 equal pieces and add them to the wine mixture remaining in the bowl. Turn the pieces over in the marinade to coat them thoroughly. Cover the bowl and place it in the refrigerator for one to two hours.

Add the remaining wine to the mixture in the saucepan. Blend the cornstarch to a smooth paste with a little cold water. Stir the paste into the liquid in the pan and heat it slowly, stirring continuously, until it boils and thickens. Remove the pan from the heat, then stir in the mixed herbs and the sesame seeds. Cover the pan and set it over very low heat to keep the sauce hot while you cook the kabobs.

Lightly oil four skewers. Drain the monkfish and thread the pieces onto the skewers, alternating them with the shrimp and scallops. Cook the kabobs over medium-hot coals for three to five minutes on each side; turn the kabobs gently, otherwise the pieces of seafood may break.

Spread the shredded lettuce on a large platter and pour the sauce into a warmed pitcher. Arrange the kabobs on the lettuce and serve them immediately, accompanied by the sauce.

EDITOR'S NOTE: *To toast sesame seeds, sprinkle a layer of seeds in a heavy-bottomed pan, cover the pan, and cook the seeds over high heat. When they begin to pop, keep the pan on the heat for one minute more but shake it constantly.*

Tarragon-Marinated Salmon with Skewered New Potatoes

Serves 8
Working time: about 1 hour
Total time: about 14 hours (includes marinating)

Calories **305**
Protein **26g.**
Cholesterol **85mg.**
Total fat **17g.**
Saturated fat **4g.**
Sodium **395mg.**

2¼ lb. salmon fillet (either one side or two)
½ oz. fresh tarragon, chopped
1 tbsp. salt
2 tbsp. light brown sugar
1 tbsp. vodka
1½ tsp. crushed black peppercorns
¾ lb. very small new potatoes
1 tsp. grape-seed or safflower oil
dried fennel twigs or seeds, to burn on the coals (optional)
fennel leaves for garnish

Wipe the salmon and run a finger along the fillet to feel for any remaining small bones: Remove these bones with a pair of tweezers. Lay the salmon in a large, shallow, nonreactive dish. In another, small, nonreactive dish, mix the chopped tarragon, salt, sugar, vodka, and 1 teaspoon of the crushed black peppercorns. Using the back of a spoon, spread this tarragon marinade all over the flesh side of the salmon. (If you are using two sides of salmon, sandwich the flesh sides together.) Cover the salmon loosely with a damp cloth, and let it marinate in the refrigerator at least 12 hours, or up to 48 hours.

Soak six bamboo skewers in cold water for 10 minutes, then drain them. Cook the new potatoes in boiling water until they are just tender—10 to 15 minutes.

Drain the potatoes and return them to the saucepan. Add the grape-seed or safflower oil and the remaining crushed peppercorns, and toss the potatoes until they are evenly coated in oil and peppercorns. Thread the potatoes evenly onto the drained, soaked skewers, and set them aside.

Lightly oil the rack. Wipe off all the marinade from the salmon and cook it, flesh side down, over hot coals for one minute. Turn the salmon over and grill it for six to nine minutes more, until it is almost cooked through but not quite opaque near the bone.

After about three minutes, place the skewered potatoes on the rack and heat them through until they are browned. At the same time, throw the dried fennel twigs or seeds, if you are using them, onto the coals to produce aromatic smoke.

Transfer the cooked salmon to a large serving dish. Arrange the new potatoes around the salmon, and garnish the dish with fennel leaves. To serve the fish, carve off thin slices, keeping the knife almost parallel with the fillet.

SUGGESTED ACCOMPANIMENT: *cucumber, grape, and curly endive salad with a yogurt dressing.*

Grilled Tuna Steaks

Serves 6
Working time: about 30 minutes
Total time: about 5 hours (includes marinating)

Calories **275**
Protein **35g.**
Cholesterol **80mg.**
Total fat **16g.**
Saturated fat **5g.**
Sodium **105mg.**

3 tuna steaks (about ½ lb. each)
8 scallions, chopped
2-inch piece fresh ginger, grated
4 garlic cloves
1 large onion, chopped
1 lime, juice only
¼ cup white wine vinegar
2 tbsp. virgin olive oil
1 tsp. finely crushed black peppercorns
⅛ tsp. salt
¾ cup plain low-fat yogurt
lime slices for garnish

Cut the tuna steaks in half and remove the bone from the middle of each steak. Place the pieces in a shallow, nonreactive dish.

Put the chopped scallions, grated ginger, garlic cloves, and chopped onion into a food processor or blender. Add the lime juice, wine vinegar, and oil, and process the ingredients to a smooth purée. Stir the crushed peppercorns and salt into the purée, then pour two-thirds of it over the tuna pieces, coating them evenly; reserve the remaining purée for use in the sauce. Cover the tuna pieces and let them marinate in the refrigerator for at least three hours, or up to 12 hours. Remove them from the refrigerator at least one hour before they are to be cooked, to allow them to reach room temperature.

Before cooking the tuna, soak six bamboo skewers in water for 10 minutes. Thread one skewer through each piece of tuna about 1 inch from the straight, cut edge, to keep the piece flat as it cooks. Cook the tuna over hot coals for five to six minutes on each side, until it is lightly browned and cooked through.

While the tuna is cooking, stir the remaining purée into the yogurt to make a sauce. Transfer the sauce to a serving bowl or sauceboat. Remove the skewers from the tuna pieces. Serve the tuna with the yogurt sauce, garnished with lime slices.

SUGGESTED ACCOMPANIMENT: *hot herb toast.*

Leaf-Wrapped Stuffed Herring

Serves 6
Working (and total) time: about 1 hour

Calories **310**
Protein **20g.**
Cholesterol **130mg.**
Total fat **20g.**
Saturated fat **4g.**
Sodium **170mg.**

1 tsp. unsalted butter
1 small onion, finely chopped
4½ oz. fresh or canned shad roe, broken into pieces
1 tart apple, peeled, cored, finely diced, and put into acidulated water
½ lemon, juice only
¼ cup fresh white breadcrumbs
3 tbsp. rolled oats
1 tbsp. apple juice, cider, or water
2 tbsp. finely chopped fresh dill
freshly ground black pepper
3 heads Boston lettuce
6 herring (about 6 oz. each), gutted and boned
¼ tsp. salt
2 tbsp. Dijon mustard
12 sprigs dill

First make the shad-roe stuffing. Melt the butter in a heavy-bottomed, nonreactive saucepan, then add the chopped onion and cook it gently, stirring occasionally, until it is soft but not browned—about five minutes. Add the roe to the pan and cook for two to three minutes, stirring constantly, until all the roe is opaque and broken up. Drain the apple and add it to the roe mixture. Stir in the lemon juice, and cook the stuffing gently until the apple is soft but not mushy—about five minutes. Remove the pan from the heat and allow the stuffing to cool slightly.

Mix the breadcrumbs with 2 tablespoons of the rolled oats, moisten them with the apple juice, cider, or water, and add them to the stuffing with the dill and some freshly ground black pepper. Mix the stuffing ingredients together well.

Select and wash 24 large lettuce leaves; reserve the lettuce hearts for use in a salad. Keeping the leaves whole, trim out any tough stems. Plunge the leaves into a large saucepan of boiling water, a few at a time, for two to three seconds, then drain them immediately and refresh them under cold running water. Drain the leaves again and set them aside.

Season the inside of the herring with the salt and some pepper. Divide the stuffing among the fish, spreading it evenly inside the body cavity. Press the sides of each fish firmly together to enclose the stuffing. Spread 1 teaspoon of the mustard evenly over the skin of each herring, then coat them in the remaining rolled oats, pressing it gently all over the fish but leaving the head and tail exposed.

For each herring in turn, lay four blanched lettuce leaves on the work surface, overlapping them neatly to make an oblong of leaves large enough to wrap around the body of the fish. Top the lettuce with two dill sprigs, and lay the oats-coated herring on the dill. Wrap the lettuce around the fish, leaving the head and tail exposed but covering the body completely.

Lightly oil the rack or the grilling basket, if you are using one. Lay the fish on the rack, with the seam in the lettuce wrapping underneath. (The seam will seal itself quickly during cooking.) Cook the fish for 5 to 10 minutes on each side, according to how plump they are. Check that the fish are cooked by cutting into the middle of the plumpest herring: If the fish flakes easily, it is done. Serve the fish immediately.

SUGGESTED ACCOMPANIMENTS: *baked potatoes; lettuce hearts dressed with sour cream and dill; thinly sliced rye or oatmeal bread.*

EDITOR'S NOTE: *To bone a herring, use a pair of kitchen scissors to snip through the backbone at both ends. Make sure that the belly is slit right down to the tail, then lay the fish, belly side down, on the work surface and press firmly down the length of the body. Turn the fish over and pull away the backbone, starting at the tail end. Use the point of a knife to gently ease away any bones that cling to the fish; pick off any stray bones with a pair of tweezers.*

Whole Anise-Orange Turbot

Serves 4
Working (and total) time: about 25 minutes

Calories **250**
Protein **20g.**
Cholesterol **80mg.**
Total fat **15g.**
Saturated fat **4g.**
Sodium **125mg.**

1½ tsp. ground fennel seed
1 whole turbot (about 3¼ lb.), gills removed
⅓ cup plain low-fat yogurt
1 orange, 4 slices reserved for garnish, peel and ½ teaspoon finely grated zest of remainder
⅛ tsp. salt
ground white pepper
6 dried fennel stalks
2 tsp. anise-flavored liqueur
curly endive leaves for garnish

Sprinkle a little of the ground fennel seed in the gill cavity of the turbot. In a small bowl, mix the yogurt, grated orange zest, salt, and some white pepper with the remaining ground fennel seed, and set the mixture aside until it is needed.

Set the rack at its lowest position and oil it lightly. Place the turbot on the rack and grill the fish, dark-skin side down, over hot coals for two and a half minutes. Remove the fish from the grill and place it on a work surface. Using the point of a sharp knife, cut the skin free at the tail and head ends of the fish. Strip off all the dark skin.

Return the fish to the grill, placing the white-skin side down, and grill the fish for about one and a half minutes. Remove the fish from the grill. Transfer it to the work surface and strip off the white skin.

Lightly oil a grilling basket. Coat one side of the fish with half of the yogurt mixture, and place it, coated side down, on one half of the grilling basket. Spread the remaining yogurt mixture over the second side of the turbot. Close the basket and place the fish on the grill with the thick side down. (The flesh is thicker on the side that was covered by dark skin.)

Grill the fish for two minutes, then turn the basket over and grill the second side for one minute. Repeat this process twice more. Throw the orange peel and fennel stalks onto the coals to produce aromatic smoke. Pour 1 teaspoon of the anise-flavored liqueur over the thick side of the fish and grill it for two minutes. Turn the fish and pour the remaining teaspoon of liqueur over the thin side. Grill the fish for one minute. The flesh should be opaque all over and flake away easily from the bone: Test the fish at its thickest part with a small knife. Grill it for a little longer if necessary, but do not overcook it.

Transfer the fish to a warmed platter and serve it at once, garnished with the four orange slices and the curly endive leaves.

SUGGESTED ACCOMPANIMENTS: *grilled new potatoes; fennel bulbs wrapped in foil and cooked on the grill.*

EDITOR'S NOTE: *Turbot are sold already gutted, but you will have to ask the fish dealer to remove the gills.*

Skewered Cheese and Tofu Patties

Serves 4
Working time: about 45 minutes
Total time: about 55 minutes

alories **240**
otein **15g.**
holesterol **30mg.**
otal fat **12g.**
aturated fat **5g.**
odium **435mg.**

1 tsp. safflower oil
1 medium onion, finely chopped
¾ cup fresh white breadcrumbs
½ lb. smoked tofu
4 oz. Edam cheese, coarsely grated (about 1¼ cups)
freshly ground black pepper
½ tsp. dry mustard
2 tbsp. chopped fresh parsley
12 fresh sage leaves, coarsely chopped
2 tbsp. unbleached all-purpose flour

Soak eight bamboo skewers in water for 10 minutes.

Meanwhile, heat the oil in a small, heavy-bottomed, nonstick skillet. Add the onion and cook it over medium heat until it is transparent—about eight minutes. Stir in the breadcrumbs. Remove the pan from the heat and set the mixture aside to cool. Chop the tofu finely in a food processor, then add the Edam cheese, black pepper, mustard, parsley, and sage. Add the breadcrumb mixture to the processor bowl and process briefly, until all the ingredients are evenly combined.

Divide the mixture into 24 equal portions. Mold each portion into a small, oval patty. Thread these patties onto the bamboo skewers: Take a patty in one hand and thread a skewer gently through it lengthwise, holding it firmly in shape as you do so. Keep the remaining patties covered with a damp cloth while you are working to prevent them from drying out. Sprinkle the flour on the work surface and carefully roll the skewers in it, so that all the patties are coated evenly in flour; brush off any excess flour.

Place a griddle or baking sheet on the grill and brush it lightly with oil. Arrange the skewers on the griddle or baking sheet and cook the patties for six to eight minutes, turning them frequently, until they are golden brown all over. Serve the patties immediately.

SUGGESTED ACCOMPANIMENT: *a salad of shredded lettuce hearts and onion rings, with a yogurt and parsley dressing.*

Greek Vegetable, Fruit, and Cheese Kabobs

Serves 8
Working time: about 1 hour
Total time: about 2 hours

Calories **170**
Protein **7g.**
Cholesterol **25mg.**
Total fat **10g.**
Saturated fat **5g.**
Sodium **335mg.**

¼ lb. eggplant, cut into eight 1-inch cubes
¼ tsp. salt
8 new potatoes (about ¾ lb.), scrubbed
2 onions, quartered
2 sweet red or orange peppers, seeded, each cut into 8 squares
1 small unpeeled cucumber, cut into 8 thick slices
8 large mushrooms, wiped clean
2 nectarines, pitted and quartered
7 oz. feta cheese, cut into 8 cubes
2 tbsp. virgin olive oil
fresh grape leaves for garnish (optional)
Minted sauce
1¼ cups plain low-fat yogurt
3 tbsp. chopped fresh mint
1 garlic clove, crushed (optional)

Sprinkle the eggplant with the salt and set it aside for 30 minutes. Meanwhile, cook the potatoes and quartered onions in a pan of simmering water for 15 to 20 minutes, until they are just tender. Drain the vegetables and allow them to cool.

Rinse the eggplant and put it in a large saucepan of boiling water. Return the water to a boil, lower the heat, and simmer the eggplant for two minutes. Add the peppers and cook for one minute, then add the cucumber and cook for one minute. Drain the vegetables and allow them to cool. Combine the ingredients for the sauce and put it into a serving bowl.

Put the cooked vegetables on a tray with the mushrooms, nectarines, and cheese, and sprinkle them with the olive oil. Lightly brush eight metal skewers with oil, and thread each skewer with one of each item from the tray. Lightly oil the rack, and cook the kabobs over hot coals, turning them frequently, until they are tender and lightly charred—about 15 minutes.

Serve the kabobs on a platter lined with grape leaves, if desired, and accompanied by the sauce.

Chickpea Croquettes with Sesame Sauce

Serves 6
Working time: about 40 minutes
Total time: about 2 hours and 35 minutes (includes soaking)

Calories **265**
Protein **14g.**
Cholesterol **45mg.**
Total fat **12g.**
Saturated fat **3g.**
Sodium **210mg.**

¾ cup dried chickpeas, picked over
1 tbsp. safflower or peanut oil
1 small onion, finely chopped
2 garlic cloves, crushed
2 tsp. ground cumin
1 tsp. ground coriander
2 oz. cheddar cheese, grated (about ⅔ cup)
¼ cup fresh whole-wheat breadcrumbs
2 tbsp. chopped fresh parsley
1 tbsp. chopped fresh mint
1 tbsp. fresh lemon juice
1 egg, beaten
⅛ tsp. salt
freshly ground black pepper
1 egg white, beaten
⅔ cup dry whole-wheat breadcrumbs
6 small firm tomatoes (about 1 lb.), quartered
Sesame sauce
2 tbsp. tahini
1½ tbsp. fresh lemon juice
1 tbsp. low-sodium soy sauce

Rinse the chickpeas under cold running water, then put them in a large, heavy-bottomed saucepan and pour in enough cold water to cover them by about 3 inches. Discard any that float to the surface. Cover the pan, leaving the lid ajar, and slowly bring the liquid to a boil over medium-low heat. Boil the chickpeas for two minutes, then turn off the heat and soak them for at least one hour. (Alternatively, soak the peas overnight in cold water.)

Drain the peas; return them to the pan and cover them with at least twice their volume of fresh water. Bring the liquid to a boil, lower the heat to maintain a strong simmer, and cook the peas until they are tender—about one hour.

Meanwhile, make the sauce. In a small bowl, mix the tahini and lemon juice, then gradually add the soy sauce and 4 tablespoons of water, stirring well. Soak 12 wooden skewers in water for about 10 minutes.

Heat the oil in a heavy-bottomed skillet over medium heat, and sauté the chopped onion with the garlic until the onion is tender—about five minutes. Add the cumin and coriander, and cook the mixture for two to three minutes more.

To make the croquettes, put the chickpeas into a food processor and grind them until they are smooth. Transfer the ground chickpeas to a bowl, and add the onion mixture, cheese, fresh breadcrumbs, parsley, mint, lemon juice, beaten whole egg, salt, and some pepper. Mix the ingredients together well, then form the mixture into 36 equal-size balls. Dip each one in the beaten egg white and coat it with dry breadcrumbs.

Thread three croquettes onto each of the 12 skewers, alternating them with tomato quarters. Place the skewers over hot coals and cook them for about three minutes on each side, or until they are golden brown. Serve the croquettes hot with the sesame sauce.

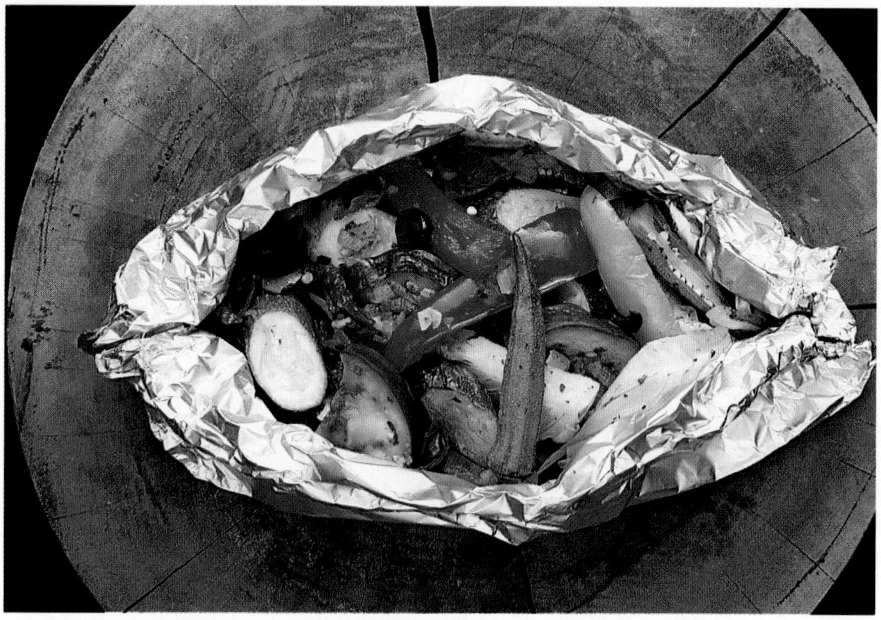

Marinated Mixed Vegetables Cooked in Foil

Serves 6
Working time: about 35 minutes
Total time: about 2 hours and 15 minutes

Calories **75**
Protein **2g.**
Cholesterol **0mg.**
Total fat **5g.**
Saturated fat **1g.**
Sodium **45mg.**

1 small eggplant (about 6 oz.), stem removed, cut diagonally into ¾-inch-thick slices
1 tbsp. salt
1 tbsp. fresh lemon juice
6 oz. small young okra
1 small fennel bulb, cut into 6 wedges, feathery top reserved and chopped
1 medium zucchini (about 6 oz.), sliced diagonally into ¾-inch pieces
1 sweet red pepper (about 6 oz.), seeded, deribbed, and cut into 12 strips
1 sweet orange pepper (about 6 oz.), seeded, deribbed, and cut into 12 strips

Herb and lemon marinade

2 tbsp. virgin olive oil
12 small shallots
1 garlic clove
6 sun-dried tomatoes (glossary), drained and quartered
1 lemon, juice only
1½ tsp. chopped fresh parsley
1½ tsp. fresh thyme
1½ tsp. chopped fresh oregano
2 pitted black olives, sliced into thin rings
¼ tsp. salt
freshly ground black pepper

Place the eggplant slices in a colander, sprinkle the salt over them, and set them aside to drain for 30 minutes to eliminate their natural bitterness. Rinse the eggplant slices well and pat them dry with paper towels.

Add the lemon juice to a nonreactive pan of boiling water. Drop the okra into the pan, cook them for five seconds, then add the fennel wedges and cook them for 10 seconds. Drain the vegetables, refresh them under cold running water, and drain them again. When the okra are cool, halve them lengthwise. Place the eggplant, okra, fennel, zucchini, and sweet-pepper strips in a large bowl.

To prepare the marinade, heat the olive oil in a heavy-bottomed, nonreactive skillet over low heat, and cook the shallots until they are golden brown—about eight minutes. Add the garlic and cook it for 20 seconds, then remove the pan from the heat. Stir in the sun-dried tomato quarters, and let the mixture infuse and cool for about 15 minutes. Add the lemon juice, parsley, thyme, oregano, olives, salt, and some pepper, and mix in the reserved fennel top. Pour the marinade over the vegetables, toss them gently, and cover the bowl. Let the vegetables marinate for at least one hour at room temperature, or overnight in the refrigerator, turning them several times.

Cut six rectangles of foil, each measuring about 24 by 12 inches, and fold them in half crosswise. Pile one-sixth of the marinated vegetable mixture in the center of a foil square. Bring the top and bottom edges of the square together, fold them over twice to seal them, then fold in the sides of the square, to make a parcel. Make five more parcels in the same way.

Cook the parcels over medium-hot coals for 20 to 30 minutes. Unfold the parcels to serve the vegetables.

Grilled Vegetables

VEGETABLES, GRILLED WHOLE OR HALVED, OR QUARTERED AND SKEWERED, MAKE A DELICIOUS AND SIMPLE ACCOMPANIMENT TO ANY MEAT OR FISH DISH. THE SELECTION AND QUANTITIES SHOWN BELOW ARE SIMPLY SUGGESTIONS THAT YOU MAY IMPROVISE UPON.

Serves 24
Working time: about 40 minutes
Total time: about 1 hour and 40 minutes (includes marinating)

Calories **50**
Protein **1g.**
Cholesterol **0mg.**
Total fat **4g.**
Saturated fat **1g.**
Sodium **50mg.**

48 shallots, blanched
3 fennel bulbs, trimmed, halved, and blanched
12 baby corn, trimmed, cut in half crosswise, and blanched
24 cherry tomatoes, stems removed
4 sweet green peppers
4 sweet yellow peppers
2 tbsp. safflower oil
3 red onions, halved
3 white onions, halved

Marinade for shallots

½ tbsp. virgin olive oil

1 tbsp. fresh lemon juice
1 tbsp. very finely chopped fresh parsley
⅛ tsp. salt
ground white pepper
Marinade for fennel
1 tbsp. virgin olive oil
1 garlic clove, crushed
1 tbsp. chopped fresh marjoram
⅛ tsp. salt
ground white pepper

In a large bowl, mix together the ingredients for the marinade for the shallots. Add the shallots to the mixture, and stir to coat them thoroughly. Cover the bowl and let the shallots marinate for one hour.

Meanwhile, in another, small bowl, mix together the ingredients for the marinade for the fennel. Lay the blanched fennel in a shallow dish, and brush the marinade all over the fennel. Cover the dish and let the fennel marinate for one hour.

Thread the pieces of corn and the cherry tomatoes alternately onto two long metal skewers. Thread the marinated shallots onto as many skewers as you need.

Brush the peppers with a little of the safflower oil, and put them on the grill first. Cook them for 20 to 25 minutes over medium-hot coals, turning them frequently until they are blistered and evenly tender. After 10 minutes, place the halved red and white onions and fennel bulbs on the rack. Brush the onions with the remaining safflower oil, and the fennel with any remaining marinade. Cook the onions and fennel for 10 to 15 minutes, turning them once, until they are lightly browned and tender.

Five to 10 minutes before these vegetables are ready, place the skewered shallots, tomatoes, and baby corn on the rack; turn the skewers once or twice during cooking. Move the vegetables to the edges of the rack as they finish cooking. Serve all the vegetables freshly cooked.

EDITOR'S NOTE: *Most vegetables are suitable for grilling, although firm vegetables need to be blanched first, and the flavor of some can be enhanced by marination. Cook the vegetables over medium-hot coals.*

Baked Apples with Ginger

THESE SPICE-STUFFED APPLES MAY BE BAKED EITHER ON THE RACK ABOVE THE COALS OR IN THE ASHES. IF YOU BAKE THEM IN THE ASHES, DOUBLE-WRAP THEM IN FOIL AND COOK THEM FOR 30 TO 40 MINUTES.

Serves 8
Working time: about 30 minutes
Total time: about 1 hour and 15 minutes

Calories **165**
Protein **2g.**
Cholesterol **5mg.**
Total fat **3g.**
Saturated fat **1g.**
Sodium **85mg.**

8 firm tart apples (about 5 oz. each)
3½ oz. peeled cooked chestnuts (about 1 cup) or hazelnuts (about ¾ cup), coarsely chopped
½ cup fresh whole-wheat breadcrumbs
6 tbsp. raisins, chopped
1 oz. preserved stem ginger, finely diced
2 tbsp. fresh lemon juice
2 tbsp. maple syrup
1 tsp. pumpkin-pie spice
1 tbsp. unsalted butter, melted
⅓ cup sour cream (optional)

Wash the apples and core them, making the hole through the center of the apple about 1 inch in diameter. Keeping the apples whole, lightly score the skin around the circumference of each one with a small, sharp knife.

Put the chopped chestnuts or hazelnuts, the breadcrumbs, raisins, ginger, lemon juice, maple syrup, and pumpkin-pie spice into a large bowl. Knead these ingredients lightly with one hand to amalgamate them.

Cut eight squares of foil, each one large enough to wrap around an apple. Brush one side of the foil squares with the melted butter. Place an apple in the center of the buttered side of each foil square, and press an eighth of the stuffing into the hollowed center of the apple. Wrap the apples in the foil.

Arrange the wrapped apples on the rack over medium-hot coals and cook them for about 45 minutes. Test the apples by piercing them with a thin skewer: If it meets little resistance, they are done.

Serve the apples hot, with a little sour cream, if you like.

EDITOR'S NOTE: *To peel and cook chestnuts, first cut a cross in the hull of each chestnut and cook them in boiling water for 10 minutes. Shell and peel them while they are warm, then return them to the pan and simmer them until they are tender—20 to 30 minutes.*

Grilled Bananas with Raspberry Coulis

Serves 8
Working (and total) time: about 20 minutes

Calories **110**
Protein **3g.**
Cholesterol **0mg.**
Total fat **trace**
Saturated fat **trace**
Sodium **10mg.**

7 oz. fresh raspberries (about 2 cups), or frozen whole raspberries, thawed
2 tbsp. confectioners' sugar
½ tsp. arrowroot
2 passionfruits, strained juice only, or 2 tbsp. Kirsch
8 large ripe bananas

First make the coulis. In a blender or food processor, blend the raspberries with the confectioners' sugar until they are reduced to a purée. Press the purée through a fine sieve to remove all the seeds, then pour it into a saucepan. Stir the arrowroot into the purée and heat it gently, stirring continuously, until it boils and thickens. Remove the pan from the heat and stir in the passionfruit juice or Kirsch. Either cover the sauce and keep it warm or set it aside to cool while you grill the bananas.

With the point of a small, sharp knife, cut through the skin along the length of a banana in two places on opposite sides; do not cut into the flesh. Peel off the top half of the skin, leaving the banana and the bottom half of the skin intact. Repeat this process with the remaining bananas.

Place the bananas, skin side down, on the rack 4 to 6 inches above medium-hot coals. When the skins are black—after about five minutes—carefully turn the bananas over and cook them for one minute more.

Serve the bananas hot, in their skins, with a little of the raspberry coulis—either hot or cold—poured over them. Serve the remaining coulis separately.

Fruit Rings Cooked in Foil

Serves 6
Working (and total) time: about 30 minutes

Calories **85**
Protein **1g.**
Cholesterol **0mg.**
Total fat **0g.**
Saturated fat **0g.**
Sodium **5mg.**

2 red-skinned apples, cored, each cut into 6 rings and dropped into acidulated water
2 ripe pears, peeled, cored, each cut into 6 rings and dropped into acidulated water
2 oranges, peeled, each cut crosswise into 6 slices
1 grapefruit, peeled and cut crosswise into 6 slices
2 tbsp. light brown sugar

Cut six rectangles of foil measuring about 18 by 12 inches, and fold them in half crosswise.

Drain the apple and pear rings. In the center of each piece of foil, pile two rings each of apple and pear, two slices of orange, and one slice of grapefruit. Sprinkle 1 teaspoon of sugar over each pile of fruit, then fold the sides of the foil up and pinch the edges to enclose the fruit in six neat parcels.

Place the foil parcels on the rack over medium-hot coals and cook them for four minutes. Serve the fruit hot, either in the foil parcels or on individual plates with the juices poured over.

Rum-Flavored Fruit Kabobs

Serves 6
Working time: about 20 minutes
Total time: about 30 minutes

Calories **125**
Protein **1g.**
Cholesterol **0mg.**
Total fat **trace**
Saturated fat **trace**
Sodium **5mg.**

3 tbsp. dark rum
3 tbsp. light brown sugar
2 tbsp. fresh lemon juice
3 kiwi fruits, peeled and quartered
6 dark-skinned plums, halved and pitted
3 small nectarines, quartered
2 bananas, peeled, each cut into 6 chunks
12 strawberries, hulled
1 orange, juice only
1 tbsp. honey

Place the rum, sugar, and lemon juice in a large, shallow, nonreactive dish. Add the kiwi, plums, nectarines, and bananas to the liquid, and turn them to coat them evenly. Let the fruit marinate for about 10 minutes. Meanwhile, soak six bamboo skewers in water for 10 minutes. Juxtaposing different fruits, thread two strawberries and two pieces of each of the other fruits onto each of the skewers; reserve the marinade. Set the skewers aside while you prepare a rum sauce.

Pour the reserved marinade into a small, nonreactive saucepan, and stir in the orange juice and honey. Bring the sauce slowly to a boil, and boil it until it is reduced by half—about five minutes. Remove the saucepan from the heat and allow the sauce to cool.

Lightly oil the rack. Brush the kabobs with a little of the rum sauce and cook them over medium-hot coals for four minutes, turning them once. Serve the fruit kabobs immediately, with any remaining rum sauce poured over them.

EDITOR'S NOTE: *Other fruit, such as oranges, grapefruit, peaches, or mangoes, may be substituted for any of the ingredients listed here.*

3

Menus to Match the Occasion

Ideally, every picnic and barbecue should be planned as an entity, so that all the courses not only suit the occasion but also complement the other dishes. This chapter suggests menus for four very different types of outdoor meal—two of the menus are for picnics, and two are for barbecues.

The first menu is for an occasion as formal as a picnic can be—a meal that might be enjoyed at the races, say, or after an alfresco concert. The robust American barbecue *(page 123)*, on the other hand, invites you to an easygoing cookout with just a nip of autumn in the air. Two menus owe their inspiration to regional cuisines: The Middle Eastern picnic *(page 116)*, a tempting selection of appetizers and snacks, and the Caribbean fish barbecue *(page 112)* impart the romance of tropical sunshine or sultry nights to any suburban garden.

Whether in the park or on the patio, truly carefree meals require careful planning. Common sense dictates that as much preparation as possible be done substantially in advance, and a brief introduction to each menu suggests which dishes may be prepared ahead. Some, such as trout in aspic *(page 109)*, must be made the day before an afternoon picnic. The salad of lettuce and nasturtium flowers *(page 110)*, however, is best made shortly before packing the picnic and should be dressed only just before serving.

Because the party atmosphere is not conducive to strict self-control, it is especially important to serve fresh, healthy food. These menus reveal the possibility of creating meals that are low in saturated fats and sodium, while still retaining all the fun of a feast.

A silver platter of trout stuffed with crab and ginger and glazed with aspic forms a dramatic centerpiece for this elegant picnic. Two salads, one of sweet peppers and rice and one of lettuce and nasturtium flowers, accompany the trout. The main dish is preceded by a chilled soup with croutons, and a passionfruit and raspberry roulade completes the meal.

FORMAL ENGLISH PICNIC

Chilled Melon and Cucumber Soup
Trout In Aspic
Sweet-Pepper Rice Ring
Salad of Lettuce and Nasturtium Flowers
Passionfruit and Raspberry Roulade

Prepare the ingredients for the lettuce and nasturtium flower salad on the day of the picnic, and keep them chilled until you are ready to leave. The other dishes may be made ahead of time and stored in the refrigerator until you need to pack them.

When packing, remember to include a tureen and ladle for the soup, and suitable serving dishes for the two salads and the roulade. To avoid breakages in transit, use plenty of tissue paper when wrapping the china and glassware, and keep silverware safe from scratches by rolling individual place settings in napkins.

If you plan to serve champagne or another chilled wine, take an ice bucket with you, and fill a wide-mouthed thermos with ice cubes. The ice cubes will remain frozen for up to eight hours and can be transferred to the ice bucket at the picnic site.

Chilled Melon and Cucumber Soup

Serves 6
Working time: about 20 minutes
Total time: about 4 hours (includes chilling)

Calories **100**
Protein **10g.**
Cholesterol **10mg.**
Total fat **3g.**
Saturated fat **1g.**
Sodium **60mg.**

1¼ lb. ripe honeydew melon, seeded, flesh cut into cubes
1¼ lb. cucumbers (3 medium), peeled, seeded, and cut into cubes
½ tsp. salt
½ bunch chopped fresh chervil
2½ cups unsalted chicken stock (recipe, page 139)
2 tbsp. heavy cream
ground white pepper
3 slices white bread (about 3 oz.), crusts removed
1 tbsp. polyunsaturated margarine

Put the melon and cucumber cubes into a heavy-bottomed saucepan with the salt and half of the chervil. Cover the pan and set it over low heat. Cook the cubes until they have softened and the juices are flowing—15 to 20 minutes. Add the chicken stock and continue cooking for 20 minutes more.

Purée the contents of the saucepan in a food processor or blender, then pour the soup into a clean bowl and set it aside to cool. Stir the cream into the cooled soup with some ground white pepper, cover the bowl, and refrigerate the soup for at least three hours to chill it thoroughly.

Cut the bread into dice, then melt the margarine in a heavy-bottomed saucepan over low heat. Add the diced bread to the saucepan, tossing it until it has browned on all sides. Allow the croutons to cool, then transfer them to an airtight container. Put the remaining chopped chervil into a small plastic bag.

Transport the soup to the picnic in a chilled thermos. To serve it, shake the thermos to blend the soup evenly, then pour the soup into a tureen. Sprinkle the chervil over the surface and serve the croutons separately, in a small bowl.

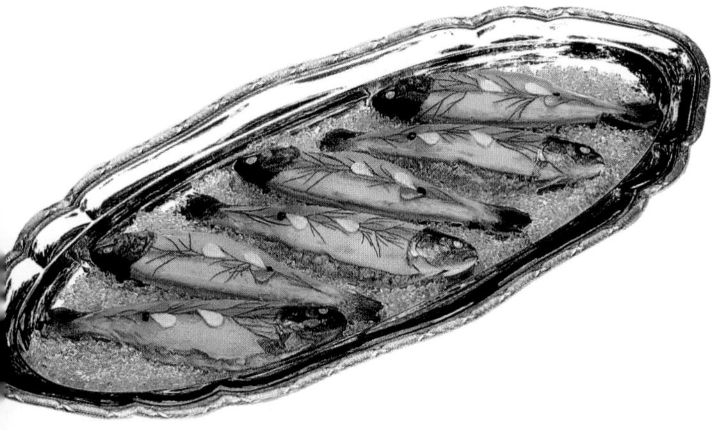

Trout in Aspic

Serves 6
Working time: about 1 hour and 30 minutes
Total time: about 7 hours and 15 minutes
(includes chilling)

alories **250**
rotein **35g.**
holesterol **120mg.**
otal fat **11g.**
aturated fat **2g.**
odium **305mg.**

6 trout (about ½ lb. each), gutted, fins removed
2 tbsp. polyunsaturated margarine
4 scallions, trimmed and chopped
2-inch piece fresh ginger, peeled and grated
6 oz. crabmeat, picked over
1 tsp. finely grated fresh horseradish, or 2 tsp. prepared horseradish
½ tsp. salt
freshly ground black pepper
1 lemon, strained juice only
1 quart unsalted vegetable stock (recipe, page 139)
¼ cup (6 pkg.) powdered gelatin
2 eggs, whites and washed shells only
1 tbsp. red wine vinegar
dill sprigs for garnish
petals cut from thinly sliced daikon radish and blanched lemon zest for garnish (optional)
small pieces of olive for garnish (optional)

Rinse the trout under cold running water, then pat them dry on paper towels. Using a small, sharp knife, bone each trout in turn. First lengthen the slit in the belly of the trout so that it extends the full length of the fish, from head to tail. Put the trout on the work surface on its back, to expose the inside. Use the tip of the knife to free the rib bones, one at a time, then run the knife down both sides of the spine, underneath the ribs, to free the flesh from the backbone. With a pair of scissors, sever the backbone at the head and tail ends of the trout. Ease out the spine and its attached ribs, and use a pair of tweezers to remove any small bones that remain. Bone the five remaining trout using the same technique.

Preheat the oven to 425° F.

To make the stuffing, melt the margarine in a small, heavy-bottomed skillet over medium heat. Add the scallions and cook them gently for about five minutes, until they are soft. Stir in the ginger and cook for one minute more. Remove the pan from the heat and allow the contents to cool for 10 minutes, then add the crabmeat, horseradish, a little of the salt, and some black pepper, and mix the ingredients together well. Fill the body cavity of each trout with some of the crab mixture, then reshape the fish neatly.

Lay a large sheet of foil on a baking sheet, and grease the foil with a little polyunsaturated margarine. Place the trout on the foil in a single layer, and sprinkle them with the lemon juice and the remaining salt. Fold the foil over to enclose the fish but do not seal the parcel completely. Cook the trout in the oven until the flesh feels firm and is opaque—15 to 20 minutes. Remove them from the oven and open the foil a little to allow the steam to escape. Set the trout aside to cool for one hour at room temperature, then refrigerate them for three hours, or until they are completely cold.

To make the aspic, first rinse a large saucepan and fill it with cold water. Put a wire whisk, a large metal sieve, and a large square of cheesecloth into the saucepan. Bring the water to a boil. Remove the whisk, sieve, and cheesecloth from the pan; pour the boiling water into a large bowl to scald it, then pour off the water. Place the sieve over the bowl and line the sieve with the cheesecloth.

Pour the vegetable stock into the saucepan and add the gelatin, egg whites and shells, and vinegar. With the scalded whisk, beat the stock over medium heat until the egg whites form a thick foam on the surface. Stop whisking, then bring the mixture to a boil so that the foam rises to the top of the saucepan—do not allow it to boil over. Remove the saucepan from the heat and allow the foam to settle back down. Repeat this process twice more, then allow the mixture to stand for five minutes.

Very gently and carefully pour the aspic through the lined sieve into the bowl, without allowing the foam floating on top of the liquid to break up. Let it drain thoroughly, then allow the aspic to cool. Refrigerate it until it begins to thicken—20 to 30 minutes.

Carefully remove the skin from one side of each trout, then place the trout, skinned side up, on a wire rack set over a large tray. Spoon a little of the partially set aspic over each trout to coat it evenly. Pour the excess aspic that has drained into the tray back into the bowl. Refrigerate the trout for 15 minutes to firmly set the aspic. Meanwhile, keep the bowl of aspic at room temperature to prevent it from setting.

Remove the trout from the refrigerator. Dip the sprigs of dill, and the daikon-radish and lemon-zest petals and the pieces of olive, if you are using them, in aspic and use them to garnish the fish decoratively. Return the trout to the refrigerator for 10 minutes to allow the garnish to set firmly in place, then coat them with more liquid aspic, again pouring the excess from the tray back into the bowl. Refrigerate the trout and the bowl of aspic until both are firmly set—about one ▶

hour. Cover the trout with plastic wrap and keep them refrigerated until you are ready to pack the picnic.

Carefully remove the trout from the wire rack and arrange them on a large serving platter. Cover them loosely with wax paper. Chop the remaining set aspic and place it in a covered container. Pack the chopped aspic in a cooler.

To serve at the picnic site, remove the wax paper and arrange the chopped aspic around the trout.

Sweet-Pepper Rice Ring

Serves 6
Working time: about 30 minutes
Total time: about 1 hour

Calories **125**
Protein **3g.**
Cholesterol **0mg.**
Total fat **3g.**
Saturated fat **1g.**
Sodium **135mg.**

½ tsp. salt
¾ cup long-grain rice
1 small sweet red pepper
1 small sweet green pepper
1 small sweet yellow pepper
1 tbsp. virgin olive oil
1 tbsp. white wine vinegar
1 garlic clove, crushed
¼ cup finely chopped fresh parsley
freshly ground black pepper
red-, green-, and yellow-pepper rings for garnish

Bring a saucepan of water to a boil with ¼ teaspoon of the salt. Add the rice, stir it once, then cover the pan and reduce the heat to low. Simmer the rice for 20 minutes, until it is cooked but still slightly firm. Drain it thoroughly and set it aside to cool.

Meanwhile, peel the peppers following the technique on page 138, then seed and derib them, retaining their juice. Cut the peppers into small dice.

Put the oil, vinegar, garlic, and parsley into a large bowl, and add the remaining salt and some black pepper. Mix the ingredients well. Add the diced peppers to the dressing with 1 tablespoon of their juice, then add the cooked rice, and combine thoroughly.

Fill a ring mold with the rice salad, pressing the mixture down firmly. Cover the mold with plastic wrap and refrigerate it until you are ready to pack the picnic. Put the pepper rings for garnish into a plastic bag and chill them too.

To serve, turn the rice salad out onto a serving dish and arrange the pepper rings in the center.

Salad of Lettuce and Nasturtium Flowers

Serves 6
Working (and total) time: about 20 minutes

Calories **25**
Protein **1g.**
Cholesterol **10mg.**
Total fat **2g.**
Saturated fat **1g.**
Sodium **75mg.**

1 small head Boston lettuce, or two small heads Bibb lettuce, leaves washed and dried
1 head red-leaf lettuce, leaves washed and dried
12 nasturtium flowers

Mustard-lemon dressing

¼ cup sour cream
2 tbsp. fresh lemon juice
2 tsp. Dijon mustard
¼ tsp. salt
freshly ground black pepper
2 tbsp. finely cut chives

Tear or cut the lettuce leaves into pieces and put them into a lidded plastic container. Place the nasturtium flowers in a separate covered container. Refrigerate both until you are ready to go to the picnic.

To make the dressing, put all ingredients into a screw-top jar and shake them together vigorously. Chill the dressing until it is needed, then pack it inside a cooler to take to the picnic.

At the picnic, shake the dressing once more, then pour it into the bottom of a serving bowl. Place the salad greens in the bowl and arrange the flowers on top. Just before serving, toss the salad with the mustard-lemon dressing.

Passionfruit and Raspberry Roulade

Serves 6
Working time: about 40 minutes
Total time: about 1 hour and 25 minutes

:alories **225**
rotein **7g.**
:holesterol **80mg.**
otal fat **8g.**
aturated fat **2g.**
odium **155mg.**

4 passionfruits
⅓ cup sour cream
3 tsp. powdered gelatin
1 egg white
2 tbsp. sugar
confectioners' sugar
½ lb. fresh raspberries (2 cups)

Hazelnut sponge

¾ cup hazelnuts, roasted, skinned, and finely ground
5½ tbsp. cake flour
2 eggs
7 tbsp. sugar
2 egg whites

Preheat the oven to 375° F. Lightly oil a 9-by-13-inch jelly-roll pan, line the pan with parchment paper, and oil the paper.

To make the sponge, put the hazelnuts and cake flour into a small bowl and mix them together well. Put the whole eggs and 4 tablespoons of the sugar into a large bowl, then place the bowl over a saucepan of gently simmering water, taking care that the bottom of the bowl does not touch the water.

Using a hand-held electric mixer, beat the eggs and sugar until the mixture becomes thick and pale. Remove the bowl from the heat and continue beating until the mixture is cool and falls from the beaters in a thick ribbon trail. Beat the egg whites until they are stiff, then gradually beat in the remaining sugar until the meringue is stiff and shiny. Carefully fold the hazelnuts and flour into the whole-egg mixture, then fold in the egg whites.

Pour the mixture into the prepared pan and spread it evenly. Gently tap the pan on the work surface to level the top. Bake the sponge for 15 to 20 minutes, until it is well risen, lightly browned, and springy to the touch. Remove the pan from the oven and place it on a wire rack. Cover the sponge loosely with foil and let it cool in the pan for about 45 minutes.

In the meantime, make the filling. Cut the passionfruits in half and spoon out their centers into a small fine sieve set over a bowl. Press the seeds with the back of the spoon to extract the juice. Stir the sour cream into the passionfruit juice until the mixture is smooth. Put 2 tablespoons of cold water in a small bowl; sprinkle the gelatin evenly over the surface and set it aside to soften. Beat the egg white until it will hold stiff peaks, then gradually beat in the sugar until the mixture is stiff and shiny.

Set the bowl of gelatin over a saucepan of gently simmering water, and stir until the gelatin has dissolved. Quickly beat the gelatin solution into the passionfruit mixture, then gradually fold it into the beaten egg white. Refrigerate the mixture until it is on the point of setting—about 10 minutes.

Lay a large sheet of parchment paper on the work surface and sift an even layer of confectioners' sugar over it. Invert the sponge rectangle onto the confectioners' sugar and remove the lining paper. Sprinkle the raspberries evenly over the rectangle, then spread the passionfruit mixture evenly over the raspberries. Starting from one of the short sides, roll up the sponge and filling: Lift one end of the underlying paper to start off the roulade, and nudge it along by gradually lifting the rest of the paper.

Wrap the roulade loosely in wax paper and place it in a covered container. Chill it until it is needed, and transport it to the picnic in a cooler. At the picnic site, transfer the roulade to a rectangular dish; cut it into slices for serving.

SUGGESTED ACCOMPANIMENT: *a bowl of fresh raspberries.*

EDITOR'S NOTE: *To roast hazelnuts, place them on a baking sheet in a preheated 350° F. oven for 10 minutes, stirring them from time to time to ensure that they brown evenly. While the hazelnuts are still warm, rub them in a dishtowel to remove the skins. Allow the nuts to cool completely before grinding them.*

CARIBBEAN FISH BARBECUE

Grilled Squid with Hot Paprika Sauce
Sea Bass Cooked with Saffron, Thyme, and Lemon
Shark, Onion, and Pepper Brochettes
Two-Potato Salad
Green Salad with Hearts of Palm and Snow Peas
Tropical Fruit Salad

Begin the preparation for this seafood barbecue 24 hours in advance by placing the shark cubes in their marinade. You may also, if you wish, prepare the hot paprika sauce and parboil the baby onions. Complete the preparation on the day of the barbecue but do not dress the salads until you are about to serve them. Have everything ready before you start to cook.

About 20 minutes before you wish to begin serving, place the sea bass on the grill. Allow it to cook for 10 minutes, then add the squid and mushroom skewers to the rack. They will need only 10 minutes' cooking; transfer them to a plate when they are done and serve them as a first course with the hot paprika sauce. Meanwhile, turn the sea bass over for its final 20 minutes' cooking, and add the shark brochettes to the rack halfway through this time.

Accompany the dishes with jugs of a Caribbean-style beverage, such as the mixture of fresh orange and pineapple juices illustrated here. If you like, spike the drink with a little Jamaican rum, and serve it in hollowed-out pineapple shells.

A large sea bass flavored with saffron, lemon, and thyme is flanked by platters of shark brochettes and squid and mushrooms with a hot paprika sauce. This seafood barbecue is accompanied by a yogurt-dressed salad of sweet and new potatoes, and a crisp green salad. A bowl of ripe tropical fruit steeped in passion-fruit juice completes the meal.

Grilled Squid with Hot Paprika Sauce

Serves 12
Working (and total) time: about 1 hour

Calories **75**
Protein **9g.**
Cholesterol **130mg.**
Total fat **3g.**
Saturated fat **1g.**
Sodium **95mg.**

1½ lb. squid, cleaned and skinned, tentacles reserved

48 small mushrooms, wiped clean

Hot paprika sauce

2 tbsp. virgin olive oil

1 garlic clove, crushed
1 lb. ripe tomatoes (3 medium), peeled, seeded (technique, page 138), and chopped
2 tsp. red wine vinegar
2 tsp. paprika
1 tsp. hot red-pepper sauce
6 oz. canned red pimientos, coarsely chopped

In a heavy-bottomed, nonreactive skillet, heat the oil over medium heat. Add the garlic and tomatoes and cook them, stirring constantly, for 10 minutes. Strain off and discard 1¼ cups of the juice. Add the vinegar to the skillet and simmer the mixture for 3 minutes more. Pour the mixture into a food processor or blender, add the paprika, hot red-pepper sauce, and chopped pimientos, and process until smooth. Transfer the sauce to a bowl and set it aside.

Cut each pouch into three or four pieces and the tentacles into groups of four. Thread the squid and mushrooms onto skewers. Place the skewers flat on the grill, spreading out the tentacles, and cook for five minutes on each side, until they are golden brown.

Remove the squid and mushrooms from their skewers and mix them together. Serve the sauce separately.

Shark, Onion, and Pepper Brochettes

Serves 12
Working time: about 45 minutes
Total time: about 25 hours (includes marinating)

Calories **120**
Protein **8g.**
Cholesterol **25mg.**
Total fat **8g.**
Saturated fat **2g.**
Sodium **85mg.**

2 tbsp. virgin olive oil
⅓ cup fresh lime juice
1 tbsp. gin
¼ tsp. salt
freshly ground black pepper
1½ lb. shark fillet, skinned and cut into 1¼-inch cubes
½ lb. boiling onions, simmered in boiling water for 8 to 10 minutes, until tender
2 sweet orange peppers, seeded, deribbed, and cut into 1¼-inch pieces
2 sweet yellow peppers, seeded, deribbed, and cut into 1¼-inch pieces
bamboo leaves for garnish (optional)

First prepare a marinade for the shark cubes. In a large shallow, nonreactive dish, combine 1 tablespoon of the olive oil with the lime juice, gin, salt, and some black pepper. Add the shark cubes to the dish, and turn them over thoroughly in the marinade to coat all the surfaces. Arrange the cubes in a single layer, cover the dish, and place it in the refrigerator for at least 24 hours. Turn the cubes over from time to time while they are marinating.

Divide the shark cubes, onions, and pieces of orange and yellow pepper into 12 equal portions. Thread each portion onto a long metal skewer, alternating the ingredients, then brush the filled skewers with the remaining olive oil.

Place the skewers on the rack over medium-hot coals and cook them for about 10 minutes, turning them over halfway through the cooking time. Pile the cooked skewers onto a serving platter, lined with a few bamboo leaves, if you are using them.

Sea Bass Cooked with Saffron, Thyme, and Lemon

Serves 12
Working time: about 30 minutes
Total time: about 1 hour and 10 minutes

Calories **150**
Protein **27g.**
Cholesterol **115mg.**
Total fat **3g.**
Saturated fat **trace**
Sodium **155mg.**

one 5-lb. sea bass, gutted and scaled
1 tsp. virgin olive oil
½ tsp. powdered saffron
½ tsp. salt
freshly ground black pepper
1 lemon, sliced
1 large bunch fresh thyme, stalks trimmed
tied bundles of chives for garnish
lemon slices and lime wedges for garnish

Rinse the fish under cold running water and pat it dry with paper towels. Make four ¼-inch-deep slashes in the flesh on both sides of the fish. Using a small pastry brush, oil each slash with a little of the olive oil, and paint on some saffron powder.

Place the fish in an oiled fish basket, and season the stomach cavity with the salt and some freshly ground black pepper. Place the lemon slices and the bunch of thyme in the stomach cavity, arranging them so that the natural stomach shape is retained.

Close the fish basket and place it on the rack. Cook the fish over medium-hot coals for 20 minutes on each side, or until it is firm to the touch. Transfer the cooked fish to a large platter, and serve it garnished with the chive bundles, lemon slices, and lime wedges.

Two-Potato Salad

Serves 12
Working time: about 30 minutes
Total time: about 1 hour and 15 minutes

Calories **80**
Protein **2g.**
Cholesterol **0mg.**
Total fat **trace**
Saturated fat **trace**
Sodium **35mg.**

1 lb. sweet potatoes, scrubbed
1 lb. new potatoes, scrubbed, halved if large
1 bunch scallions, trimmed and cut diagonally into thirds
2 tsp. Dijon mustard
⅔ cup plain low-fat yogurt
ground white pepper
2 tbsp. capers, rinsed well, dried, and coarsely chopped

Put the sweet potatoes and new potatoes into separate heavy-bottomed saucepans, and pour in sufficient cold water to cover the potatoes in each pan by 1 inch. Bring both pans to a boil, then lower the heat and simmer the vegetables until they are tender—15 to 20 minutes for the new potatoes and 25 to 30 minutes for the sweet potatoes.

Drain the potatoes and set them aside, on separate plates, until they are cool enough to handle. Peel the sweet potatoes and cut them into slices. Arrange the sweet-potato slices in a serving dish with the new potatoes and the scallion pieces.

In a small bowl, stir the mustard into the yogurt and add some ground white pepper. Pour this dressing over the potatoes and scallions, and sprinkle the capers over the top.

Green Salad with Hearts of Palm and Snow Peas

Serves 12
Working (and total) time: about 30 minutes

Calories **45**
Protein **2g.**
Cholesterol **0mg.**
Total fat **3g.**
Saturated fat **trace**
Sodium **20mg.**

4 heads Bibb lettuce or other small lettuce, cut in half, leaves washed and dried
four 7½-oz. cans hearts of palm, drained and rinsed well, each heart cut crosswise into equal pieces
2 cups watercress sprigs, trimmed, washed, and dried
2 cucumbers, halved lengthwise, seeded, and cut into 2-inch-long sticks
1¼ lb. snow peas, strings removed, blanched, refreshed under cold running water
Lemon vinaigrette
2 tbsp. safflower oil
2 tbsp. fresh lemon juice
freshly ground black pepper

First prepare the lemon vinaigrette. In a small bowl, whisk together the oil and lemon juice with a fork, and season the dressing with plenty of black pepper.

Pile all the salad ingredients into a large bowl. Just before serving, pour on the dressing and toss the salad.

Tropical Fruit Salad

Serves 12
Working (and total) time: about 40 minutes

Calories **115**
Protein **3g.**
Cholesterol **0mg.**
Total fat **2g.**
Saturated fat **trace**
Sodium **60mg.**

6 ripe passionfruits

1 honeydew melon, halved and seeded, flesh scooped into balls with a melon baller

1 cantaloupe, halved and seeded, flesh scooped into balls with a melon baller

1 pineapple, peeled and cored, flesh cut into chunks

3 guavas, halved lengthwise, seeded, each half sliced crosswise

2 pink grapefruits, peeled and segmented

3 papayas, peeled and seeded, flesh cut into chunks

2 large mangoes, peeled, flesh cut lengthwise into slices, pits discarded

Cut the passionfruits in half crosswise. Using a teaspoon, scoop out the seeds and pulp from each fruit into a fine sieve set over a bowl. With the back of the spoon, press all the juice into the bowl; discard the seeds and fibrous pulp remaining in the sieve.

Place all the prepared fruits in a large serving bowl and pour on the passionfruit juice. Gently mix and turn the fruits in the bowl to ensure that they are all coated with juice. Store the fruit salad in the refrigerator until it is needed.

EDITOR'S NOTE: *The skin of a ripe passionfruit is very dark in color and has a wrinkled, shriveled appearance. Avoid passionfruit that has pale, plump-looking skin; the flesh will taste bitter and acidic.*

MIDDLE EASTERN PICNIC

Coriander Pork Skewers
Kibbeh with Yogurt-Mint Sauce
Falafel with Red-Pepper Relish
Carrots Cooked with Honey and Spices
Tabbouleh
Fruit and Nut Triangles
Turkish Delight

A *mezze*—a selection of Middle Eastern appetizers and snacks—provides a novel theme for a picnic. Because the dishes in this *mezze* are served cold, they can be prepared in advance and kept in the refrigerator until you are ready to leave. The Turkish delight is best made the day before, to ensure that it has time to set. Most of the items will benefit from being transported in a cooler, especially the *kibbeh* and sauce, the pork skewers, and the Turkish delight.

To complete your *mezze,* you may want to include pita bread or one of the many other types of Middle Eastern bread—such as those flavored with olives, cheese, onions, and herbs—that can be bought in Greek and Turkish bakeries and delicatessens. Iced mint tea goes well with these dishes.

Tender pork skewers, spicy lamb and couscous balls, and falafel diamonds with a red-pepper relish provide the focal points to this mezze. Tabbouleh—a salad of bulgur, mint, and parsley—and carrots cooked with honey and spices accompany them. Triangles of pastry topped with fruit and nuts, and cubes of Turkish delight complete the meal.

Coriander Pork Skewers

Serves 6
Working time: about 25 minutes
Total time: about 1 hour and 30 minutes
(includes marinating)

Calories **185**
Protein **19g.**
Cholesterol **45mg.**
Total fat **10g.**
Saturated fat **3g.**
Sodium **120mg.**

¾ lb. pork loin, trimmed of fat
1 garlic clove, crushed
2 tsp. coriander seeds, crushed
¼ tsp. ground allspice
¼ tsp. paprika
2 tbsp. safflower oil
⅓ cup dry red wine
¼ tsp. salt
1 tbsp. light brown sugar

Cut the meat lengthwise into 12 equal strips. Place the strips of meat in a large, shallow container, and add the garlic, coriander, allspice, paprika, and oil. Mix the ingredients together well, then cover the container and let the meat marinate in a cool place for at least one hour, or for up to 24 hours.

Thread each strip of meat onto a wooden skewer and lay the skewers in a large, heavy-bottomed, nonreactive, nonstick skillet or in a heavy-bottomed roasting pan. Using a plastic spatula, scrape down any marinade remaining in the shallow container and spread it on top of the skewers.

Cook the skewers over medium heat for about five minutes, or until they are lightly browned, turning them once. In a small bowl, whisk together the wine, salt, and sugar. Add this mixture to the pan, cover it, and simmer the pork skewers in the juices for 10 minutes. Transfer the skewers to a plate and continue to cook the pan juices over high heat until they have reduced to a syrupy glaze—three to four minutes. Drizzle the glaze over the pork skewers and set them aside to cool.

For transport to the picnic, wrap the skewers in foil or arrange them in a covered container. Pack the skewers inside a cooler.

Kibbeh with Yogurt-Mint Sauce

Serves 6
Working time: about 25 minutes
Total time: about 1 hour and 25 minutes
(includes soaking)

Calories **155**
Protein **13g.**
Cholesterol **30mg.**
Total fat **6g.**
Saturated fat **2g.**
Sodium **115mg.**

½ cup couscous
¼ tbsp. safflower oil
1 small onion, very finely chopped
1 garlic clove, crushed
¼ tsp. ground cinnamon
1 tsp. ground cumin
7 oz. lean lamb, finely ground
¼ tsp. salt
freshly ground black pepper
lemon slices, halved, for garnish
flat-leaf parsley sprig for garnish

Yogurt-mint sauce

⅔ cup plain low-fat yogurt
1½ tbsp. chopped fresh mint leaves, plus 2 mint leaves, cut into strips, for garnish
¼ tsp. caraway seeds
¼ cucumber, peeled and grated
freshly ground black pepper

Put the couscous into a flameproof bowl and pour on ½ cup of boiling water. Let the couscous soak for 15 minutes, or until all the liquid has been absorbed; stir occasionally, to prevent lumps from forming.

Heat the oil in a small, heavy-bottomed skillet. Add the onion, garlic, cinnamon, and cumin, and sauté the mixture gently for two minutes, stirring frequently. Stir the mixture into the soaked couscous, then stir in the lamb, the salt, and some black pepper. Mix all the ingredients together thoroughly.

Preheat the oven to 375° F. and lightly oil a baking sheet. Divide the meat mixture into 12 equal portions. Take one portion and squeeze it firmly in your hand to compact it, then roll it into a ball between your palms; neaten the shape by rolling the ball on a cutting board. Shape the remaining mixture into balls in the same way, then place all 12 on the baking sheet.

Bake the *kibbeh* until they are a light golden color—about 45 minutes. Transfer them to a plate to cool, then chill them until they are needed.

For the yogurt-mint sauce, combine the yogurt, chopped mint, caraway seeds, and cucumber in a bowl and add a little black pepper. Chill the sauce until you are ready to leave for the picnic.

Pack the *kibbeh* and the yogurt sauce, in separate covered containers, in a cooler. Place the garnishes—the lemon slices, the parsley sprig, and the mint strips—in small plastic bags, and put them into the cooler too. At the picnic, arrange the *kibbeh* in a serving dish and garnish them with the lemon slices and parsley sprig. Transfer the yogurt sauce to a small bowl, and scatter the mint strips over the surface.

Falafel with Red-Pepper Relish

Serves 6
Working time: about 40 minutes
Total time: about 2 hours and 50 minutes
(includes soaking)

Calories **190**
Protein **19g.**
Cholesterol **20mg.**
Total fat **7g.**
Saturated fat **1g.**
Sodium **190mg.**

½ cup dried chickpeas, picked over
¼ cup coarsely chopped onion
1 garlic clove, coarsely chopped
¼ tsp. ground cumin
½ tsp. garam masala (glossary)
¼ tsp. chili powder
½ cup fresh whole-wheat breadcrumbs
1 tbsp. chopped fresh parsley
¼ tsp. salt
freshly ground black pepper
1½ tbsp. beaten egg
fig leaves for garnish (optional)

Red-pepper relish

1 tsp. safflower oil
½ sweet red pepper, seeded, deribbed, and finely chopped
1 small onion, finely chopped
1 garlic clove, crushed
2 tbsp. malt vinegar or cider vinegar
½ tsp. dry mustard
2 tsp. sugar
⅛ tsp. hot red-pepper sauce

Rinse the chickpeas under cold running water, then put them in a large, heavy-bottomed saucepan and pour in enough cold water to cover them by about 3 inches. Discard any that float to the surface. Cover the pan, leaving the lid ajar, and slowly bring the liquid to a boil over medium-low heat. Boil the chickpeas for two minutes, then turn off the heat and soak them for at least one hour. (Alternatively, soak the chickpeas overnight in cold water.)

Drain the chickpeas; return them to the pan and cover them with at least twice their volume of fresh water. Bring the liquid to a boil, lower the heat to maintain a strong simmer, and cook the chickpeas until they are tender—about one hour.

Drain the chickpeas and put them into a food processor with the onion and garlic. Process them for about one minute, until the mixture is smooth. Turn the mixture into a bowl and add the cumin, garam masala, and chili powder, half the breadcrumbs, all of the parsley, the salt, some black pepper, and ½ tablespoon of the beaten egg. Mix all the ingredients together thoroughly.

Preheat the oven to 375° F. Lightly oil a nonstick baking pan. Gather the chickpea mixture into a ball, and working on a damp board, shape it into a long roll. Cut the roll into six equal portions, then use a metal spatula to form each portion into a diamond shape on the board. Slide the spatula under one of the diamonds, lift it off the board, and then brush the top and sides with beaten egg and cover them with breadcrumbs, pressing the crumbs on gently. Turn the diamond over and coat the bottom with beaten egg and breadcrumbs. Coat the remaining diamonds in the same way, and place all six in the baking pan.

Bake the falafel for 15 minutes, then turn them over and bake them for 15 minutes more. Let them cool. Cover the falafel and chill them until they are needed.

For the relish, heat the oil in a heavy-bottomed, nonreactive skillet, and cook the red pepper, onion, and garlic over low heat for one minute. Add the vinegar, dry mustard, sugar, and hot red-pepper sauce to the pan with 5 tablespoons of water, then cover the pan and simmer for 10 minutes. Remove the lid and simmer for five minutes more, then pour the contents of the pan into the food processor and process briefly, until the ingredients are just combined. Allow the relish to cool, then chill it until it is needed.

When you are ready to go to the picnic, pack the falafel into a covered container and spoon the relish into a separate container with a tightfitting lid. Put the fig leaves, if you are using them, into a plastic bag. Transport all the items in a cooler.

To serve the dish, spread the fig leaves on a platter and place the falafel on top. Transfer the relish to a serving bowl.

Carrots Cooked with Honey and Spices

Serves 6
Working time: about 5 minutes
Total time: about 15 minutes

Calories **35**
Protein **1g.**
Cholesterol **0mg.**
Total fat **0g.**
Saturated fat **0g.**
Sodium **210mg.**

1 lb. carrots, sliced diagonally
1 small onion, finely chopped
2 tbsp. honey
2 tbsp. wine vinegar
1 tsp. ground cumin
½ tsp. ground cinnamon
½ tsp. salt
2 tbsp. chopped fresh parsley

Place the carrots, onion, honey, vinegar, cumin, cinnamon, and salt in a heavy-bottomed, nonreactive saucepan with ½ cup of water. Set the pan over high heat and bring the liquid to a boil. Lower the heat a little, and cook the carrots fairly rapidly, uncovered, until most of the liquid has evaporated but the carrots are still slightly crunchy—about 10 minutes. Allow the mixture to cool.

Transfer the carrots to a covered, nonreactive container, and chill them until you are ready to leave for the picnic. Place the chopped parsley in a small plastic bag and close the bag with a twist tie.

At the picnic site, turn the carrots into a serving bowl and sprinkle on the chopped parsley.

Tabbouleh

Serves 6
Working time: about 15 minutes
Total time: about 45 minutes (includes soaking)

Calories **75**
Protein **3g.**
Cholesterol **0mg.**
Total fat **3g.**
Saturated fat **1g.**
Sodium **10mg.**

½ cup bulgur
¾ cup loosely packed fresh mint leaves, finely chopped
2 cups loosely packed fresh parsley, finely chopped
1 onion, finely chopped
3 tbsp. fresh lemon juice
1 tbsp. virgin olive oil
tomato wedges for garnish

Put the bulgur into a bowl and add sufficient boiling water to cover it. Let the bulgur soak for 30 minutes, adding water as necessary to keep the grains covered. Pour the bulgur into a fine sieve and allow it to drain thoroughly; press it down with the back of a spoon to force out as much moisture as possible.

Turn the drained bulgur into a mixing bowl, and add the mint, parsley, onion, lemon juice, and oil. Stir all the ingredients together thoroughly. Turn the tabbouleh into a covered, nonreactive container, and chill it until it is needed. Chill the tomato wedges in a separate container.

At the picnic, transfer the tabbouleh to a serving bowl and garnish it with the tomato wedges.

Fruit and Nut Triangles

Serves 6
Working time: about 25 minutes
Total time: about 45 minutes

Calories **205**
Protein **4g.**
Cholesterol **0mg.**
Total fat **12g.**
Saturated fat **5g.**
Sodium **100mg.**

¾ cup unbleached all-purpose flour
1 tbsp. sugar
4 tbsp. polyunsaturated margarine
2 tbsp. chopped walnuts
2 tbsp. chopped pine nuts
2 tbsp. chopped pistachio nuts
3 tbsp. semolina flour
2 tbsp. honey
7 tbsp. golden raisins

3 tbsp. chopped dates
3 tbsp. chopped dried apricots
1 tsp. rose water
1 walnut half for decoration

Preheat the oven to 400° F.

Lightly grease and flour an 8-inch round tart pan with a removable bottom.

Sift the flour and sugar into a large bowl, and rub in the margarine with your fingertips or the back of a wooden spoon until the mixture resembles breadcrumbs. Using a wooden spoon, mix 1½ teaspoons of ice water into the dry ingredients to form a soft dough. Gather the dough into a ball and knead it briefly on a lightly floured surface to smooth it. Alternatively, prepare the dough in a food processor.

Press the dough evenly into the bottom of the prepared tart pan, and prick it all over with a fork. Spread out the chopped walnuts, pine nuts, and pistachio nuts on a baking sheet. Cook the nuts and the pastry shell in the oven for 10 minutes, stirring the nuts occasionally. Remove both from the oven, but leave the oven on. Run the tip of a sharp knife around the edge of the pastry shell to loosen it.

While the pastry and nuts are cooking, prepare the topping. Place the semolina flour, honey, golden raisins, dates, and apricots in a small, heavy-bottomed saucepan with ½ cup of water. Stir the ingredients together and bring them just to a boil. Lower the heat and simmer the mixture for about eight minutes, or until it has formed a thick purée. Remove the pan from the heat, and stir in the rose water and all of the chopped roasted nuts. Spread the fruit and nut filling over the pastry shell in an even layer, and return it to the oven to bake for 20 minutes.

Allow the baked sweet pastry to cool in its pan, then cut it into 12 triangles. Cover the pan with plastic wrap and store the triangles in the refrigerator until you are ready to leave for the picnic. Transport the triangles in the pan and also take along a walnut half, for decoration. At the picnic site, arrange the fruit and nut triangles on a round serving dish, and place the walnut half in the center.

Turkish Delight

Serves 6
Working time: about 20 minutes
Total time: about 3 hours and 35 minutes

Calories **70**
Protein **3g.**
Cholesterol **0mg.**
Total fat **3g.**
Saturated fat **2g.**
Sodium **5mg.**

2 cups unsweetened white grape juice
2 tbsp. walnuts
1½ tbsp. powdered gelatin (2 pkg.)
½ tbsp. orange-flower water
½ tsp. pure vanilla extract
walnut oil
2 tbsp. unsweetened coconut flakes

Preheat the oven to 350° F.

Pour the grape juice into a wide, heavy-bottomed saucepan and boil it gently until it has reduced to 1 cup. Transfer the grape juice to a flameproof bowl and set it aside.

Spread out the walnuts on a baking sheet and roast them in the oven for 15 minutes, stirring them occasionally. When they are cool enough to handle, chop them coarsely.

Sprinkle the gelatin over 5 tablespoons of cold water in a small, flameproof bowl. Set the gelatin aside for two minutes to allow the granules to soften and swell, then put the bowl over a pan of gently simmering water and stir until the gelatin has completely dissolved—about three minutes. Stir the gelatin solution, the orange-flower water, and the vanilla extract into the reduced grape juice. Chill the mixture until it is on the point of setting—about 15 minutes.

Brush a square pan 4 by 4 by 1 inch with a little walnut oil. Stir the chopped walnuts into the partially set grape gelatin, then turn the mixture into the prepared pan. Chill the grape gelatin until it is firmly set—at least three hours, and preferably overnight.

Unmold the set gelatin onto a cutting board and divide it into 12 equal squares. Dip the squares in the coconut flakes, pressing them on gently to ensure that each square is evenly coated. Store the squares in the refrigerator, packed in a covered container, until you are ready to leave for the picnic. Carry the container to the picnic site in a cooler.

AMERICAN BARBECUE

Toasted Onion Dip
Chicken Drumsticks in Barbecue Sauce
Citrus-Marinated Round Steak
Fruited Cabbage Salad
Garlic Potato Fans and Grilled Corn on the Cob
Iced Peach Yogurt with Hot Blueberry Compote

The iced yogurt dessert for this barbecue can be prepared a day or two in advance and stored in the freezer. The steak, too, can begin its marination the day before. Both the onion dip and the cabbage salad will benefit from thorough chilling, so make those ahead of time if you can. The foil parcels—of corn, of garlic potatoes, and of fruit compote—can all be assembled in advance and set aside, ready to be cooked at the appropriate time.

About one and a half hours before you plan to serve, place the potatoes on the grill, and add the corn parcels after 40 minutes. Set the vegetables aside once they are cooked—they will remain hot in their foil wrappings. Next, begin to grill the chicken drumsticks; after 10 minutes, move them to the edges of the rack for the remainder of their cooking time and cook the steaks in the center of the rack, over the hottest coals. When the chicken and meat are cooked, the vegetables may be reheated briefly.

Shortly before you wish to serve the dessert, place the parcels of fruit on the grill to cook in the residual heat of the fire.

A smooth onion dip with crudités is served as a prelude to this American barbecue. The main course of chicken drumsticks and citrus-marinated steak is accompanied by a colorful salad of fruit and crisp, shredded cabbage in a light yogurt dressing. Garlic potatoes and juicy corn on the cob round out the meal, which concludes with bubbling-hot parcels of fruit compote topped with iced peach yogurt.

Toasted Onion Dip

Serves 12
Working time: about 30 minutes
Total time: about 2 hours and 30 minutes
(includes chilling)

Calories **45**
Protein **5g.**
Cholesterol **trace**
Total fat **2g.**
Saturated fat **trace**
Sodium **30mg.**

3 large Spanish onions, 2 coarsely chopped
⅔ cup low-fat ricotta cheese
6 oz. low-fat cream cheese
6 tbsp. finely cut chives
freshly ground black pepper

Preheat the oven to 375° F., and line a baking sheet with aluminum foil.

Put the coarsely chopped onions into a heavy-bottomed saucepan and cover them with cold water. Bring the water to a boil, cover the pan, and simmer the onions gently until they are very soft and tender—30 to 40 minutes.

Meanwhile, cut the remaining onion into slices ¼ inch thick and spread them out on the prepared baking sheet. Toast the onion slices in the oven for about 20 minutes, turning them so that they brown evenly and removing them as they brown; do not let the onions burn. Alternatively, toast the onion slices under a preheated, medium-hot broiler, again watching carefully to be sure that they do not burn. Set the toasted onion slices aside.

When the chopped onions are cooked, drain them well and allow them to cool. Transfer them to a food processor and blend them to a smooth purée. Add the cheeses and process the mixture briefly to combine the ingredients. Turn the dip into a bowl.

Crumble the toasted onion slices. Reserve 1 tablespoon for garnish, and add the remainder to the bowl with the chives and some black pepper. Gently fold these ingredients into the dip. Cover the bowl and chill the dip for at least one hour. Just before serving, sprinkle the surface with the reserved toasted onion.

SUGGESTED ACCOMPANIMENT: *a selection of crunchy fresh vegetables for dipping.*

Chicken Drumsticks in Barbecue Sauce

inutes
30 minutes

alor
rote
holeste...
otal fat **5g.**
aturated fat **2g.**
odium **95mg.**

d diced
d
two 14-oz. cans tomatoes, chopped
3 tbsp. dark brown sugar
1 tbsp. Worcestershire sauce
1 tsp. paprika
freshly ground black pepper
12 chicken drumsticks (about 4½ oz. each)

To make the barbecue sauce, put all the ingredients except the drumsticks into a heavy-bottomed saucepan. Cover the pan and simmer the ingredients over low heat for one hour, or until the vegetables are very tender. Remove the pan from the heat. When the mixture has cooled, purée it in a food processor. Press the purée through a sieve into a clean pan, discarding the solids that remain in the sieve. Cook the sauce, uncovered, at a strong simmer, stirring it occasionally, until it is thick and the quantity has reduced by half—about 30 minutes.

Brush the chicken drumsticks with some of the sauce and arrange them on a lightly oiled rack over hot coals. Cook the drumsticks for 10 minutes, turning them frequently and basting them with more of the sauce each time they are turned. Move the drumsticks to the outer edges of the rack and continue to cook for another 10 to 15 minutes, again turning them frequently and basting them with the sauce.

Insert a skewer in the thickest part of the flesh of one of the drumsticks; if the juices run clear, the drumsticks are ready. Pile the cooked drumsticks on a serving plate. Transfer the remaining barbecue sauce to a bowl and serve it with the drumsticks.

SUGGESTED ACCOMPANIMENT: *scallions.*

Citrus-Marinated Round Steak

Serves 12
Working time: about 25 minutes
Total time: about 5 hours and 30 minutes
(includes marinating)

Calories **170**
Protein **24g.**
Cholesterol **50mg.**
Total fat **8g.**
Saturated fat **3g.**
Sodium **40mg.**

3 tbsp. fresh orange juice
2 tbsp. fresh lime juice
1 tsp. fresh lemon juice
2 tbsp. virgin olive oil
1 or 2 garlic cloves, finely chopped
1 tbsp. green peppercorns, rinsed and coarsely crushed
1 tbsp. fresh thyme, or 1 tsp. dried thyme leaves
2-lb. round steak, about 1 to 1½ inches thick, trimmed of all fat and cut into 2 equal pieces

In a shallow, nonreactive dish that is just large enough to hold the steaks comfortably, mix together the orange juice, lime juice, lemon juice, olive oil, garlic, peppercorns, and thyme. Put the steaks into the dish and turn them over to coat both sides with the marinade. Cover the dish tightly and let the meat marinate in the refrigerator for at least four hours, or overnight, turning the steaks occasionally during this time.

Remove the meat from the refrigerator about one hour before you plan to cook it. Reserving the marinade, lay the steaks on the grill over hot coals, and cook them for four to five minutes on each side for medium-rare meat; increase the cooking time to six to seven minutes on each side for medium to well-done meat. Baste the steaks with the reserved marinade when turning them.

Transfer the cooked steaks to a cutting board and let them rest for five minutes. To serve, slice each steak into six portions.

Fruited Cabbage Salad

Serves 12
Working time: about 25 minutes
Total time: about 1 hour

Calories **105**
Protein **4g.**
Cholesterol **trace**
Total fat **3g.**
Saturated fat **1g.**
Sodium **45mg.**

3 cups finely shredded red cabbage
3 cups finely shredded white cabbage
2 cups finely shredded Chinese cabbage
1 red onion, cut into fine slivers
½ lb. seedless green grapes, halved if large
2 tart apples, cored, diced, and sprinkled with a little fresh lemon juice
1 tbsp. caraway seeds

Honey dressing

⅓ cup cider vinegar
3 tbsp. honey
1 tbsp. Dijon mustard
2 tbsp. corn or safflower oil
¾ cup plain low-fat yogurt
freshly ground black pepper

First make the dressing. In a small bowl, combine the vinegar, honey, and mustard, and whisk them together. Gradually whisk in the oil, followed by the yogurt. Season the dressing with some black pepper.

In a large mixing bowl, combine the red, white, and Chinese cabbages, the onion, the grapes, and the apples. Pour the dressing over the salad, and sprinkle on the caraway seeds. Toss the salad until the fruit and vegetables are evenly coated with the dressing.

Cover the bowl and chill the salad for at least 30 minutes before serving it. Toss the salad again before transferring it to a serving dish.

Garlic Potato Fans and Grilled Corn on the Cob

Serves 12
Working time: about 30 minutes
Total time: about 2 hours and 30 minutes

Calories **385**
Protein **9g.**
Cholesterol **0mg.**
Total fat **8g.**
Saturated fat **1g.**
Sodium **15mg.**

1 large garlic clove, lightly crushed
¼ cup corn or safflower oil
12 baking potatoes (about ½ lb. each), scrubbed
12 ears corn, unhusked

At least one hour before cooking the potatoes, com bine the garlic and oil in a cup. Set the garlic aside t allow it to steep in the oil.

Make crosswise cuts about ½ inch apart in th potatoes, cutting about two-thirds of the wa through. Place each potato on a double-thicknes square of foil that is large enough to wrap around i Brush the garlic-flavored oil over the potatoes so tha it can seep down into the cuts. Wrap the foil securel around the potatoes.

Place the foil parcels on the grill, over hot coals Roast the potatoes for about one hour, turning ther occasionally so that they cook evenly.

To prepare the corn on the cob, pull back the husk on each ear and remove the silk, keeping the husk attached to the ear. Fold the husks back up around th corn, then wrap each ear securely in a double thicknes of foil. Place the foil-wrapped corn on the rack an cook it for 15 to 20 minutes, turning it occasionally s that it cooks evenly.

To serve, remove the foil from the corn, then ver carefully peel back and trim off one side of the husks The corn inside will be extremely hot. Open out the fo around the potatoes, and pinch their sides to open u the cuts. Pile the vegetables on a platter.

Iced Peach Yogurt with Hot Blueberry Compote

Serves 12
Working time: about 1 hour and 15 minutes
Total time: about 5 hours (includes freezing)

alories **165**
otein **5g.**
nolesterol **trace**
otal fat **1g.**
turated fat **trace**
odium **70mg.**

4 cups plain low-fat yogurt
1½ lb. ripe peaches, peeled and pitted
⅔ cup sugar
1 orange, juice only
2 egg whites

Hot blueberry compote

1¾ lb. fresh or thawed frozen blueberries or blackberries
3 tbsp. cornstarch
½ cup fresh orange juice
1 tsp. finely grated orange zest
½ tsp. freshly grated nutmeg or ground nutmeg
2 tbsp. Kirsch

Line a large fine sieve with a double thickness of paper towels and set it over a bowl. Place the yogurt in the sieve and let it drain for one and a half hours.

Meanwhile, purée the peaches in a food processor: There will be about 2½ cups of purée. Pour the peach purée into a bowl, and add ½ cup of the sugar and all of the orange juice. Stir the mixture until the sugar has dissolved. Add the drained yogurt to the purée, scraping it carefully off the paper towels, and stir it in. Beat the egg whites until they are foamy. Gradually beat the remaining sugar into the egg whites, and continue beating until the egg whites are stiff. Lightly fold the egg whites into the peach purée.

Pour the mixture into a 9-by-13-inch metal baking pan, cover the pan with foil, and put it into the freezer. When the mixture has set around the edges—after 30 to 40 minutes—transfer it to a food processor and process it briefly to break down the frozen parts. Return the mixture to the pan, cover it as before, and put it back into the freezer. Process the mixture for a second time when it has again set around the edges, then return it to the freezer, covered, until it is completely frozen—two to three hours.

Alternatively, pour the mixture into the container of an electric ice-cream maker and insert the paddle. Cover the yogurt mixture and freeze it until the paddle stops turning, then remove the paddle and let the yogurt ripen in the freezer for one hour more.

Transfer the iced yogurt to the refrigerator about 30 minutes before you plan to serve it, or about one hour before serving if it has been stored in the freezer for more than 24 hours.

To make the compote, put the blueberries or blackberries into a bowl and toss them with the cornstarch. Add the orange juice and zest, the nutmeg, and the Kirsch, and toss them with the fruit until they are thoroughly combined.

Cut out twelve 10-by-5-inch strips of foil and fold each one in half crosswise into a 5-inch square. Cut out 12 squares of parchment paper slightly smaller than the foil squares. Place a paper square on each foil square. Press one pair of squares, with the foil underneath, into a cereal bowl to mold it, then spoon in a portion of the blueberry mixture. Wrap the paper and foil around the fruit, sealing the parcel well. Make 11 more parcels in the same way.

After the main course has been cooked, place the parcels of fruit mixture on the grill and cook them for 10 to 15 minutes, depending on the heat left in the coals. Shake each parcel halfway through the cooking time to redistribute the contents. To check that the compote is ready, open up a parcel: The juices should be thickened and the berries piping hot.

To serve, open up the parcels and top the compote with scoops of the iced peach yogurt. Serve the desserts in their parcels.

EDITOR'S NOTE: *To make peaches easier to peel, first immerse them in boiling water for two minutes to loosen the skins.*

4 A hollowed-out squash shell provides the perfect serving vessel for this creamy salad of chicken, baby corn, and spaghetti squash (recipe, opposite).

An Indoor Aid to Outdoor Meals

The marriage of modern technology with the most ancient traditions of cooking is nowhere more surprising than in the contribution of the microwave oven to outdoor eating. In fact, the well-known advantages of microwave cooking prove particularly useful to anyone preparing meals to eat alfresco.

Bright, festive foods are ideal for picnics. Cooked in a microwave oven, vegetables retain their original, vivid colors. The three-pepper flan on page 131 brings a touch of Mediterranean brilliance to the most overcast of picnics. Moreover, because it saves you time in the kitchen, the microwave frees you to enjoy the sun. Even apparently time-consuming composite dishes become short work with a microwave oven. For the elegant chicken salad on the right, for instance, a whole spaghetti squash cooks in just 10 to 12 minutes, while the strips of chicken breast require only three minutes' cooking time.

Another salad—the Atlantic kedgeree on page 136—highlights the microwave oven's renowned capacity to produce moist, tender fish. And because microwave cooking destroys few vitamins and minerals, you can be assured of a nutritious meal for healthful outdoor eating. Even at a barbecue—where old-fashioned cooking over coals takes center stage—the microwave oven plays an invaluable supporting role. Before the fire is ready, a cook can prepare the sauces and relishes *(pages 132 and 133)*.

A few simple techniques help ensure perfect results. If you are covering a dish with plastic wrap, turn back one corner to prevent the buildup of steam. Use wrap that is free of plasticizers so that potentially harmful substances do not leach out into the hot food.

The recipes in this chapter include instructions for turning the food; if your microwave oven has a turntable, these instructions may be ignored. Soups and sauces require occasional stirring to ensure even cooking. And remember that microwaved food is not necessarily done when the oven turns off. Many recipes call for additional "standing time" of up to half the total cooking time.

The recipes in this book have been tested in 650-watt and 700-watt ovens. Most of the dishes are cooked on "high," or 100 percent power; the term "medium" refers to 50 percent power.

Golden Chicken Salad in a Spaghetti Squash

Serves 4
Working time: about 35 minutes
Total time: about 2 hours and 35 minutes (includes cooling)

Calories **205**
Protein **26g.**
Cholesterol **65mg.**
Total fat **6g.**
Saturated fat **3g.**
Sodium **440mg.**

¼ cup sweet white wine
1-inch piece fresh ginger, sliced
⅛ tsp. powdered saffron
¾ lb. skinned and boned chicken breasts, cut into 1½-by-½-inch strips
¼ lb. baby corn, fresh or frozen, trimmed if necessary
2 small spaghetti squashes (about 1½ lb. each)
¼ cup sour cream
¼ tsp. freshly grated nutmeg or ground nutmeg
⅛ tsp. salt
ground white pepper
1½ tsp. yellow mustard seeds

Place the wine, ginger, and saffron in a dish, and stir to distribute the saffron. Add the chicken and stir to coat all the strips in the wine mixture. Cover the dish with plastic wrap pulled back at one edge, and microwave the chicken on high for two and a half to three minutes, until all the strips are cooked; stir twice during the cooking time. Let the chicken cool in the liquid—about two hours.

Meanwhile, place the baby corn in a dish with 3 tablespoons of cold water. Cover the dish as before, and microwave the corn on high for three minutes, stirring halfway through the cooking time. Let the corn rest for two minutes, then uncover and drain it.

Wash the squashes and pierce each one in three or four places with a thin skewer. Place both squashes in the microwave oven on a double layer of paper towels. Cook them on high for 16 minutes, or until they are slightly soft to the touch and aromatic, rearranging them two or three times during cooking. Let the squashes rest for five minutes.

Remove the chicken strips from their cooking liquid and set them aside. Microwave the liquid, uncovered, on high until it has reduced to 1 tablespoon—three to four minutes; watch carefully while you do this, to avoid boiling the liquid dry. Strain the reduced liquid into a bowl, discarding the ginger. Let the liquid cool for one minute, then stir in the sour cream, nutmeg, salt, and some white pepper.

Place the mustard seeds in a narrow, deep dish, and cook them on high for two minutes, or until they start ▶

to pop and release their aroma. Reserve about a quarter of the seeds for garnish, and place these in a small screw-top jar. Lightly crush the remainder with a mortar and pestle, and stir them into the dressing.

Cut each spaghetti squash in half lengthwise. Use a fork to scrape out the seeds and fiber from the middle of each portion of squash; discard the seeds and fiber. Fork out the strands of squash, and pile them into a large mixing bowl; reserve the squash shells.

Gently mix the chicken and corn with the squash. Pour in the dressing, and continue to mix until all the ingredients are thoroughly combined.

Pile the mixture lightly into the four squash shells, and cover them with plastic wrap. Chill the shells until they are needed.

Transport the squash to the picnic site in a cooler, inside covered containers packed with paper towels. When you unwrap the shells, sprinkle the reserved mustard seeds over them, and add a little extra grated nutmeg if you like.

Chilled Beet Soup

Serves 6
Working time: about 25 minutes
Total time: about 3 hours and 25 minutes (includes chilling)

Calories **60**
Protein **2g.**
Cholesterol **5mg.**
Total fat **1g.**
Saturated fat **trace**
Sodium **205mg.**

¼ lb. tomatoes (2 small), quartered
¾ lb. beets, peeled and grated
1 carrot, grated
1 onion, grated
1 small potato, peeled and grated
2 bay leaves
4 cups unsalted vegetable stock (recipe, page 139)
⅓ cup sour cream
⅓ cup plain low-fat yogurt
½ tsp. salt
freshly ground black pepper

Place the tomatoes in a bowl with 3 tablespoons of cold water. Cover the bowl with plastic wrap pulled back at one edge, and microwave the tomatoes on high for three to four minutes, until they are pulpy. Sieve the tomatoes.

Place the beets, carrot, onion, and potato in a large bowl. Stir in the sieved tomatoes, the bay leaves, and half of the stock. Cover the bowl as before, and microwave the soup on high for 25 to 30 minutes, until the vegetables are tender; stir the mixture twice during the cooking time. Remove the bay leaves from the soup, then stir in the remaining stock and let the soup cool—30 to 45 minutes.

Ladle a little of the cooled soup into a small bowl, and stir the sour cream and yogurt into it. When the yogurt mixture is smooth, add it to the rest of the soup and stir to mix it in evenly. Add the salt and some pepper. Chill the soup for two hours, then transfer it to a chilled thermos.

Three-Pepper Flan

Serves 6
Working (and total) time: about 1 hour

Calories **220**
Protein **8g.**
Cholesterol **75mg.**
Total fat **12g.**
Saturated fat **3g.**
Sodium **185mg.**

1½ cups whole-wheat flour
4 tbsp. polyunsaturated margarine
1 tbsp. smooth peanut butter
1 small sweet red pepper, seeded, deribbed, and cut into thin rings
1 small sweet green pepper, seeded, deribbed, and cut into thin rings
1 small sweet yellow pepper, seeded, deribbed, and cut into thin rings
2 eggs
1 cup skim milk
¼ tsp. salt
freshly ground black pepper
1 tbsp. chopped cilantro

Put the flour into a mixing bowl and add the margarine and peanut butter. Using your fingertips, lightly rub the margarine and peanut butter into the flour until the mixture resembles fine breadcrumbs. Make a well in the center of the dry ingredients. Using a wooden spoon, mix in 8 to 10 teaspoons of ice water to form a soft but not sticky dough.

Gather the dough into a firm ball, and knead it briefly on a lightly floured surface until it is smooth. Roll out the dough into a circle large enough to line an 8-inch quiche dish. Taking care not to stretch the dough, line the dish, then chill it for 20 minutes.

Lay a piece of paper towel over the pastry shell, pressing it lightly onto the bottom. Microwave the pastry shell on high for three and a half minutes, or until the pastry has lost its wet, glossy appearance and looks dry; give the dish a half-turn after two minutes. Remove the paper towel and let the pastry cool.

Place the pepper rings in a bowl, and sprinkle 1 tablespoon of cold water over them. Cover the bowl with plastic wrap, leaving one edge open to let steam escape. Microwave the pepper rings on high for two minutes, or until they are soft. Allow them to stand for five minutes, then arrange them evenly in the pastry shell.

Beat the eggs and milk together with the salt and a generous grinding of black pepper. Stir in the chopped cilantro, and pour the mixture over the peppers in the pastry shell. Microwave the flan on medium for 15 minutes, giving it a quarter-turn every two minutes. If the filling is not quite set at the end of this time, cook the flan, in short bursts of power, for 15 to 30 seconds more.

Remove the flan from the oven and let it cool completely, in its dish, before covering it with foil or plastic wrap for transport to the picnic.

Five Colorful Accompaniments

These quick-to-prepare sauces and relishes make a wholesome range of accompaniments to the picnic and barbecue recipes in this volume. All of them keep well and may be made in advance. Store them in the refrigerator, either in a covered bowl or in a screw-top jar, for up to three days. If you wish to freeze any of these condiments, allow them to cool fully and then transfer them to plastic containers. Once thawed, they should be stirred thoroughly before serving.

Nutritionally, these accompaniments are greatly superior to their commercially prepared equivalents. A tablespoon of one of them will provide between 20 and 30 calories, or 15 calories in the case of the Mexican chili relish. The green garlic sauce contains about 5 milligrams of cholesterol per tablespoon; the other four have negligible amounts. A portion of any one of these condiments contains only a trace of saturated fat and little sodium.

Mexican Chili Relish

Makes 2 cups
Working time: about 25 minutes
Total time: about 1 hour (includes cooling)

6 oz. frozen corn
2 celery stalks, finely chopped
1 small onion, finely chopped
2 small green chili peppers, seeded and finely chopped (cautionary note, page 63)
1 tbsp. sugar
⅓ cup white wine vinegar
1 sweet green pepper,seeded, deribbed, and finely diced
1 sweet red pepper,seeded, deribbed, and finely diced
1 tsp. fennel seeds, crushed
1 tbsp. mustard seeds, crushed
1 tsp. cornstarch

Place the corn in a small bowl with 1 tablespoon of water. Cover the bowl with plastic wrap pulled back at one edge, and microwave it on high for one minute. Drain the corn and refresh it under cold running water.

Place the celery, onion, chili peppers, sugar, and vinegar in a bowl, and microwave them on high for four minutes, stirring twice. Add the corn, diced sweet peppers, and the crushed fennel and mustard seeds, and stir to mix all the ingredients together. Cover the bowl with plastic wrap, pulling back one edge as before. Microwave the mixture on high for two minutes, or until it is hot, stirring once. Blend the cornstarch to a smooth paste with 2 tablespoons of cold water, and stir it into the hot mixture. Microwave the relish on high for another two minutes, or until it has thickened, stirring it twice. Transfer the relish to a serving bowl and let it cool.

Goes well with steaks and hamburgers, and with all types of sausages.

Green Garlic Sauce

Makes 1¼ cups
Working (and total) time: about 20 minutes

½ tbsp. unsalted butter
4 shallots, coarsely chopped
3 garlic cloves, coarsely chopped
1 oz. pickled gherkins, rinsed and sliced (about 3 tbsp.)
1 tbsp. capers, rinsed
1 cup medium-dry white wine
1 tsp. sugar
¾ cup loosely packed fresh parsley
2 or 3 sprigs tarragon

Place the butter in a dish, and microwave it on high for 30 seconds to melt it. Add the chopped shallots and garlic, and stir them into the melted butter. Microwave them on high for two minutes, or until the shallots are soft; stir once during this time. Mix in the gherkins, capers, wine, and sugar, and cover the dish with plastic wrap pulled back at one edge. Microwave on high for two minutes, stirring once.

Transfer the ingredients to a food processor or blender. Add the parsley and tarragon, then blend the mixture until it is almost smooth. Transfer the sauce to a serving bowl, and reheat it on high for one minute. Alternatively, let the sauce cool completely and serve it cold.

Goes well with lamb and any whitefish, or can be used as a sauce for pasta.

Sweet-and-Sour Sauce

Makes 2½ cups
Working time: about 20 minutes
Total time: about 30 minutes

1 tsp. sesame oil
1 bunch scallions, white parts chopped, a few green tops sliced for garnish
1-inch piece fresh ginger, finely chopped
1 sweet yellow pepper, seeded, deribbed, and diced
2 tbsp. low-sodium soy sauce
1 tbsp. white wine vinegar
3 tbsp. medium-dry sherry
1 small fresh pineapple (about 2¾ lb.), peeled, cored, and cut into ½-inch dice
1 tbsp. sesame seeds
1 tbsp. cornstarch

In a large bowl, mix the oil and the white parts of the scallions. Microwave them on high for two minutes, stirring once. Stir in the ginger, yellow pepper, soy sauce, vinegar, and sherry. Add ⅓ cup of water, stir, and cover the bowl with plastic wrap, leaving one edge open to allow steam to escape. Microwave the sauce on high for one minute, or until it is hot.

Stir in the pineapple and sesame seeds. Blend the cornstarch to a smooth paste with 2 tablespoons of cold water, and stir it into the sauce. Cover the bowl as before, and microwave the sauce on high for five minutes, or until it has thickened, stirring it several times during cooking. Transfer the sauce to a serving bowl and serve it, either hot or cold, garnished with a few slices of green scallion tops.

Goes well with chicken and pork dishes.

Barbecue Sauce

Makes 2 cups
Working (and total) time: about 20 minutes

1 large red onion, chopped
1 slice bacon, trimmed of all fat and coarsely chopped
1 tsp. virgin olive oil
2 bay leaves
1 tbsp. red wine vinegar
1 tbsp. molasses or dark brown sugar
1 tsp. paprika
2 tbsp. tomato paste
1 tbsp. grainy mustard
2 tsp. Worcestershire sauce
1 cup fresh orange juice
½ tsp. very finely chopped orange zest for garnish

Mix the onion, bacon, oil, and bay leaves in a large bowl, and microwave them on high for three minutes, stirring once. Add the vinegar, molasses or brown sugar, paprika, tomato paste, mustard, Worcestershire sauce, and orange juice. Stir all the ingredients together, and cover the bowl with plastic wrap, leaving one edge open to allow steam to escape. Microwave the mixture on high for two minutes.

Remove the bay leaves, then transfer the contents of the bowl to a food processor or blender, and process until a smooth sauce is formed. Pour the sauce into a serving bowl, and reheat it on high for one minute. Alternatively, allow the sauce to cool and serve it cold. Before serving the sauce, sprinkle the finely chopped orange zest over the surface.

Goes well with all types of barbecued meat and vegetables.

Curried Mango Relish

Makes 2½ cups
Working time: about 20 minutes
Total time: about 30 minutes

1 fresh green chili pepper, seeded and coarsely chopped (cautionary note, page 63)
2 tsp. safflower oil
2 garlic cloves, crushed
¼ tsp. ground turmeric
1 tsp. ground coriander
1 tsp. ground cumin
2 ripe mangoes (about 1¼ lb. each), pitted and peeled, flesh coarsely chopped
2 tsp. white wine vinegar
⅔ cup plain low-fat yogurt

In a large bowl, mix the chopped chili pepper with the oil, garlic, turmeric, coriander, and cumin. Microwave the mixture on high for one minute, stirring halfway through. Stir in the chopped mangoes and the vinegar. Cover the bowl with plastic wrap, leaving one edge open to allow steam to escape. Microwave on high for three minutes, stirring once. Mash the mixture with a potato masher until it is pulpy, and then allow it to cool for five minutes.

Stir ½ cup of the yogurt into the relish, and chill it until it is required. Just before serving, transfer the relish to a serving bowl and swirl the remaining yogurt over the surface.

Goes well with cold chicken, barbecued fish, and meat—particularly lamb.

Greek-Style Celery and Tomato Salad

Serves 4 as a main course or 6 as a side dish
Working time: about 25 minutes
Total time: about 2 hours
(includes cooling)

Calories **150**
Protein **6g.**
Cholesterol **30mg.**
Total fat **11g.**
Saturated fat **4g.**
Sodium **410mg.**

1 lb. ripe tomatoes (about 3 medium) quartered, plus 6 tomatoes, peeled (technique, page 138) and quartered
1 tbsp. tomato paste
1 large head of celery, trimmed, sliced diagonally into 1-inch pieces
1 garlic clove, crushed
1 tbsp. virgin olive oil
3 tbsp. fresh lemon juice
2 bay leaves
1/8 tsp. ground coriander
4 scallions, trimmed and chopped
freshly ground black pepper
1/4 lb. feta cheese, cut into 1/2-inch cubes
4 black olives, pitted and cut into sixths lengthwise
2 tsp. chopped flat-leaf parsley, plus flat-leaf parsley sprigs for garnish (optional)
1 tsp. chopped fresh oregano

Place the unpeeled tomato quarters in a bowl with 2 tablespoons of cold water. Cover the bowl with plastic wrap pulled back at one edge, and microwave the tomatoes on high for six minutes, or until they are pulpy; stir them once during this time. Sieve the tomato pulp, and stir the tomato paste into it.

Place the celery in a large bowl, and add the sieved tomatoes, garlic, oil, lemon juice, bay leaves, and coriander. Stir to mix the ingredients, then cover the bowl with plastic wrap as before. Microwave on high for eight minutes, stirring once.

Stir in the scallions and peeled tomato quarters, and cook on high for two minutes more, or until the celery is tender but still crisp. Add some pepper and let the mixture cool for one and a half to two hours.

Remove the bay leaves, and transfer the celery and tomato salad to a covered container. Pack the feta cheese, olive slices, parsley sprigs, if you are using them, chopped parsley, and oregano separately.

At the picnic site, arrange the salad in a serving dish, and scatter on the feta cheese, olive slices, and chopped parsley and oregano. Garnish the salad with the parsley sprigs, if you wish.

SUGGESTED ACCOMPANIMENT: *crusty brown rolls.*

Mushroom and Parsley Pâté

Serves 6
Working time: about 25 minutes
Total time: about 24 hours (includes chilling)

Calories **85**
Protein **4g.**
Cholesterol **0mg.**
Total fat **3g.**
Saturated fat **1g.**
Sodium **205mg.**

1 tbsp. polyunsaturated margarine
2 garlic cloves, crushed
1 large onion, finely chopped
1¼ lb. mushrooms, wiped clean and coarsely chopped
¾ cup loosely packed fresh parsley, chopped, plus parsley sprigs for garnish
freshly ground black pepper
1 tbsp. mango chutney, chopped
2 tbsp. white wine vinegar
¼ tsp. salt
⅔ cup fresh whole-wheat breadcrumbs

Place the margarine in a large bowl and microwave it on high for 30 seconds, or until it has melted. Stir the garlic and onion thoroughly into the margarine, and cook them on high for two minutes.

Stir in the mushrooms, and cook the mixture on high for five minutes. Add half of the chopped parsley and some pepper, mix them in, and cook on high for five minutes more. Stir the chutney, wine vinegar, and salt into the mushroom mixture, making sure that all the ingredients are thoroughly combined. Microwave on high for five minutes more. or until all the liquid has evaporated. Mix in the breadcrumbs and the remaining chopped parsley.

Spoon the pâté into a round dish measuring about 6 inches in diameter and 3 inches in depth. Press the mixture down lightly with the back of the spoon. Let the pâté cool, then cover the dish with a tightfitting lid or with plastic wrap, taped down securely. Chill the pâté for about 24 hours to allow the flavors to develop fully. Serve garnished with the parsley sprigs.

SUGGESTED ACCOMPANIMENT: *toast points.*

Atlantic Kedgeree

Serves 6
Working time: about 45 minutes
Total time: about 2 hours and 30 minutes
(includes cooling)

Calories **280**
Protein **23g.**
Cholesterol **90mg.**
Total fat **2g.**
Saturated fat **trace**
Sodium **170mg.**

1 lb. mussels, scrubbed and debearded
1½ cups long-grain rice
3 celery stalks, sliced
4 cups unsalted vegetable stock (recipe, page 139)
5 oz. green beans, trimmed, cut into 1-inch lengths
¾ lb. cod or haddock fillets
½ sweet orange pepper, seeded, deribbed, and sliced into thin strips
½ sweet yellow pepper, seeded, deribbed, and sliced into thin strips
6 oz. peeled cooked shrimp
freshly ground black pepper
2 tbsp. fresh lemon juice (optional)
1 tbsp. finely cut chives
samphire (glossary) or parsley sprigs for garnish (optional)

Place the mussels in a large bowl. Sharply tap any that are open; if they remain open, discard them. Cover the bowl with plastic wrap pulled back at one edge, and microwave the mussels on high for five to six minutes, shaking the bowl or stirring the mussels after three minutes. Let them cool, then discard any that remained closed during cooking. Remove the mussels from their shells. Strain any cooking liquid through a cheesecloth-lined sieve into a bowl, and set it aside.

Place the rice and celery in a large bowl. Bring the stock to a boil, then add it to the bowl along with the reserved mussel-cooking liquid. Cover the bowl with plastic wrap as before, and microwave the rice on high for 10 minutes. Stir in the beans. Set the cooked rice aside to cool; any stock that was left at the end of the cooking time will be absorbed as it does so.

Put the cod or haddock on a plate, thinner pieces toward the center, and cover it with plastic wrap pulled back at one corner. Cook the fish on high for three to four minutes, until the flesh flakes easily. Flake the fish, discarding the skin and any bones. Set the flaked fish aside to cool.

Meanwhile, place the orange- and yellow-pepper strips in a bowl. Cover the bowl with plastic wrap as before, and microwave the strips on high for one and a half minutes, or until they are tender. Pour off any juices, and let the peppers cool.

Combine the beans and rice with the fish, peppers, mussels, and shrimp. Season the mixture with some pepper, and add the lemon juice, if you are using it.

Transfer the kedgeree to a container with a tight-fitting lid. Place the chives and the samphire or parsley garnish, if you are using it, in plastic bags, and put all items in a cooler. At the picnic site, arrange the kedgeree on a serving platter, sprinkle on the chives, and garnish the dish with the samphire or parsley sprigs.

Smoked Haddock Roulade

Serves 6
Working time: about 50 minutes
Total time: about 1 hour and 20 minutes

alories **130**
otein **12g.**
holesterol **100mg.**
otal fat **6g.**
aturated fat **2g.**
odium **460mg.**

6 oz. smoked haddock or cod fillet, skinned
2 eggs
1 egg white
¼ cup unbleached all-purpose flour
freshly ground black pepper
1 tbsp. freshly grated Parmesan cheese

Watercress filling

1½ tbsp. polyunsaturated margarine
3 tbsp. unbleached all-purpose flour
½ cup skim milk
2 cups loosely packed watercress, finely chopped
1 tbsp. finely cut chives

First make the watercress filling. Put the margarine, flour, and milk into a 1-quart container, and beat the mixture until the flour is evenly dispersed in the milk. Microwave the sauce on high for three minutes, or until it is thick and smooth, stirring it briskly every 30 seconds. Stir in the chopped watercress and chives. Cover the surface of the filling with a circle of damp wax paper to prevent a skin from forming. Set the filling aside to cool to room temperature, then chill it until it is needed.

Lay the haddock or cod fillet on a plate and cover it with plastic wrap, pulling back one edge to allow steam to escape. Microwave the fish on high for three minutes, or until the flesh flakes easily; give the plate a quarter-turn after one and a half minutes. Flake the fish and remove any bones, then lightly mash the flakes with a fork.

Next make the sponge layer. Line the bottom of an 8-by-8-inch baking dish with parchment paper. Put the eggs and egg white into a bowl, and set the bowl over a saucepan of simmering water. Using an electric hand-held mixer, beat the eggs until they are thick and creamy and have doubled in volume—about 15 minutes. Sift the flour over the egg mixture. Season the flaked fish with some freshly ground black pepper, and add the fish to the bowl. Using a rubber spatula, carefully fold in the flour and fish.

Turn the mixture into the prepared baking dish, spreading it in an even layer right into the corners. Microwave the mixture on high for four minutes, or until it is just firm to the touch; give the dish a half-turn after two minutes.

Sprinkle the Parmesan cheese over a sheet of wax paper, and invert the cooked sponge layer onto the paper. Peel off the parchment paper. Spread the watercress filling evenly over the sponge layer to within 1½ inches of the edges. Roll the sponge layer and filling into a cylinder, using the following technique: Lift one end of the underlying wax paper to start the roulade off, and nudge it along by gradually lifting the rest of the paper.

Wrap the roulade loosely in wax paper, and set it aside to cool. Once it is cold, wrap the roulade carefully in a double thickness of foil or wax paper. Chill it until it is needed. To avoid crushing the roulade, place it in a covered, rigid container, and carry this to the picnic inside a cooler. Take with you a sharp knife and a board so that the roulade can be sliced for serving.

SUGGESTED ACCOMPANIMENTS: *radishes; cucumbers; olives.*

Peeling and Seeding a Tomato

1 *PEELING THE TOMATO. Core the tomato by cutting a conical plug from its stem end. Cut a shallow cross in the base. Immerse the tomato in boiling water for 10 to 30 seconds, then plunge it into cold water. When the tomato has cooled, peel the skin away from the cross in sections.*

2 *SEEDING THE TOMATO. Halve the peeled tomato. Gently squeeze one of the halves, forcing out its seeds and juice. Rotate the tomato 90 degrees and squeeze once more. Remove any seeds from the inner chambers. Repeat the process with the other half.*

Peeling a Sweet Pepper

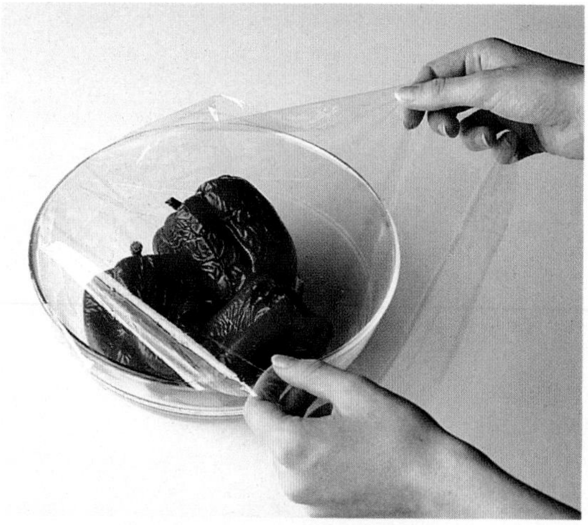

1 *LOOSENING THE SKIN. Place the pepper 2 inches below a preheated broiler. Turn the pepper as its sides become scorched; turn until the skin has blistered on all sides. Transfer the pepper to a bowl and cover with plastic wrap, or put it into a paper bag and fold it shut; the trapped steam will loosen the pepper's skin.*

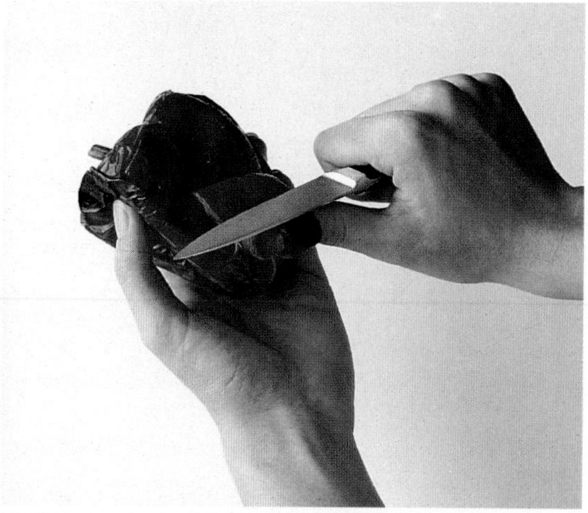

2 *REMOVING THE SKIN. With a small, sharp knife, peel off the pepper's skin in sections, working from top to bottom. The pepper may then be seeded and deribbed.*

Chicken Stock

Makes 2 to 3 quarts
Working time: about 20 minutes
Total time: about 3 hours

4 to 5 lb. uncooked chicken trimmings and bones (preferably wings, necks, and backs), the bones cracked with a heavy knife
2 carrots, scrubbed, sliced into ½-inch rounds
3 celery stalks, sliced into 1-inch lengths
2 large onions, cut in half, one half stuck with 2 cloves
2 sprigs fresh thyme, or ½ tsp. dried thyme leaves
1 or 2 bay leaves
10 to 15 parsley stems
5 black peppercorns

Put the trimmings and bones into a heavy stockpot and pour in enough water to cover them by 2 inches. Slowly bring the liquid to a boil, skimming off the scum that rises to the surface. Boil for 10 minutes, skimming and adding a little cold water from time to time to help precipitate the scum.

Add the carrots, celery, onions, thyme, bay leaves, parsley, and peppercorns, and submerge them in the liquid. If necessary, add enough additional water to cover the vegetables and bones. Reduce the heat to low. Simmer the mixture for two to three hours, skimming once more during the process.

Strain the stock and allow it to stand until it is tepid, then refrigerate it overnight or freeze it long enough for the fat to congeal. Spoon off and discard the layer of fat.

Tightly covered and refrigerated, the stock may safely be kept for three to four days. Stored in small, tightly covered freezer containers and frozen, the stock may be kept for as long as six months.

EDITOR'S NOTE: *The chicken gizzard and heart may be added to the stock. Wings and necks—rich in gelatin—produce a particularly gelatinous stock, ideal for sauces and jellied dishes. The liver should never be used.*

Vegetable Stock

Makes about 2 quarts
Working time: about 25 minutes
Total time: about 1 hour and 30 minutes

3 celery stalks (with leaves), finely chopped
3 carrots, scrubbed, sliced into ⅛-inch rounds
3 large onions (about 1½ lb.), coarsely chopped
2 large broccoli stems, coarsely chopped (optional)
1 medium turnip, peeled and cut into ½-inch cubes
5 garlic cloves, coarsely chopped
½ cup loosely packed parsley leaves and stems, coarsely chopped
10 black peppercorns
2 sprigs fresh thyme, or 1 tsp. dried thyme leaves
2 bay leaves

Put the celery, carrots, onions, broccoli, if you are using it, turnip, garlic, parsley, and peppercorns into a heavy stockpot. Pour in enough water to cover them by 2 inches. Slowly bring the liquid to a boil over medium heat, skimming off any scum that rises to the surface. When the liquid reaches a boil, add the thyme and bay leaves. Stir the stock once and reduce the heat to low; cover the pot, leaving the lid slightly ajar. Let the stock simmer undisturbed for one hour.

Strain the stock into a large bowl, pressing down lightly on the vegetables to extract all their liquid. Discard the vegetables. Allow the stock to stand until it is tepid, then refrigerate or freeze it.

Tightly covered and refrigerated, the stock may safely be kept for five to six days. Stored in small, tightly covered freezer containers and frozen, the stock may be kept for as long as six months.

Veal Stock

Makes about 3 quarts
Working time: about 30 minutes
Total time: about 4 hours and 30 minutes

3 lb. veal breast or shank meat, cut into 3-inch pieces
3 lb. veal bones (preferably knuckles), cracked
2 onions, quartered
2 celery stalks, sliced
1 carrot, sliced
8 black peppercorns
3 unpeeled garlic cloves crushed (optional)
1 tsp. fresh thyme, or ¼ tsp. dried thyme leaves
1 bay leaf

Fill a large pot halfway to the top with water. Bring the water to a boil, add the veal meat and bones, and blanch them for two minutes to clean them. Drain the meat and bones in a colander, discarding the liquid. Rinse the meat and bones under cold running water, and return them to the pot.

Add the onions, celery, carrot, peppercorns, and garlic, if you are using it. Pour in enough water to cover the contents of the pot by about 3 inches, and bring the water to a boil over medium heat. Lower the heat to maintain a simmer, and skim any impurities from the surface. Add the thyme and bay leaf, and simmer very gently for four hours, skimming occasionally.

Strain the stock into a large bowl; let the solids drain thoroughly before discarding them. Allow the stock to stand until it is tepid, then refrigerate it overnight or freeze it long enough for the fat to congeal. Spoon off and discard the layer of fat.

Tightly covered and refrigerated, the stock may safely be kept for three to four days. Stored in small, tightly covered freezer containers and frozen, the stock may be kept for as long as six months.

EDITOR'S NOTE: *Any combination of veal meat and bones may be used to make this stock; ideally, the meat and bones together should weigh about 6 pounds. Ask your butcher to crack the bones.*

Glossary

Acidulated water: a dilute solution of lemon juice in water, used to keep certain vegetables and fruits from discoloring after they are peeled.
Al dente: an Italian term meaning "to the tooth." It is used to describe perfectly cooked pasta: chewy but with no flavor of flour.
Asian fish sauce (also called nuoc mam and nam pla): a thin, brown, salty liquid made from fermented fish. It is used in Southeast Asian cooking to bring out the flavors of a dish. If fish sauce is not available, substitute a mixture of one part anchovy paste to four parts water.
Balsamic vinegar: a mild, intensely fragrant wine-based vinegar made in northern Italy; traditionally it is aged in wooden casks.
Baste: to help brown and flavor a food, and keep it from drying out, by brushing it with marinade, pan juices, or other liquid during cooking.
Bâton (also called bâtonnet): a piece of vegetable that has been cut in the shape of a stick; bâtons are slightly larger than julienne.
Blanch: to plunge food into boiling water, which is then drained off as soon as it has returned to the boil. Blanching softens vegetables and fruits and can also mellow strong flavors.
Calorie (or kilocalorie): a measure of the energy a food supplies when it is broken down in the body.
Canelle knife: a kitchen utensil used to create small grooves in vegetables for decorative purposes.
Caul fat: the weblike fatty membrane that surrounds a pig's stomach. When wrapped around a lean ground meat filling, it melts during cooking and moistens the meat.
Celeriac (also called celery root): the knobby, tuberous root of a plant in the celery family.
Ceps (also called porcini): wild mushrooms with a pungent, earthy flavor that survives drying or long cooking. Dried ceps should be soaked in hot water before they are used.
Chili peppers (also called chilies): a variety of hot or mild red or green peppers. Fresh or dried, most chili peppers contain volatile oils that can irritate the skin and eyes; they must be handled with extreme care *(cautionary note, page 63).*
Cholesterol: a waxlike substance manufactured in the human body and also found in foods of animal origin. Although a certain amount of cholesterol is necessary for proper body functioning, an excess can accumulate in the arteries, contributing to heart disease. See also Monounsaturated fats; Polyunsaturated fats; Saturated fats.
Coral: the edible roe, or eggs, of the scallop, lobster, or crab.
Crème fraîche: a slightly ripened, sharp-tasting French cream.
Daikon radish: a long, white Japanese radish.
Debeard: to remove the fibrous threads from a mussel. These tough threads, called the beard, are produced by the mussel to attach itself to stationary objects. See also Mussel.
Dietary fiber: a plant-cell material that passes undigested through the human body but that promotes healthy digestion of other food matter.
Fat: a basic component of many foods, comprising three types of fatty acid—saturated, monounsaturated, and polyunsaturated—in varying proportions. See also Monounsaturated fats; Polyunsaturated fats; Saturated fats.
Fiber: see Dietary fiber.
Fillet: a full-length section of meat or fish cut from the ribs and backbone. Can be used to describe the act of removing a fillet from a cut of meat or a fish.
Five-spice powder: a pungent blend of ground Sichuan pepper, star anise, cassia, cloves, and fennel seeds; available in Asian markets.
Garam masala: an aromatic mixture of ground spices used in Indian cooking. It usually contains coriander, cumin, cloves, ginger, and cinnamon. It is sold in Asian markets and some supermarkets.
Gelatin: a virtually tasteless protein, available in powdered form or in sheets. Dissolved gelatin is used to set chilled molded dishes and desserts so that they retain their shape when unmolded.
Ginger: the spicy, buff-colored rhizome, or rootlike stem, of the ginger plant, used as a seasoning either in fresh form or dried and powdered. Dried ginger makes a poor substitute for fresh.
Hot red-pepper sauce: a hot, unsweetened chili sauce.
Julienne: the French term for food cut into thin strips.
Juniper berries: the berries of the juniper tree, used as the key flavoring in gin. They lend a resinous tang to marinades and sauces for game and other meats.
Kirsch (also called Kirschwasser): a clear cherry brandy distilled from small black cherries grown in Switzerland, Germany, and the Alsace region of France; often used to macerate fruit desserts.
Lemon balm: an aromatic plant of the mint family, having lemon-scented leaves used as a seasoning.
Lemon grass (citronella): a long, woody, lemon-flavored stalk that is shaped like a scallion. Lemon grass is available in Asian markets. To store, refrigerate in plastic wrap for up to two weeks; lemon grass may also be frozen for storage.
Mango: a fruit grown throughout the tropics, with sweet, succulent, yellow-orange flesh that is extremely rich in vitamin A. Like papaya, it may cause an allergic reaction in some individuals.
Marinade: a mixture of aromatic ingredients in which meat, vegetables, or fruit are allowed to stand before cooking to enrich their flavor. Some marinades will tenderize meat.
Medallion: a round or oval-shaped slice of lean meat for grilling or sautéing.
Monounsaturated fats: one of the three types of fats found in foods. Monounsaturated fats are believed not to raise blood-cholesterol levels.
Mussel: a bivalve mollusk with bluish black shells found along Atlantic and Pacific coasts as well as in the Mediterranean. The mussel's sweet flesh varies from beige to orange-yellow in color when cooked. See also Debeard.
Noisettes: boned lamb from the loin, rolled, tied, and cut into rounds for grilling or sautéing.
Nonreactive pan: a cooking vessel whose surface does not chemically react with food. Materials used include stainless steel, enamel, glass, and some alloys. Untreated cast iron and aluminum may react with acids, producing off colors or tastes.
Olive oil: any of various grades of oil extracted from olives. Extra virgin olive oil has a full, fruity flavor and the lowest acidity. Virgin olive oil is slightly higher in acidity and lighter in flavor. Pure olive oil, a processed blend of olive oils, has the highest acidity and the lightest taste.
Paprika: a slightly sweet, spicy powder produced by grinding dried red peppers. The best type of paprika is Hungarian. Available in various colors and strengths.
Parboil: to partially cook a food in liquid to prepare it for a second cooking method that would otherwise leave it underdone.
Parchment paper: a reusable paper treated with silicone to produce a nonstick surface. It is used to line pans and baking sheets, and to wrap foods for baking.
Passionfruit: a juicy, fragrant, egg-shaped tropical fruit with wrinkled skin, yellow flesh, and small black seeds. The seeds are edible; the skin is not.
Phyllo (also spelled "filo"): a paper-thin flour-and-water pastry popular in Greece and the Middle East. It can be made at home or bought, fresh or frozen, from delicatessens and some supermarkets.
Plantain: a starchy variety of banana that is normally cooked before it is eaten. Although the skin turns yellowish brown and then black as the plantain ripens, the flesh remains creamy yellow or slightly pink.
Poach: to cook gently in simmering liquid. The temperature of the poaching liquid should be approximately 200° F., and its surface should merely tremble.
Polyunsaturated fats: one of the three types of fats found in foods. They exist in abundance in such vegetable oils as safflower, sunflower, corn, and soybean. They are also found in seafood. Certain highly polyunsaturated fatty acids called omega-3s occur exclusively in seafood and marine animals. Polyunsaturated fats lower the level of cholesterol in the blood.
Proof: to cause dough to rise by the addition of yeast or some other leavening agent.
Purée: to reduce food to a smooth consistency by mashing it, passing it through a sieve, or processing it in a blender or food processor.
Radicchio: a purplish red Italian chicory with a chewy texture and slightly bitter taste.
Radish sprouts: the young shoots of the radish plant, eaten as a vegetable.
Recommended Dietary Allowance (RDA): the average required daily amount of an essential nutrient as determined for healthy people of various ages by the National Research Council.
Reduce: to boil down a liquid to concentrate its flavor or thicken its consistency.
Refresh: to rinse a briefly cooked vegetable under cold water to arrest its cooking and set its color.
Rice-paper wrappers: brittle wrappers for small portions of food, made from rice flour and sold in stores specializing in Southeast Asian foods. They

·e softened by dipping them in hot water.
ice wine: Chinese rice wine (shao-hsing) is rewed from rice and wine. Japanese rice wine ake) has a different flavor but may be used as a ubstitute. If rice wine is not available, use dry herry in its place.
oe: refers primarily to fish eggs, but edible roe is lso found in scallops, crabs, and lobsters.
oulade: a light sponge cake baked in a shallow, ectangular pan, then turned out, spread with lling, and rolled up.
afflower oil: the vegetable oil that contains the ighest amount of polyunsaturated fats.
affron: the dried, yellowish red stigmas (or hreads) of the saffron crocus, which yield a owerful yellow color as well as a pungent flavor. owdered saffron has less flavor than the threads.
amphire (also called sea fennel): a European ucculent plant of the parsley family, growing in efts of rock near the sea.
aturated fats: one of the three types of fats ound in foods. They exist in abundance in animal roducts and in coconut and palm oils; they raise e level of cholesterol in the blood. Because high lood-cholesterol levels may cause heart disease, aturated fat consumption should be restricted to ss than 15 percent of the calories provided by the aily diet.
ausage casing: natural casings, stronger than ommercial casings, are the cleaned intestines of mb, hog, or beef. Usually sold preserved in brine r dry salt, they can be ordered from butchers or pecialist suppliers and should be soaked before se. Lamb casings are generally used for thin ausages, hog or beef casings for thicker ones.
ear: to brown meat by exposing it briefly to very igh heat, sealing in the natural juices.
esame paste: see Tahini.
hallot: a refined cousin of the onion, with a ubtle flavor and papery, red-brown skin.
hrimp: a crustacean that lives in Atlantic and acific waters. Although there are hundreds of pecies, the most popular are white, brown, and ink shrimp. Also available are northern shrimp, aught in the North Atlantic and North Pacific, and ock shrimp, so named because of their tough hells. Rock shrimp are found primarily around lorida. Virtually all commercially caught shrimp is mmediately beheaded and frozen. It is sold ccording to count per pound; the range is from ewer than 10 per pound to more than 70. Shrimp can be cooked in or out of the shells. Shrimp is moderately high in cholesterol but very low in fat.
Shrimp paste: a pinkish brown to dark brown shrimp sauce sold in blocks. It is available from Asian markets.
Sichuan pepper (also called Chinese pepper, Japanese pepper, or anise pepper): a dried shrub berry with a tart, aromatic flavor that is less piquant than black pepper.
Simmer: to maintain a liquid at a temperature just below its boiling point so that the liquid's surface barely ripples.
Skim milk: milk from which almost all the fat has been removed.
Sodium: a nutrient essential to maintaining the proper balance of fluids in the body. In most diets, a major source of the element is table salt, which is 40 percent sodium. Excess sodium may contribute to high blood pressure, which increases the risk of heart disease. One teaspoon of salt, with 2,132 milligrams of sodium, contains about two-thirds of the maximum "safe and adequate" daily intake recommended by the National Research Council.
Soy sauce: a savory, salty brown liquid made from fermented soybeans and available in both light and dark versions. One tablespoon of ordinary soy sauce contains 1,030 milligrams of sodium; lower-sodium variations, such as those used in the recipes in this book, may contain half that amount.
Spaghetti squash: a yellow-skinned squash whose cooked flesh resembles strands of spaghetti.
Stock: a savory liquid prepared by simmering meat, bones, trimmings, aromatic vegetables, herbs, and spices in water. Stock forms a flavor-rich base for sauces and soups.
Sun-dried tomatoes: tomatoes that have been naturally dried in the sun to concentrate their flavor and preserve them; some are then packed in oil with seasoning and herbs. Many sun-dried tomatoes are of Italian origin.
Tahini (also called sesame paste): a nutty-tasting paste made from ground sesame seeds. Light tahini, made from raw sesame seeds, and dark tahini, made from roasted seeds, are sold in health-food stores and Middle Eastern delicatessens.
Tamarind concentrate: the brown, acid-flavored pulp from the seed pod of the tamarind tree, available from Asian specialty stores.
Tarragon: a strong herb with a sweet anise taste. In combination with other herbs—especially rosemary, sage, or thyme—it should be used sparingly, to avoid a clash of flavors. Because heat intensifies tarragon's flavor, cooked dishes require smaller amounts.
Tenderloin: the tenderest muscle in an animal's carcass, located inside the loin.
Tofu: a low-fat, high-protein curd made from soybeans. It looks like white cheese.
Tomato paste: a concentrated tomato purée, available in cans and tubes.
Total fat: an individual's daily intake of polyunsaturated, monounsaturated, and saturated fats. Nutritionists recommend that total fat constitute no more than 30 percent of a person's total caloric intake. The term as used in this book refers to the combined fats in a given dish or food.
Turmeric: a spice used as a coloring agent and occasionally as a substitute for saffron. It has a musty odor and a slightly bitter flavor.
Vanilla sugar: sugar flavored by placing a whole vanilla pod in a closed container of sugar for about a week.
Virgin olive oil: see Olive oil.
Water bath (also called bain-marie): a large pan partially filled with hot water and placed in a preheated oven as a cooking vessel for foods in smaller containers. The combination of ambient hot water and air cooks the food slowly and evenly.
Whole-wheat flour: wheat flour that contains the whole of the wheat grain with nothing added or taken away. It is nutritionally valuable as a source of dietary fiber and it is higher in B vitamins than white flour.
Worcestershire sauce: a hot sauce containing vinegar, molasses, chili peppers, and tropical fruits and spices.
Yeast: a microorganism that feeds on sugars and starches to produce carbon dioxide and thus leaven bread. Yeast is sold either fresh or dried; fresh yeast will keep for six weeks in the refrigerator.
Yeast, fast-rising: a recently developed strain of yeast that reduces the amount of time necessary for rising.
Yogurt: a smooth-textured, semisolid cultured milk product made with varying percentages of fat. Yogurt makes a good substitute for sour cream in cooking. Yogurt may also be combined with sour cream to produce a sauce or topping that is lower in fat and calories than sour cream alone.
Zest: the flavored outermost layer of citrus-fruit peel; it should be cut or grated free of the white pith that lies beneath it.

Picture Credits

Credits from left to right are separated by semicolons; from top to bottom by dashes.

:over: John Elliott. 4: James Murphy—Chris naggs; Martin Brigdale. 5: top right, David ohnson—Andrew Williams—Martin Brigdale. 6: acqui Hurst. 10-12: John Elliott. 13: James ackson. 14-16: David Johnson. 17: James Jackson. 8-21: John Elliott. 22: Chris Knaggs. 23: James ackson. 24, 25: Chris Knaggs. 26: John Elliott. 27: ames Murphy. 28, 29: Chris Knaggs. 30: James Murphy. 31: Chris Knaggs. 32: John Elliott. 33: ames Murphy. 34: Chris Knaggs. 35: James Murphy. 36: John Elliott. 37: James Murphy. 38: ohn Elliott. 39: Andrew Whittuck. 40, 41: John lliott. 42: David Johnson. 43: John Elliott. 44: David Johnson. 46, 47: Chris Knaggs. 48: John lliott. 49: James Murphy. 50: David Johnson. 51: James Jackson. 52-54: Chris Knaggs. 55: David Johnson. 56: James Murphy. 57: David Johnson. 58-62: John Elliott. 63: Andrew Williams—Andrew Whittuck. 64: John Elliott. 65: James Jackson. 66: John Elliott. 67, 69: Martin Brigdale. 70: Andrew Williams. 71: David Johnson. 72: John Elliott. 73: Andrew Williams. 74: Andrew Whittuck. 75: James Jackson. 76: Andrew Whittuck. 77: John Elliott. 78: David Johnson. 79: Andrew Whittuck. 80-82: Andrew Williams. 83, 84: David Johnson. 85: Andrew Williams. 86: Martin Brigdale. 88, 89: Andrew Whittuck. 90: John Elliott. 91: David Johnson. 92, 93: Andrew Whittuck. 94: Andrew Williams. 95: James Jackson. 96: Andrew Whittuck. 97, 98: John Elliott. 99-101: Andrew Williams. 102, 103: John Elliott. 105: Andrew Williams. 106-111: James Murphy. 112-115: Martin Brigdale. 116, 117: Martin Brigdale; Andrew Williams. 118-121: Andrew Williams. 122-127: John Elliott. 128: David Johnson. 130: James Jackson. 131: David Johnson. 132, 133: Martin Brigdale. 134-136: John Elliott. 137: David Johnson. 138: Taran Z. Photography.

Props: The editors thank the following outlets and manufacturers; all are based in London. 18: plate, Hutschenreuther (U.K.) Ltd. 50: napkin, Next Interior. 65: napkin, Ewart Liddell. 71: pottery, Winchcombe Pottery, The Craftsmen Potters Shop. 90: plate, Hutschenreuther (U.K.) Ltd. 92: china, Line of Scandinavia. 94: china, Villeroy & Boch. 98: plate, Daphne Carnegy, The Craftsmen Potters Shop. 106-107: linen, Ewart Liddell; hamper, Fortnum & Mason; silver platter and cutlery, Mappin & Webb Silversmiths; china, Villeroy & Boch; glasses, Chinacraft Ltd. 135: plate, Tony Grant; casserole, Owen Thorpe, The Craftsmen Potters Shop. 137: plates, Villeroy & Boch.

Acknowledgments

The editors wish to thank the following: Paul van Biene, London; Maureen Burrows, London; Stuart Cullen, London; Jonathan Driver, London; Neil Fairbairn, Wivenhoe, Essex; Bridget Jones, Guildford, Surrey; James Knight of Mayfair, London; Lidgates of Holland Park, London; Perstorp Warerite Ltd., London; Sharp Electronics (U.K.) Lt London; Mhairi Sharpley, Chesham, Bucks; Jane Stevenson, London; Toshiba (U.K.) Ltd., London.

Index